Stitch by Stitch

Volume 13

TORSTAR BOOKS

NEW YORK · TORONTO

Stitch by Stitch

TORSTAR BOOKS INC.
41 MADISON AVENUE
SUITE 2900
NEW YORK, NY 10010

Knitting and crochet abbreviations

approx = approximately
beg = begin(ning)
ch = chain(s)
cm = centimeter(s)
cont = continue(ing)
dc = double crochet
dec = decreas(e)(ing)
dtr = double triple
foll = follow(ing)
g = gram(s)
grp = group(s)
hdc = half double crochet

in = inch(es)
inc = increas(e)(ing)
K = knit
oz = ounce(s)
P = purl
patt = pattern
psso = pass slipped stitch over
rem = remain(ing)
rep = repeat
RS = right side
sc = single crochet
sl = slip

sl st = slip stitch
sp = space(s)
st(s) = stitch(es)
tbl = through back of loop(s)
tog = together
tr = triple crochet
WS = wrong side
wyib = with yarn in back
wyif = with yarn in front
yd = yard(s)
yo = yarn over

A guide to the pattern sizes

		10	12	14	16	18	20
Bust	in	32½	34	36	38	40	42
	cm	83	87	92	97	102	107
Waist	in	25	26½	28	30	32	34
	cm	64	67	71	76	81	87
Hips	in	34½	36	38	40	42	44
	cm	88	92	97	102	107	112

Torstar Books also offers a range of acrylic book stands, designed to keep instructional books such as *Stitch by Stitch* open, flat and upright while leaving the hands free for practical work.

For information write to Torstar Books Inc., 41 Madison Avenue, Suite 2900, New York, NY 10010.

Library of Congress Cataloging in Publication Data
Main entry under title:

Stitch by stitch.

Includes index.
1. Needlework. I. Torstar Books (Firm)
TT705.S74 1984   746.4   84-111
ISBN 0-920269-00-1 (set)

987654

© Marshall Cavendish Limited 1986

Printed in Belgium

ISBN 0-920269-13-3   (Volume 13)

Contents

Crochet / COURSE 57

More about surface crochet

The raised lines worked onto the surface of a plain crochet fabric can be combined with other crochet stitch patterns to create more interesting, textured fabrics, similar in appearance to the traditional Aran patterns found in knitting. For the devotee of crochet who finds it more satisfying and easier to work with a crochet hook than with knitting needles, this is an ideal way of making fabrics suitable for bulky cardigans and country-style sweaters in the yarns traditionally associated with Aran knitting.

The raised lines must be worked precisely and carefully so that clear, geometric shapes are achieved on the background fabric, which can be worked in either single crochet, half doubles or doubles. For example, when working a diamond shape as a center panel on the sleeve front of a plain sweater, it is important to make sure that each diamond consists of the same number of stitches, moved exactly the same number of stitches to the right or left.

Raised slip stitch

This simple method of working a raised line of crochet stitches onto a basic background fabric is similar to the technique used for working lines onto a filet background (see Volume 6, page 8). You can use either one or two strands of yarn for the slip stitches, depending on the effect you wish to achieve. Two strands create a really bulky effect which stands out clearly in relief against the background fabric when used with knitting worsted or Aran yarns. This technique would be unsuitable for working with a bulky yarn, when only one strand should be used.

To work a sample like the one shown in the step-by-step pictures, make a square of single crochet using a knitting worsted or Aran yarn. Use two strands of yarn for the slip stitches, which have been worked in a contrasting color for clarity.

1 Hold the yarn at the back of the work and insert the hook into the base of the fabric from front to back. Draw through two strands of yarn from back to front.

2 Now insert the hook into the fabric in the middle of the first row and draw through another loop, then draw this loop through the first to complete the slip stitch. This small stitch worked at the base of the fabric holds the yarn in place.

3 Now insert the hook into the middle of the next row and work a slip stitch as before. Continue to work up the fabric in a straight line, placing the hook slightly to the right, then the left, each time, as the stitches do not lie immediately above each other on every row.

4 Here a second line of raised slip stitches has been worked beside the first, working from the top to the bottom of the fabrics so that the stitches lie in opposite directions on the background fabric.

5 To move the stitches to the right or the left, insert the hook one row up, placing it either one stitch to the right or one stitch to the left each time.

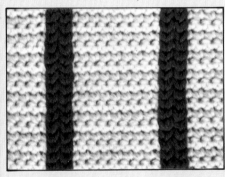

6 Use double lines to divide a plain background into panels so that cables or diamonds can be worked into the panels for a complete Aran-style fabric.

7 To work the raised slip stitches on a half double fabric, join the yarn at the base in the same way as before. Work up the fabric in the same way, but insert the hook into the middle of one row, then the base of the next row each time, so that the slip stitches cover the fabric completely and do not pull it out of shape.

8 Similarly when working over a double fabric make sure that you work into the middle of one row, then the base of the next row each time, extending the loop as it is drawn through the fabric, before inserting the hook back into the crochet to complete the stitch so that the slip stitches do not distort the background fabric.

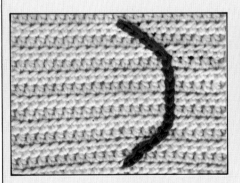

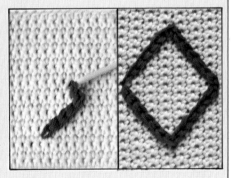

9 When working a geometric shape, complete one side of the motif, working from the bottom to the top. Here the first side of a hexagon has been worked using two strands of yarn on a half double fabric.

10 The second side of the shape is worked in the opposite direction to the first, starting from the lower edge once more.

11 When working a diamond shape where the stitches must be turned sharply to the right or the left to achieve the correct shape, work the first part of the diamond from the bottom to the right, then turn and work the first stitch to the left, level with the last stitch worked to the right, as shown above left. Completed diamond is shown above right, worked on a single crochet fabric.

Combining textured patterns with raised crochet

Crochet stitches vary a lot in height and a patterned fabric based on a double stitch could not be worked alongside a pattern based on a single crochet or half double since the stitches would either dip down or slant upward where the different patterns met. Some crochet patterns combine two different stitches, changing the height of the basic fabric. For this reason, where you wish to work a fabric consisting of different panels of stitches, it is better to choose one textured stitch (such as uneven berry stitch—see Volume 5, page 10), and combine it with a plain background fabric, using surface crochet to decorate the plain panels.

Before you start a garment make a sample piece at least 4in (10cm) square in the stitches and patterns of your choice to make sure that they can be worked side by side satisfactorily.

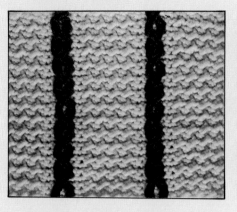

1 The surface crochet should always be worked on a flat background fabric so that you will need to allow for stitches in single crochet, half doubles or doubles between the patterned panels.

2 In this sample even seed stitch (see Volume 5, page 19) has been worked with panels of single crochet. Single cables have been worked on the single crochet panels, leaving one stitch at each side so that they stand out clearly against the background crochet.

3 Here, panels of uneven berry stitch (see Volume 5, page 10) have been combined with single crochet. Outline the berry stitch panel with slip stitches and work diamond shapes onto the plain background fabric.

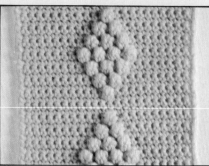

4 For a central panel which can be used down the center of a sleeve or sweater front, work berry stitches in a diamond shape up the center of the fabric as shown here.

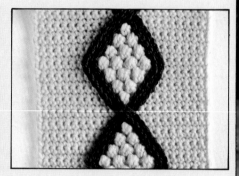

5 Outline the berry stitches with double lines of raised single crochet (see Volume 12, page 28) to complete the Aran effect.

How to plan a raised crochet design

When working several different surface crochet shapes on a plain background, you will need to plan your design on graph paper before you start to make sure that the different shapes fit evenly across the fabric and that where neck shaping is to be worked any central panels are centered on each side of the neck shaping.

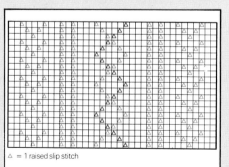

△ = 1 raised slip stitch

1 Use each square to represent a row or stitch on the graph paper in the normal way as shown here. The diamond shapes have been marked in two colors. Work the line marked in red first, followed by the line marked in blue, taking the second line over the first.

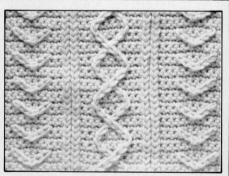

2 Here the graph has been translated into fabric form, using the same color for both the background fabric and the surface crochet. Where the second line crosses the first on the diamond shape, take the yarn over the first raised line where they meet, working into the next stitch to the right or left of the first line.

Crochet cardigan

An elegant Aran-style cardigan encrusted with bobbles and diamonds. It looks stunning with either pants or a skirt.

Size
To fit 34-36in (87-92cm) bust.
Length, 32¼in (82cm).
Sleeve seam, 16¾in (43cm).

Materials
55oz (1550g) of a knitting worsted
Sizes H and I (5.00 and 6.00mm)
crochet hooks
7 buttons

Gauge
15 sc and 18 rows to 4in (10cm) worked on a size I (6.00mm) hook.

Bobble panel
Note: Each bobble panel is worked over 9 sts and 20 rows.
1st row (RS) 1 sc into each of next 9 sts.
2nd-5th rows As 1st.
6th row (WS) 1 sc into each of next 3 sts, sl st into next st, keeping last loop of each dc on hook, work 3dc into next st, yo and draw through all 4 loops on hook—called 1 bobble or 1 B—sl st into next st, 1 sc into each of next 3 sts.
7th row 1 sc into each of next 4 sts, sl st into next st, 1 sc into each of next 4 sts.
8th row 1 sc into each of next 2 sts, (sl st into next st, 1 B into next st) twice, sl st into next st, 1 sc into each of next 2 sts.

9th row 1 dc into each of next 3 sts, (sl st into next st, 1 sc into next st) twice, 1 sc into each of next 2 sts.
10th row 1 sc into next st, (sl st into next st, 1 B into next st) 3 times, sl st into next st, 1 sc into next st.
11th row 1 sc into each of next 2 sts, (sl st into next st, 1 sc into next st) 3 times, 1 sc into next st.
12th row (Sl st into next st, 1 B into next st) 4 times, sl st into next st.
13th row 1 sc into next st, (sl st into next st, 1 sc into next st) 4 times.
14th row As 10th. 15th row As 11th.
16th row As 8th. 17th row As 9th.
18th row As 6th. 19th row As 7th.
20th row As 1st.

Back
Using size I (6.00mm) hook make 71 ch.
1st row 1 sc into 3rd ch from hook, 1 sc into each ch to end. Turn. 70 sts.
2nd row 1 ch to count as first sc, skip first st, 1 sc into each st to end. Turn. Rep last row 3 times more. **
6th row 1 ch, 1 sc into each of next 16sc, patt 9 sts as 6th row of bobble panel, 1 sc into each of next 18sc, patt 9 sts as 6th row of bobble panel, 1 sc into each sc to end. Turn.
Cont in patt as set keeping sts in sc at

each side of the 2 bobble panels and keeping bobble panels correct throughout, until work measures 19¾in (50cm); end with a WS row.
Place a marker at each end of last row to denote beg of armholes.
Shape raglan armholes
Dec one st at each end of next and every other row until 24 sts rem. Fasten off.

Left front
Using size I (6.00mm) hook, make 33 ch. Work as for back to **. 32 sts.
6th row 1 ch, 1 sc into each of next 5sc, work 9 sts as 6th row of bobble panel, 1 sc into each of next 17sc. Turn.
7th row 1 ch, 1 sc into each of next 16sc, work 9 sts as 7th row of bobble panel, 1 sc into each sc to end. Turn.
Cont in patt as set until work measures 6in (15cm); end with a WS row.
Divide for pocket
Next row 1 ch, 1 sc into each of next 8sc, turn and cont on these sts for 6in (15cm); end with a RS row. Fasten off.
Rejoin yarn to rem sts and cont in patt for 6in (15cm); with a RS row. Now work across all sts, keeping bobble patt until work measures same as back to armhole; end with a WS row.
Shape raglan armhole
Dec one st at beg of next and every other row until 15 sts rem; end with a WS row.
Shape neck
Next row Dec one st, patt to last 3 sts, turn. 11 sts.
Dec one st at each end of foll 4 alternate rows, then at armhole edge only on foll alternate row. 2 sts rem. Fasten off.

Right front
Work as given for left front, reversing all shaping, position of panel and pocket shaping so that 6th row will read:
6th row 1 ch, 1 sc into each of next 16sc, work 9 sts as 6th row of bobble panel, 1 sc into each of next 6sc. Turn.

Sleeves
Using size I (6.00mm) hook make 40ch and work first 5 rows as for back. 39 sts.
6th row 1 ch, 1 sc into each of next 14sc, patt 9 sts as 6th row of bobble panel, 1 sc into each sc to end. Turn.
Cont in patt as set, inc one st at each end of next and every foll 8th row until there are 55 sts. Cont straight until sleeve measures 14½in (37cm); end with a WS row.
Shape raglan armhole
Keeping bobble panel correct, dec one st at each end of next and every other row until 9 sts rem. Fasten off. *continued*

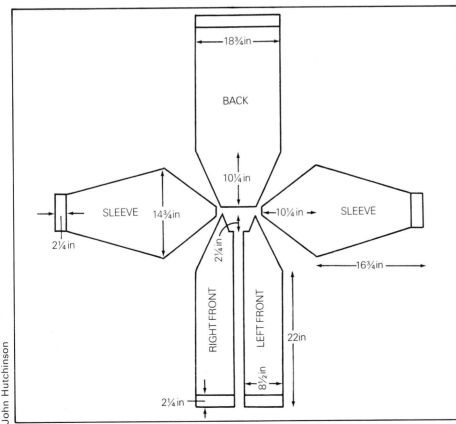

BACK
18¾in
10¼in
SLEEVE 14¾in
2¼in
RIGHT FRONT
LEFT FRONT
10¼in
SLEEVE
16¾in
22in
2¼in
8½in
2¼in

Lower band
Using size I (6.00mm) hook make 11 ch.
Base row 1sc into 3rd ch from hook, 1sc into each ch to end. Turn. 10 sts.

Beg ribbed patt.
Patt row 1ch, skip first st, * sc into horizontal loop below next st, rep from * to end, 1sc into turning chain. Turn.

Rep patt row until work measures 35½in (90cm) from beg. Fasten off.

Cuffs (make 2)
Work as given for lower band for 8in (20cm). Fasten off.

Button band
Work as for lower band until band fits along front edge. Fasten off.
Mark 7 button positions on this band, the first to come 5th row from lower edge, the last 5 rows from the top and the others evenly spaced between.

Buttonhole band
Work as given for button band, making buttonholes thus:
1st buttonhole row 1ch, 1sc into each of next 3sc, 3ch, skip next 3sc, 1sc into each sc to end. Turn.
2nd buttonhole row Work 1sc into each sc and 3sc into 3ch space. Turn.

Collar
Using size H (5.00mm) hook make 20ch. Work first 8 rows as for lower band. 19sc. Cont to work in ribbed patt throughout.
***Shape collar
Next row 1sc, 1sc into each of next 5sc, turn and patt to end.
Next row 1ch, 1sc into each of next 11sc, turn and patt to end.
Work 8 rows in patt across all sts.***
Rep from *** to *** until inner edge of collar measures 13¾in (35cm); end by working 8 rows straight. Fasten off.

Pocket borders (make 2)
Using size H (5.00mm) hook make 9ch and work as for lower band for 6in (15cm). Fasten off.

Pocket linings (make 2)
Using size H (5.00mm) hook make 21 ch.
Base row 1sc into 3rd ch from hook, 1sc into each ch to end. Turn. 20 sts. Cont in sc until pocket lining measures 6in (15cm). Fasten off.

To finish
Using size H (5.00mm) hook work surface crochet following step-by-step instructions for raised single crochet in Volume 12, page 28, and raised slip stitch on page 4, working raised sc to form diamond trellis around each bobble pattern and a raised slip stitch cable up each front.
Join raglan seams. Using size H (5.00mm) hook and using yarn double, work a row of raised sl st (see page 4) up each side of each raglan. Join side and sleeve seams. Sew on lower band and cuffs, easing to fit. Sew on front bands. Sew on collar. Sew on pocket linings and pocket borders.
Sew on buttons to correspond with buttonholes.
Press seams.

Victor Yuan

Crochet / COURSE 58

Looped-fur fabrics

Loop stitches are easy to work in crochet and can be used to make allover fun-fur fabrics in a variety of yarns, which are ideal for bulky winter coats or jackets. Worked in cotton yarn, the loops can be used to make bright-colored bathmats: beautifully soft baby blankets can be worked using a bulky baby yarn.

The fabrics can be made in a loop or stitch pattern, or the yarn can be cut into short lengths and hooked onto a basic filet crochet mesh background fabric, to make a cut-fur effect.

You can use the method given in Volume 11, page 30 in the step-by-step course on looped edgings to make the loops. Use the finger method for a thick fabric, which is ideal for all types of yarn that must be held in place firmly, including cotton or string, or use the card method for a finer effect.

For a lightweight looped effect use the method shown in the step-by-step pictures that follow.

Try experimenting with different yarns to see the effects that can be achieved when working in this way. A soft mohair could be used for a beautifully textured country-style jacket or a luxurious cape for evenings.

Single-loop fabric

Each loop in this pattern is made by drawing the yarn from behind the middle finger of the left hand, so it is important to wind the yarn correctly around the left hand to ensure that the loops are a uniform length all over the fabric. All the loops are formed with the wrong side of the work facing, so that they fall on the right side of the crochet once it has been completed.

We have used a knitting worsted and a size G (4.50mm) hook for our sample, making 30 chains to start the work.

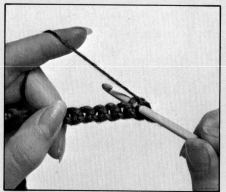

1 Work 1 row of single crochet on the foundation chain. Turn and make 1 chain for the first stitch. Insert the hook from front to back into the second stitch.

2 Wind the yarn around the fingers in the usual way, so that the yarn lies over the top of the index finger and middle finger of the left hand.

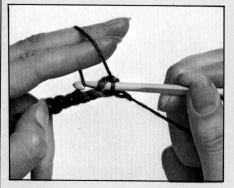

3 Place the hook around the yarn so that the hook is under and behind the middle finger of the left hand. Now draw the yarn toward the work, thus forming a loop over the first two fingers of the left hand as shown here.

4 Draw the yarn through the stitch, keeping the yarn around the fingers at the back of the work for the time being, so that the loop remains firmly in place on the right side of the work.

5 Now drop the loop from the left hand and complete the single crochet in the usual way. Here we show you the right side of the work with the completed loop hanging downward.

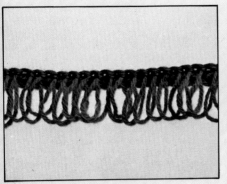

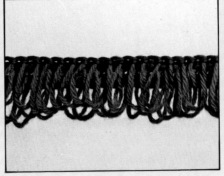

6 Continue to work a loop into each stitch all the way along the row in the same way. Here is the completed row on the right side of the work. For a smooth edge work a single crochet *only* into the turning chain.

7 Work one more row of single crochet on the right side of the work, then turn and work another loop row in exactly the same way as before, with the wrong side facing, so that the second row hangs over the first as shown here.

8 Repeat the last two rows for the pattern to make a complete loop stitch crochet fabric as shown here.

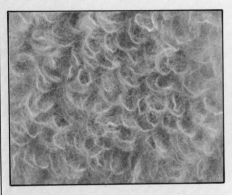

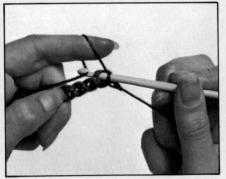

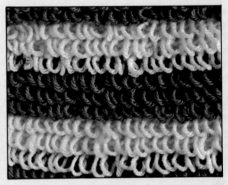

9 Here the same pattern has been worked in a mohair yarn for a fun-fur effect, ideal for warm winter coats.

10 To make a shorter loop, work in the same way as before, but taking the yarn over the index finger only, drawing the loop from below this finger as shown here.

11 Complete the single crochet as before, dropping the loop only when the yarn has been drawn through the stitch. The loops can be worked in stripes as shown here. Change color by drawing the yarn through the last stitch in the normal way.

Cut-fur fabric

In this pattern the background fabric is worked first to make a close mesh fabric onto which the loops can be hooked to complete the fur fabric. This method is more laborious than working the loops at the same time as working the background fabric, but it is ideal for making something like a bathmat or rug. The thickness of the fabric depends not only on the type of yarn used, but also on the number of strands used to make each loop, so that the fabric can be made to any thickness, depending on the garment or article to be made.

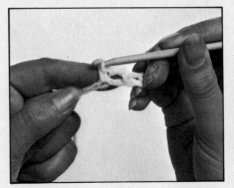

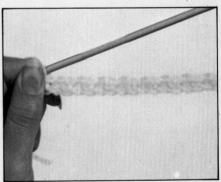

1 Start the background fabric by making an even number of chains. Now work a single crochet into the 4th chain from the hook to count as the first single crochet and one chain space. Make one chain, skip the next chain and work a single crochet into the following chain.

2 Continue to work a single crochet into every other chain, working one chain between each stitch, and working the last single crochet into the last chain.

continued

Fred Mancini

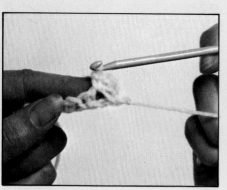

3 Turn and make two chains to count as the first single crochet and one chain space. Now work a single crochet into the first chain space.

4 Continue to work one chain followed by one single crochet worked into each chain space across the row, working the last single crochet into the turning chain.

5 To complete the pattern, repeat the last row each time, working 2 chains at the beginning of every row and working the last single crochet into the first of the two chains worked at the beginning of each row.

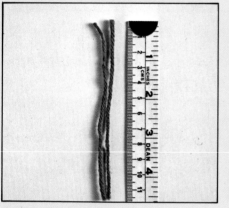

6 To make the fur fabric, cut two lengths of yarn, approximately 4¾in (12cm) each in length. We have used a contrasting color for clarity. You will need to cut two strands of yarn for each loop, or more if a thicker fabric is required.

7 Fold the two strands of yarn in half and hold the yarn at the front of the work. Now insert the hook from front to back between the turning chain and the first single crochet at the bottom right-hand corner of the 2nd pattern row.

8 Take the hook around the back of the next single crochet from right to left and to the front again to the left of this stitch.

9 Loop the doubled strands of yarn onto the hook and draw them through the single crochet from left to right, behind the single crochet and to the front or right side of the work again.

10 Wind the yarn around the hook and draw it through the two loops so that the strands are knotted at the front of the work. Straighten the loops once the stitch has been completed.

11 Now take two more strands of yarn and insert the hook into the next one chain space, taking the hook behind the next single crochet and to the front again, through the center of this stitch. Complete the knotted loop around and through this single crochet as before.

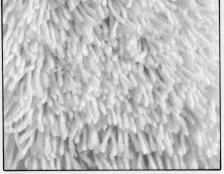

12 Continue to work a knotted loop into every one chain space across the row, working the last loop around the single crochet before the turning chain in the previous row.

13 Here two strands of yarn have been knotted through every stitch, using the same color for the background and cut fur. For a finer fabric work around every other stitch, alternating the position of the knots on every row.

14 The sample above has been worked in a random colored yarn for a multicolored effect, working the knots into every chain space for a really bulky-looking fabric. Below, the same pattern has been used for a sample worked in bright-colored string, using shorter strands of yarn to make a short-pile fabric that is ideal for mats or rugs.

Child's "sheepskin" rug

Here's a rug to delight any child—a warm and wooly sheep standing in lush green grass. It would make a terrific Christmas or birthday gift.

Materials
Bulky-weight yarn
53oz (1500g) in white (A)
15oz (400g) in green (B)
2oz (50g) in black (C)
Size H (5.50mm) crochet hook

Gauge
12 sts and 14 rows to 4in (10cm) in sc loops.
12 sts and 14 rows to 4in (10cm) in hdc loops.

Grass and legs section
Using size H (5.50mm) crochet hook and B make 124 ch.
Base row Work 1sc into the 2nd ch from hook, 1sc into each ch to end. Turn. 123sc.
1st row (WS) 1ch—to form a firm edge work into the first and last st throughout; *make a loop into the next st (see page 10) winding the yarn once around two fingers, rep from * working one loop into each st to end of row. Turn. 123 loops.
2nd row 1ch, 1sc into each st to end. Turn. 123sc.
These 2 rows form the patt. Rep them 3 times more, then work the first row again.
Divide the ball of C into four small balls for legs.
10th row 1ch, with B work 1sc into each of next 30 sts, joining in first ball of C on last sc, with C work 1sc into each of next 6sc rejoining in B on last st, with B work 1sc into each of next 42 sc, join in 2nd

ball of C, with C work 1sc into each of next 6sc, joining in B on last st, with B work 1sc into each of next 39sc. Turn.
11th-13th rows Twisting yarns when changing color to prevent a hole, cont in loop patt for grass and sc for legs, as set.
14th row 1ch, working in sc work 30B, 6C, 3B joining in third ball of C on last sc, 6C, 33B, 6C, 3B joining in fourth ball of C on last sc, 6C, 30B. Turn.
15th-27th rows Work in patt as set, ending with a WS loop row. Fasten off first and second balls of C.
28th row 1ch, work 24sc, turn.
29th-31st rows Work in patt on these 24sc as set.
32nd row 1ch, work 18sc, turn.
33rd-34th rows Work in patt on these 18sc as set.
35th row Sl st over first 3 sts, 1ch, work a loop st into each of next 15 sts, turn.
36th-38th rows Work in patt on these 15 sts as set.
39th row Sl st over first 6 sts, 1ch, work a loop st into each of next 9 sts, turn.
40th and 41st rows Work in patt on these 9 sts as set. Fasten off.
42nd row Return to the 3rd leg in C and work 1ch, 1sc into first st, 1sc into each of next 5 sts, joining in B on last st, with B work 1sc into each of next 30sc. Turn.
43rd-45th rows Work in patt on sts as set, ending with a WS loop row. Fasten off C.
46th row 1ch, 1sc into first st, 1sc into each of next 23 sts. Turn.
47th-49th rows Work in patt on these 23 sts as set. Fasten off.
50th row Return to the 4th leg in C and

work 1ch, 1sc into first st, 1sc into each of next 5 sts joining in B on last st, with B work 1sc into each of next 30 sts. Turn.
51st-53rd rows Work in patt as set, ending with a WS loop row. Fasten off C.
54th row Sl st over first 3 loop sts, 1ch, work 1sc into first st, 1sc into each of next 26 sts. Turn.
55th and 56th rows Work in patt on these 27 sts, turn.
57th row 1ch, work a loop st into each of next 24 sts, turn.
58th-63rd rows Work in patt on these 24 sts, ending with a WS loop row. Fasten off.

Sheep body section
Using size H (5.50mm) crochet hook and A make 32ch.
1st row (RS) Work 1hdc into 3rd chain from hook, 1hdc into each ch to end. Turn. 30hdc.
2nd row *Make 8 chains, work 1sc into the back loop only of next st, rep from * to end. Turn. 30ch loops.
Cont to work 1 row hdc and 1 row loop patt throughout, inc as foll:
3rd row Inc thus: 6ch, sl st into 2nd ch from hook, sl st into each of the next 2ch, 1hdc into the first loop skipped on previous row, 1hdc into each st to end. Turn. 30hdc.
4th row Inc thus: Make 14 ch, 1sc into the back loop of the 9th ch from hook, work an 8-chain loop into each of the next 5 ch, *8ch, 1sc into back loop only of next st, rep from * to end working across slipped sts. Turn. 39 loops.

5th row 2ch, 1hdc into each of next 39 sts, turn.

6th row *8ch, 1sc into back loop only of next st, rep from * to end. Turn. 39 loops.

7th row Inc as for 3rd row, then work 39hdc. Turn.

8th row Inc as for 4th row, then work loop patt to end. Turn. 48 loops.

9th row 2ch, 1hdc into each of next 48 sts. Turn.

10th row Work to end. Turn. 48 loops.

11th row As 9th.

12th row As 10th.

13th row Inc as for 3rd row, work 48hdc. Turn.

14th row Make 11ch, 1sc into the back loop of the 9th ch from hook, work an 8-chain loop into each of the next 2ch, work loop patt to end of row. Turn. 54 loops.

15th and 16th rows Work to end. Turn.

17th row Inc as for 3rd row, work to end. Turn.

18th row Inc as for 14th row, work to end. Turn. 60 loops.

19th-23rd rows Work to end. Turn.

24th row Inc as for 14th row, work to end. Turn. 63 loops.

25th-38th rows Work to end. Turn.

39th row Sl st into each of next 3 sts, 2ch, work 1hdc into each of next 60 sts. Turn.

40th-42nd rows Work to end. Turn. 60 loops.

43rd row 2ch, 1hdc into each of next 57 sts, turn.

44th-48th rows Work to end. Turn.

49th row 2ch, sl st into each of next 3 sts, 2ch, 1hdc into each of next 51 sts, turn.

50th-76th rows Work to end. Turn.

77th row Inc as for 3rd row, work 51hdc, turn.

78th row Inc as for 14th row, work to end. Turn. 57 loops.

79th and 80th rows Work to end. Turn.

81st row Inc as for 3rd row, work 57hdc. Turn.

82nd and 83rd rows Work to end. Turn.

84th row Inc as for 14th row. Work to end. Turn. 63 loops.

85th row Inc as for 3rd row, work 63hdc. Turn.

86th-88th rows Work to end. Turn. 66 sts.

89th row Inc as for 3rd row. Work to end. Turn.

90th-94th rows Work in patt on these 69 sts. Turn.

95th row Inc as for 3rd row, work to end. Turn. 69hdc.

96th-98th rows Work in patt on these 72 sts. Turn.

99th row Inc as for 3rd row, work 69hdc, turn.

100th-102nd rows Work in patt on these 72 sts, turn.

103rd row Inc as for 3rd row, work to end. Turn.

104th-108th rows Work in patt on these 75 sts. Turn.

109th row Inc as for 3rd row, work 72hdc, turn.

110th row Work across first 54 sts, turn.

111th and 112th rows Work to end. Turn.

113th row Sl st over first 3 sts, 2ch, 1hdc into each of next 45 sts, turn.

114th-116th rows Work in patt on these 45 sts. Turn.

117th row Sl st over first 3 sts, 2ch, 1hdc into each of next 39 sts, turn.

118th-120th rows Work in patt on these 39 sts. Turn.

121st row Sl st over first 3 sts, 2ch, work 1hdc into each of next 27 sts, turn.

122nd row Work in patt on these 27 sts. Turn.

123rd row 2ch, work 1hdc into each of next 24 sts, turn.

124th-126th rows Work to end. Turn.

127th row Sl st over first 3 sts, 2ch, work 1hdc into each of next 12 sts, turn.

128th-130th rows Work in patt on these 12 sts.
Fasten off.

131st row With WS facing skip next 3 sts, rejoin A to next st, work a loop st into each of next 18 sts. Turn.

132nd and 133rd rows Work to end. Turn.

134th row 2ch, 1hdc into each of next 15 sts, turn.

135th-137th rows Work to end. Turn.

138th row 2ch, work 1hdc into each of next 9 sts, turn.

139th-142nd rows Work to end. Turn.

143rd row Inc as for 14th row, work to end. Turn. 12 loops.

144th row Work to end. Turn.

145th row Inc as for 14th row, work a loop st into each of next 12 sts. Turn.

146th row Sl st over first 3 sts, 2ch, work 1hdc into each of next 12 sts. Turn.

147th-149th rows Work to end. Turn.

150th row Sl st over first 3 sts, 2ch, 1hdc into each of next 9 sts, turn.
151st-153rd rows Work to end. Turn.
154th row Sl st over first 3 sts, 2ch, work 1hdc into each of next 3 sts, turn.
155th row Work a loop st into each of these 3 sts. Fasten off.

Face
Using size H (5.50mm) hook and A, make 4ch.
1st row 1sc into 2nd ch from hook, 1sc into each of next 2ch. Turn.
2nd row 1ch, 1sc into each sc to end. Turn.
3rd row Inc 3 sts by working 4ch, sl st into 2nd ch from hook, sl st into each of next 2ch, 1sc into each sc to end. Turn.
4th row Inc 3 sts by working 4ch, 1sc into 2nd ch from hook, 1sc into each of next 2ch, 1sc into each sc and sl st to end. Turn.
5th and 6th rows 1ch, 1sc into each st to end. Turn. 9sc.
7th row As 3rd row.
8th row Inc 6 sts by working 7ch, 1sc into 2nd ch from hook, 1sc into each st to end. Turn. 18sc.
9th and 10th rows 1ch, 1sc into each st to end. Turn.
11th row As 4th row. 21sc.
12th-14th rows 1ch, 1sc into each st to end. Turn.
15th row 1ch, 1sc into each of next 18sc, turn.
16th row 1ch, 1sc into each st to end.

Turn.
17th row As 3rd row.
18th row Sl st over first 3 sts, 1ch, 1sc into each st to end. Turn. 18sc.
19th and 20th rows 1ch, 1sc into each st to end. Turn.
21st row As 3rd row.
22nd and 23rd rows 1ch, 1sc into each st to end. Turn.
24th row Inc 2 sts as for 4th row, work to within last st, inc st by working 2sc into last st. Turn. 24sc.
25th row 1ch, 1sc in each st to end. Turn.
26th row 1ch, dec one st by working 2 sts tog, 1sc into each st to within last st, inc in last st. Turn.
27th row 1ch, inc one st, 1sc into each st to end. Turn.
28th row 1ch, dec one st, 1sc into each st to within last st, inc one st. Turn.
29th row 1ch, inc one st, 1sc into each sc to within last 2sc, dec one st. Turn.
30th row 1ch, dec one st, 1sc into each st to end. Turn.
31st row 1ch, 1sc into each st to within last 2 sts, dec one st. Turn.
32nd row 1ch, dec one st, 1sc into each st to end. Turn.
33rd row 1ch, 1sc into each st to within last 2 sts, dec one st. Turn.
34th-39th rows Rep 32nd and 33rd rows 3 times.
40th row 1ch, dec one st, 1sc into each st to end.
41st row 1ch, 1sc into each st to within last 2 sts, dec one st. Turn.
42nd row 1ch, dec one st, 1sc into each st to within last 2 sts, dec one st. Turn.
43rd row As 42nd.
44th row 1ch, dec one st, 1sc into each

st to end. Fasten off.

Ear
Using size H (5.50mm) hook and A, make 11ch.
1st row 1sc into 2nd ch from hook, 1sc into each ch to end. Turn.
Cont in sc, inc one st at each end of next 7 rows. 24 sts. Work 6 rows sc without shaping.
Now dec one sc at each end of next and foll 8 alternate rows ending with a row of sc.
Next row 1ch, (dec 1sc) twice. Turn.
Next row Work 2sc tog. Fasten off.

Tail
Using size H (5.50mm) hook and A, make 22ch.
1st row 1hdc into 3rd ch from hook, 1hdc into each ch to end. Turn.
2nd row Work one 8ch loop into each st to end. Turn. 20 loops.
3rd row 2ch, 1hdc into each of next 15hdc, turn.
4th row As 2nd row. 15 loops.
5th row 2ch, 1hdc into each of next 10hdc, turn.
6th row As 2nd row. 10 loops.
7th row 2ch, 1hdc into each of next hdc, turn.
8th row As 2nd row. 5 loops.
Fasten off.

To finish
Darn in all ends. Sew face to body and body to grass section. Sew 4in (10cm) of tail to body. Fold ear in half and sew top to face. Embroider eye in satin stitch and nose and mouth in stem stitch.

35in

41in

Terry Evans

Tray hanger

Four braids, made of yarn, make a simple, pretty hanger for trays.

Size
18½in (47cm) long.
To fit a tray up to 14in (35cm) wide.

Materials
A 3½ (9cm)-diameter wooden ring
3×8½yd (8m) skeins of tapestry yarn
in each of three harmonizing or
contrasting colors
Bunch of artificial flowers
Transparent tape
Matching thread

1 From each skein of yarn cut 24 pieces, each 30in (75cm) long. Divide the cut yarn into four equal groups.
2 Use one group from each of the three different colors to make four braids.
3 Wrap a piece of tape around each end of each braid to keep strands in place.
4 Cut five more pieces of yarn, each about 10in (25cm) long. Use one piece to bind four braids firmly at one end.
5 Slip the wooden ring between the braids at the bound end, so that two braids lie on each side. Using two more pieces of yarn, bind together one braid from the front and one from the back, just below the ring. Repeat with the remaining two braids.
6 Bind the braids together at their lower ends in the same pairs as above.
7 Place the bunch of flowers where the braids are fixed to the ring and sew them neatly in place, covering the binding.
8 Hang the holder up by the wooden ring.

Crochet / COURSE 59

Mitered corners in crochet

Mitered corners are worked from the inner to the outer edge in crochet, whether they are worked as a separate band to be sewn onto the garment afterward or worked directly onto the crochet fabric. The bands, which are most effective when worked in either single crochet or half doubles, can have either a pointed or rounded corner to create a mitered neat,

firm border for any crochet fabric.
A narrow edging worked in the same color as the main fabric will neaten the edges of your fabric; a wide edging worked in one or more contrasting colors can become a feature of a cardigan, bedspread or afghan. Remember when working down the side of your fabric that you will need to work into the row end

of your fabric. As a general rule you will need to work one stitch into each row end when working into a single crochet or half double fabric; whereas for a double or triple fabric you should work two or three stitches into each row end so that the fabric lies flat once the border has been completed.

Pointed mitered corner

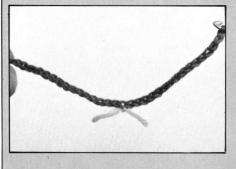

1 To work a separate band, calculate the number of chains you will need for the length of the edging, adding one extra turning chain for single crochet and half doubles. Mark the corner chain with a colored thread.

2 Work a single crochet into 3rd chain from hook, then into each single crochet to colored marker. Now make 2 chains, then work a single crochet into the next chain for the first corner group.

3 Work 1 single crochet into each chain to end. Now turn, make 1 chain and work a single crochet into each stitch to the corner 2 chain. Work 1 single crochet into each of these 2 chains. Continue in single crochet to the end of the row.

4 On the next row work back to corner in single crochet, noting that you will work one more single crochet this time before the corner is reached. Now make 2 chains as before and work to the end in single crochet with one more stitch on this side of the corner.

5 On the next row work in single crochet only, working a single crochet into each of the 2 chains made in the previous row. To make the band wider repeat the last 2 rows, noting that you will work an extra stitch on each side when working the 2-chain row. Always complete the band with a single crochet row.

6 Here the same edging has been worked directly onto a single crochet fabric. Work a single crochet into each row end down side of the fabric, 1 single crochet, 2 chains and 1 single crochet at the corner, then a single crochet into each stitch along the lower edge. The 2nd row is worked as before, with one single crochet into each stitch and 2 chains.

Frederick Mancini

Rounded mitered corner

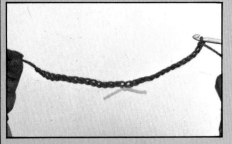

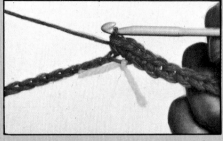

1 Calculate the number of chains needed for a separate edging in the same way as for a pointed corner (see step 1, page 17) and mark the center or corner chain as before.

2 Work 1 single crochet into 3rd chain from hook, then into each chain to the marked corner chain. Now work 3 single crochets into the corner chain. The middle of these 3 stitches will be the corner stitch on the next row.

3 Work in single crochet to the end of the row. On the next row make 1 chain, then work 1 single crochet into each stitch, including the 3 single crochets at the corner, to the end of the row.

4 On the next row work a single crochet into each stitch to the corner. Now work 3 single crochets into the corner stitch and work in single crochet to the end of the row. Note that there should be one more single crochet worked on each side of the corner in this row.

5 Turn and work in single crochet as before, without shaping, to the end of the row. To make the edging wider continue to repeat the last two rows each time, noting that you will work one more single crochet on each side of the corner when working the increase row each time.

6 Here the same edging has been worked in half doubles directly onto a crochet fabric. Work a half double into each row end or stitch, working 3 half doubles into the corner of the fabric. Work 2nd row in half doubles only, with one more stitch on each side of the corner. Repeat these two rows for width required.

V-neck shaping

V-neck shaping is usually started at the same time as the armhole shaping, although it can be made deeper or shallower.

The shaping at the neck edge must be completed at the same time as, or before, the shoulder shaping has been completed. When working a deep V-neck, you will decrease gradually at the neck edge, working the armhole shaping at the same time when necessary and then working without shaping once the neck shaping has been completed until the shoulder has been reached. For a V-neck which starts either at the same level or higher than the armhole shaping, you will have to decrease more sharply to complete the neck shaping by the time shoulder shaping has been completed. Your directions will tell you exactly how many stitches to decrease at the neck edge; our pictures are intended to act just as a general guide to help you when working a V-neck.

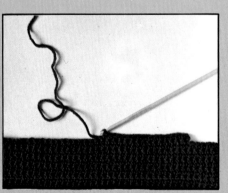

1 Each side of a V-neck is worked separately. Divide the stitches on the front of the fabric evenly by working to the center of the fabric. Leave the remaining stitches unworked. Make sure that there are the same number of stitches on each side of the V.

2 Your directions will tell you exactly how many stitches should be decreased at the neck edge, depending on the depth of the V. For a normal V-neckline starting at the same level as the armhole, one stitch is usually decreased on every 3rd or 4th row. For a neat edge work 2 stitches together inside the first or last stitch each time.

3 With the right side of the front facing return to the remaining unworked stitches. Rejoin the yarn to the next stitch by drawing a loop through then working a single crochet into the same stitch.

4 Work the second side in exactly the same way as the first, but reverse the shaping, so that stitches decreased at the beginning of the row (neck edge) on the first side will be decreased at the end of the row (neck edge) on the second side, and vice versa. It is quite easy to miscount when working armhole and neck shaping at the same time, so make sure to work armhole shaping at side edge using a row counter if necessary.

5 Where there is an odd number of stitches in a pattern, or for a more widely spaced V-shape, leave one stitch unworked in the center of the neck shaping as shown here, making sure that there are the same number of stitches on each side of the center stitch.

V-neck borders

Borders for a V-neck can either be crocheted directly onto the garment or be worked as a separate piece and sewn on afterward.

Whatever the method, single crochet or half doubles produce the best results, since they make a firm border which does not curl at the outer edge once it has been completed.

The borders can be used simply as a means of making the V-neck neater, in which case one or two rows of single crochet worked directly onto the fabric will be enough. By working several rows in a contrasting yarn using the pointed corner method (see page 17), you can make the border a prominent feature of the garment.

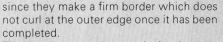

1 With the right side of the front facing, join the yarn to the top right-hand corner of the V-neck and work a single crochet into each row end down the first side, then work the last two stitches together on this side of the center point to decrease one stitch. For a double fabric work two or three stitches into each row end to maintain an even fabric.

2 Work the first two stitches together on the second side of the neck to decrease one stitch, then work a single crochet into the end of each row up the second side of the V. Always work the same number of stitches on each side of the neckline. For a wider edging continue in single crochet rows, decreasing a stitch at each side of center point on every row.

3 To make a separate V-neck band, calculate the number of chains needed to fit around neck edge and make a pointed mitered corner at the center as shown above. Overcast neck border neatly to V-neck edge, using same color yarn as main fabric (below).

Frederick Mancini

V-neck pullover and cardigan

Make this classic sweater set to wear many different ways.

Sizes

Pullover To fit 34[36:38:40]in (87[92: 97:102]cm) bust.
Length, 21[21:21¼:21¼]in (53[53:54: 54]cm).
Jacket To fit as pullover.
Length, 23[24:24½:25]in (59[61.5:62: 64]cm).
Sleeve seam, 17[17:17¾:17¾]in (43.5[43.5:45:45]cm).
Note: Directions for larger sizes are in brackets []; if there is only one set of figures it applies to all sizes.

Materials

Pullover *6[7:8:8]oz (160[180:200: 200]g) of a sport yarn in main color (A)*
3oz (60g) in contrasting color (B)
Size E (3.50mm) crochet hook
Jacket *12[13:15:16]oz (340[360: 400:420]g) in main color (A)*
3oz (60g) in contrasting color (B)
Size E (3.50mm) crochet hook

Gauge

2 patt repeats measure 1¼in (3cm) in width using size E (3.50mm) hook.

Pullover

Back

Using size E (3.50mm) hook and A, make 84[90:93:99]ch.
Base row Work 2dc into 3rd ch from hook, *skip next 2ch, 1sc and 2dc into next ch, rep from * to end, finishing 2ch, 1sc into last ch. Turn.
Patt row 2ch, 2dc into first sc, *1sc and 2dc into next sc, rep from * to end, 1sc into turning ch. Turn.
Rep patt row until work measures 10in (25.5cm). 27[29:30:32] patts.
Shape armholes
1st row Sl st across first 2dc, 1sc and 2dc into next sc, 2ch, 2dc into same sc, work in patt to end, finishing 1sc into 2nd sc from end. Turn and leave rem sts unworked.
2nd row 3ch, 1sc and 2dc into next sc, work in patt to end, finishing 1sc into top of turning ch. Turn.
Rep 2nd row 5[5:5:7] times more. 17[19:20:20] complete patts.
Next row 2ch, 2dc into first sc, work in patt, finishing with 1sc into top of turning ch. Turn.
Cont straight until armholes measure 7¾[7¾:8:8]in (19.5[19.5:20.5:20.5]cm).
Shape shoulders and neck
1st row Sl st to 3rd sc, 2ch, 2dc into same sc, 1sc and 2dc into next sc, 1sc into next

sc. Fasten off.
Return to rem sts. Do not turn work but rejoin yarn to 4th sc from other armhole edge.
Next row 2ch, *1sc and 2dc into next sc, rep from * once more, 1sc into next dc. Fasten off.

Front

Work as for back until front measures one row less than back to armholes.
Shape neck and armholes
1st row 2ch, 2dc into first sc, *1sc and 2dc into next sc, rep from * 11[12:13:14] times more, 1sc into next (center) sc, turn.
2nd row 3ch, skip sc at base of hook, 1sc and 2dc into next sc, work in patt finishing 1sc into 2nd sc from end, turn.
3rd row 3ch, 1sc and 2dc into next sc, work in patt to end finishing with 1sc into top of turning ch. Turn.
4th row 2ch, 1dc into first sc, work in patt, ending 1sc into top of turning ch. Turn.
5th row 3ch, 1sc and 2dc into next sc, work in patt, ending with 1sc into top of

turning ch. Turn.
6th row 3ch, skip sc at base of ch, work in patt, ending with 1sc into top of turning ch. Turn.
7th row 3ch, 1sc and 2dc into next sc, work in patt, finishing with 1sc into turning chain. Turn.
8th row As 4th.
3rd and 4th sizes only
Rep 5th, 6th and 7th rows once more.
All sizes
Cont to dec at neck edge only as before, until 4 complete patts rem.
Cont straight until work measures same as back to beg of shoulder shaping, ending at armhole edge.
Next row Sl st to 3rd sc, 2ch, 2dc into same sc, 1sc and 2dc into next sc, 1sc into top of turning ch. Fasten off.
Return to rem sts. Do not turn work but rejoin yarn to center sc, 3ch, patt to end. Complete as for first side, reversing shaping.
Armhole borders (make 2)
Using size E (3.50mm) hook and B, make 79[79:83:83]ch.

1st row 1sc into 2nd ch from hook, 1sc into each ch to end. Turn.

2nd row 1ch, skip first sc, 1sc into each st to end. Turn.

3rd row 1ch, 1sc into each of next 4sc, work next 2sc tog—called dec 1sc—, 1sc into each of next 4sc, dec 1sc, 1sc into each sc until 13sc rem, dec 1sc, 1sc into each of next 4sc, dec 1sc, 1sc into each st to end. Turn.

Rep 2nd and 3rd rows twice. Fasten off.

Neck border

Using size E (3.50mm) hook and B, make 106[108:112:114]ch.

1st row 1sc into 2nd ch from hook, 1sc into each of next 14[15:15:16]ch, place a colored marker here, 1sc into each of next 37[37:39:39]ch, place 2nd colored marker here, 1sc into each of next 37[37:39:39]ch, place 3rd colored marker here, 1sc into each sc to end. Turn. Beg each row with 1ch, work 6 rows sc, dec 1sc at each side of 2nd (center) marker on every row and dec 1sc **before** first marker and 1sc **after** 3rd marker on first, 3rd and 6th rows. Fasten off.

Waistband

Using size E (3.50mm) hook and B, make 18ch.

Base row 1hdc into 3rd ch from hook, 1hdc into each ch to end. Turn.

1st row 2ch, *yo, insert hook from right to left behind stem of next hdc and work 1dc—called 1dcB—rep from * to end, working last 1dcB around turning ch. Turn.

2nd row 2ch, 1hdc into each dc to end. Turn. Rep first and 2nd rows until waistband measures 15½[16:16½:17]in (39.5[41:42:43]cm); end with a first row. Fasten off.

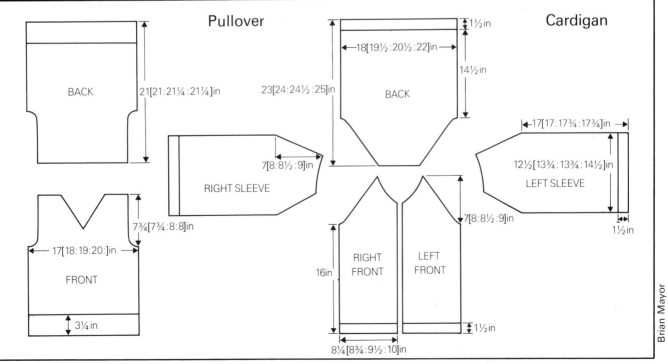

Stuart Macleod

Make another piece in the same way.

To finish
Do not press. Join shoulder seams. With RS facing place ch edge of one armhole border one stitch over main part and backstitch in place through each ch. Sew ends of border in place. Join row ends of neck edging to form center back seam. Place neck edging on RS and backstitch in place. Sew waistbands to front and back. Join side seams.

Cardigan

Back
Using size E (3.50mm) hook and A, make 90[96:102:108]ch. Work base row as for pullover back, 29[31:33:35] patts. Cont in patt until work measures 14½in (37cm).

Shape raglan armholes
1st row Sl st across to next sc, 1sc and 1dc into same sc, patt to end, working 1sc into last sc. Turn.
2nd row 3ch, skip first sc, work in patt to end. Turn.
3rd row As 2nd.
4th row 2ch, 1dc into first sc to count as first patt, patt to end, working 1sc into last sc. Turn.
Rep 2nd to 4th rows 4[5:5:6] times more, then 2nd row 8 times more. 9[9:11:11] patts. Fasten off.

Left front
Using size E (3.50mm) hook and A, make

63[69:69:72]ch.

42[45:48:51]ch. Work base row as for pullover back. 13[14:15:16] patts. Cont in patt until work measures 14½in (37cm).

Shape raglan armhole
1st row Patt to end, 1sc into last sc. Turn.
2nd row 3ch, skip sc at base of these 3ch, patt to end. Turn.
3rd row 2ch, patt to end. Turn.
4th row 2ch, 1dc into sc at base of these 2ch, patt to end. Turn.
5th row As 3rd, ending 1sc into top of turning ch.
Rep 2nd to 5th rows 3[3:3:4] times more, then 2nd row once. 7[8:9:9] patts.

Shape neck
1st row 3ch, 1sc and 2dc into next sc, patt to end.
Turn.
2nd row As 4th armhole shaping row.
3rd-5th rows As first neck shaping row.
3rd size only
Dec one more st at neck edge as before.
4th size only
Dec 2 more sts at neck edge as before.
All sizes
Cont to dec at armhole edge only until one patt rems.
Next row 3ch, 1sc into top of turning ch. Fasten off.

Right front
Work as for left front (work reversible).

Left sleeve
Using size E (3.50mm) hook and A, make 63[69:69:72]ch.

Work base row as for pullover back. 20[22:22:23] patts. Rep patt row until work measures 15½[15½:16¼:16¼]in (39.5[39.5:41:41]cm), noting that last 2 row ends are sewn to armhole.

Shape raglan
1st row 3ch, skip sc at base of these 3ch, patt to end. Turn.
2nd row As first.
3rd row 2ch, 1dc into sc at base of these 2ch (counted as one patt), patt to end working 1sc into last sc. Turn.
Rep first, 2nd and 3rd rows 5[6:6:8] times more, then first row 4[4:4:1] times more.
Next row Sl st across 1 patt, patt to end. Fasten off.

Right sleeve
Work as for left sleeve; work is reversible.

Sleeve borders (make 2)
Using size E (3.50mm) hook and B, make 59[65:65:68]ch.
1st row 1sc into 2nd ch from hook, 1sc into each ch to end. Turn.
Work 7 more row sc.
Fasten off.

Back border
Using size E (3.50mm) hook and B, make 84[90:96:102]ch and work as for sleeve edging.

Left front border
Using size E (3.50mm) hook and B, make a ch the length of lower edge on left front, place colored marker on ch, cont to make a ch to fit up left front edge to neck edge, place another colored marker here, then cont until ch is long enough to reach center back neck edge.
1st row 1sc into 2nd ch from hook, 1sc into each ch to end. Turn.
2nd row 1ch, 1sc into each sc to first marker (lower corner), 2ch, 1sc into each sc to 2nd marker, 3sc into marked st, 1sc into each sc to end. Turn.
3rd row Work in sc, working 1sc into each of 3sc at neck edge corner, 1sc into each of 2sc at corner of lower edge. Turn.
4th row 1ch, 1sc into each sc to first marker, working last sc into first sc worked into ch, 2ch, 1sc into each sc to center of 3 increased sc, 3sc into center sc, 1sc into each sc to end. Turn.
5th row As 3rd.
Rep 2nd to 4th rows once more. Fasten off.

Right front border
Work as for left front border, reversing position of neck and lower edges.

To finish
Do not press. Set in sleeves, sewing last two row ends on sleeves to first patt skipped on back and fronts. Sew on edgings as for pullover. Join side and sleeve seams.

A case for pencils

This pretty pencil case may encourage a little girl to keep all her pens and crayons together.

Finished size
$9\frac{1}{2} \times 6\frac{1}{4}$in (24×16cm).

Materials
Piece of quilted floral fabric $15\frac{1}{4} \times 9\frac{1}{2}$in (39×24cm)
Piece of solid-color vinyl fabric $14\frac{1}{2} \times 9\frac{1}{2}$in (37×24cm)
Bias binding to match vinyl fabric
Colored pencil to match vinyl fabric, about 4in (10cm) long
Matching thread; craft knife

1 Place vinyl and quilted fabric pieces together, wrong sides facing and short edges matching at one end. Pin and baste across end. The quilted fabric will be $\frac{3}{4}$in (2cm) longer at the opposite short side; this will be taken up when the layers are folded.
2 Bind the stitched short edges with bias binding: open out binding and place right side down on fabric side of case. Pin, baste and stitch along the creased line of the binding.
3 Fold binding over edge to vinyl fabric side. Pin, baste and slip stitch remaining edge of binding in place.
4 Fold the bound edge up for 6in (15cm) with vinyl inside, form the case. The flap will be about $2\frac{3}{4}$in (7cm) deep. Pin in place.
5 Place the remaining short edges (the flap) together. Trim off corners into neat curves.
6 For fastening loops, cut a 6in (15cm) piece of bias binding. Fold binding in half lengthwise, with the raw edges inside. Pin, baste and stitch down the length close to edges. Cut strip in half.
7 Fold each length of binding in half to make loops. Position on each loop on the vinyl side of the flap just inside the corners, about $3\frac{1}{2}$in (9cm) apart, with raw edges matching and loops pointing inward. Pin and baste in place.
8 Bind the remaining raw edges with bias binding. Open out bias binding and, starting at one lower corner, position the binding on front of case, right sides together and raw edges matching, leaving an extra $\frac{1}{4}$in (5mm) at each lower corner. Pin, baste and stitch along creased line of binding, catching in loops.
9 Fold binding over the edge to the back of the case. Tuck in the raw edges of binding at corners. Pin, baste and slip stitch free edge of binding to case.
10 Fold loops up over bound edge, so that

they extend beyond the bound edge. Hand-sew them to binding.
11 Fold the flap down over the case and mark the positions of the toggles on the case front.
12 With a sharp craft knife cut two pieces of pencil, each $1\frac{1}{2}$in (4cm) long.

13 Sharpen one end of each pencil piece. Carefully cut a small groove in the center of each.
14 Using the center grooves to hold the threads, sew the pencils in place with the sharpened ends pointing outward, sewing through the quilted fabric only.

Crochet / COURSE 60

Color and design in patchwork crochet

The imaginative use of color and careful planning are very important in patchwork crochet and can make the difference between a really superb, original design and an untidy, haphazard-looking fabric. When using a large number of colors you will obtain the best results by using only one shape—a square, hexagon or diamond, for example—so that the colors rather than the shapes create the patchwork effect. Conversely, if you are using several shapes for the patchwork, you should confine your design to a few colors for the best results.

Plan your design carefully before you start, mapping it out on graph paper if necessary and making sample motifs in the colors of your choice to make sure that all the colors can be combined successfully. Some colors which seem to be very bright when looked at by themselves can lose their color considerably when placed beside another bright color. Patchwork crochet fabrics are ideal for afghans and bedspreads, but you need not confine yourself to making only square or rectangular-shaped fabrics; it is possible to make many garments this way.

Hexagon

These step-by-step photographs show you how to work the hexagon shape used to make the beautiful flower motif afghan shown on page 29, but you could use the motif in many different ways for a variety of patchwork patterns.

1 Use one color for the hexagon. Make 6 chains and join into a circle with a slip stitch. Make 4 chains for the first triple. Crochet over extra yarn while working the first round to avoid darning it into the back of the motif once it has been completed.

2 Make 2 more chains and work a triple into the circle. Continue to make 2 chains followed by a triple until there are 12 triples in all, including the first 4 chains. Make 2 chains and join the last chain to the 4th of the first 4 chains with a slip stitch.

3 Now start to shape the hexagon. Slip stitch to the first 2-chain space so that the yarn is in the correct position to start the next round. Make 3 chains to count as the first double. Work 1 double, 2 chains and 2 doubles all into the same space for the first corner.

4 Work 3 doubles into the next 2-chain space, followed by a corner consisting of 2 doubles, 2 chains and 2 doubles worked into the following 2-chain space. This completes the first side of the hexagon.

5 Continue to work around the circle in the same way, with 3 doubles into one 2-chain space and a corner group into the next 2-chain space until there are 6 corners in all. Complete the round with 3 doubles worked into the last space, joining the last stitch to the 3rd of the first 3 chains with a slip stitch.

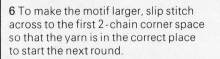

6 To make the motif larger, slip stitch across to the first 2-chain corner space so that the yarn is in the correct place to start the next round.

7 Now make the first corner as before, working 3 chains to count as the first double, then 1 double, 2 chains and 2 doubles all into the first space.

8 Now work a double into each stitch to the corner space, then another corner group into the next 2-chain corner space as before.

9 Continue around the motif in this way, making sure that there are the same number of doubles on each side of the hexagon. Join the last double to the first with a slip stitch. You should have 10 doubles between each 2-chain corner space.

10 When using more than one color in a motif, fasten off the yarn at the end of one round by drawing the yarn through the last loop. Join the new yarn to *any* corner space by making a slip knot on the hook. Draw the new yarn through the corner space and the slip loop to hold it firmly in place.

11 Continue around the motif in the correct pattern with the new yarn, working over the spare end of yarn (held at the back of the work), at the same time as working the pattern so that you will not need to darn in this end once the motif has been completed.

Fred Mancini

Finishing a patchwork fabric

Be careful when completing your patchwork fabric to ensure perfect results. It would be a shame to spoil your design at the last moment after many hours spent carefully making all the motifs needed for your design. It is worth a few extra moments spent darning any loose ends into the wrong side of the work to make sure that the back of the fabric is as neat as the front and that all the motifs are sewn together neatly and evenly.

1 Once all the motifs have been completed, darn all the loose ends into the wrong side. Take the yarn under the top loops of two or three stitches in one direction, then under two or three stitches in the other direction to secure it. Cut the yarn as close to the crochet as possible to ensure a neat fabric.

2 To sew the motifs together, use either the same yarn or, if this is too thick, a matching yarn in a finer ply. Two strands of the same yarn can also be used. Hold the motifs with *right* sides together and overcast along the top edge, drawing the yarn (not too tightly) under the top two loops of each stitch.

Stitch Wise

Two-color hexagon

Note: Change color by drawing new yarn through last 2 loops of last stitch worked in previous color and work over spare yarn when carrying it across the back of the work. Use 2 colors, A and B. Using A, make 6ch and join into a circle with a sl st.

1st round Using A, work 1ch 9sc into circle. Join with a sl st to first ch. 10sc.

2nd round Using A, work 1ch, 1sc into first st, now work 2sc into each st all around circle, changing color on every 3rd stitch. Join with a sl st to first ch. 3 blocks of 3 sts in A alternated with 3 blocks of 3 sts in B.

3rd round Keeping color sequence correct, work 1ch, 1sc into first st, 1sc into next st, 2sc into next st changing to B on last st, using B* work 2sc into next st, 1sc into next st and 2sc into next st, changing to A on last st, rep from * twice more. Join with a sl st to first ch. 5sc in each block.

4th round Keeping color sequence correct, work 1ch, 1sc into each sc to end. Join with a sl st to first ch.

5th round Keeping color sequence correct, work 1ch, 1sc into first st, *1sc into each of next 3 sts, (2sc into next st) twice, rep from * to end, working 2sc into last st in B, changing to A on last st. Join with a sl st to first ch. 7sc in each block.

6th round As 4th.

7th round Keeping color sequence correct, work 1ch, 1sc into first st, *1sc into each of next 5 sts, 2sc into next st changing color on last st, 1ch, 2sc into next st, rep from * 4 times more, 1sc into each of next 5 sts, 2sc into next st changing color on last st, 1ch. Join with a sl st to first ch. Fasten off.

Cluster square

Make 6 chains and join into a circle with a sl st.

1st round 3ch, keeping last loop of each st on hook work 2dc into circle, yo and draw through all 3 loops on hook—called Cl2—, *2ch, keeping last loop of each st on hook work 3dc into circle, yo and draw through all loops on hook—called Cl3—, rep from * 6 times more, 2ch. Join with sl st to 3rd of first 3ch.

2nd round Sl st into first 2ch sp, 3ch, Cl2 into same space, 3ch, Cl3 into same sp, *2ch, 2sc into next 2ch sp, 2ch, (Cl3, 2ch, Cl3) into next 2ch sp, rep from * twice more, 2ch, 2sc into next 2ch sp, 2ch. Join with sl st to 3rd of first 3ch.

3rd round Sl st into first 3ch corner sp, 3ch, Cl2 into same sp, 3ch, Cl3 into same sp, *1ch, 2dc into next 2ch sp, 1dc into each of next 2 sts, 2dc into next 2ch sp, 1ch,

3 Pin out the crochet, making sure the motifs are running in straight, even lines. Press the completed fabric lightly with a damp cloth if appropriate. Do not press too firmly or the crochet will become flattened, losing the texture of the stitches. Where a large piece is to be pressed, divide the work into sections.

4 Work a single crochet row all the way around the edges of your patchwork, using one of the colors used for the motifs, to make a neat, firm edge.

5 Shawls, blankets and bedspreads are enhanced by adding a deep fringe to the edge of the fabric, knotting the fringe into the single crochet row as shown above. Garments can be trimmed with either picot or shell edgings (see Volume 4, page 26 and Volume 7, page 5), crocheting onto the basic single crochet edging.

Fred Mancini

(Cl3, 3ch, Cl3) into next 2ch sp (corner), rep from * twice more, 1ch, 2dc into next 2ch sp, 1dc into each of next 2 sts, 2dc into next 2ch sp, 1ch. Join with sl st to 3rd of first 3ch.
4th round Sl st into first 2ch sp, 3ch, Cl2 into same sp, 3ch, Cl3 into same sp, *1ch, 2dc into next sp, 1dc into each of next 6 sts, 2dc into next sp, 1ch, (Cl3, 3ch, Cl3) into next 3ch corner sp, rep from * twice more, 1ch, 2dc into next sp, 1dc into each of next 6 sts, 2dc into next sp, 1ch. Join with sl st to 3rd of first 3ch. Fasten off.

Octagon

Make 6 chains. Join in circle with sl st.
1st round 2ch to count as first hdc, work 15hdc into circle. Join with sl st to 2nd of first 2 ch. 16 hdc.
2nd round 5ch to count as first dc and

2ch sp, 1dc into same st, 1dc into next st, *(1dc, 2ch, 1dc) into next st, 1dc into next st, rep from * to end. Join with sl st to 3rd of first 5ch. Eight 2-ch corner spaces.
3rd round Sl st into first 2ch sp, 4ch to count as first hdc and 2ch sp, 1hdc into same sp, 1hdc into each of next 3 sts, *(1hdc, 2ch, 1hdc) into next 2ch sp, 1hdc into each of next 3 sts, rep from * to end. Join with sl st to 2nd of first 4ch.
4th round Sl st into first 2ch sp, 5ch to count as first dc and 2ch sp, 1dc into same sp, 1dc into each of next 5 sts, *(1dc, 2ch, 1dc) into next 2ch sp, 1dc into each of next 5 sts, rep from * to end. Join with sl st to 3rd of first 5ch. Fasten off.

Triangle

Make 4ch and join into a circle with sl st.
1st round 1ch to count as first sc, work 11sc into circle. Join with a sl st to first

ch. 12sc.
2nd round 3ch to count as first dc, 4dc into same st at base of 3ch, *1hdc into next st, 1sc into next st, 1hdc into next st, 5dc into next st, rep from * once more, 1hdc into next st, 1sc into next st, 1hdc into next st. Join with a sl st into 3rd of first 3ch.
3rd round Sl st to center dc of first 5dc group, 3ch, 4dc into same place at base of 3ch, *hdc into each of next 7 sts, 5dc into next (corner) st, rep from * once more, 1hdc into each of next 7 sts. Join with a sl st to 3rd of first 3ch.
4th round Sl st to center of first 5dc corner group, 2ch to count as first hdc, (1hdc, 1ch, 2hdc) into same st, *1hdc into each st to next dc at center of next corner group, (2hdc, 1ch, 2hdc) into center dc, rep from * once more, 1hdc into each st to end. Join with sl st to 3rd of first 3ch. Fasten off.

Flower afghan

While away long winter evenings by making hexagonal motifs in coordinating and contrasting shades, and then sew them together to make a vivid patchwork blanket.

Size
Approx 69 × 54in (176 × 137cm).

Materials
23oz (640g) of a knitting worsted in main color (white)
4oz (100g) in each of 2 contrasting colors (dark pink and blue)
3oz (80g) in each of 5 contrasting colors (orange, light pink, yellow, emerald and jade)
Size F (4.00mm) crochet hook

Note *If altering the size of the afghan, allow 1oz (28.35g) of yarn for 11 motifs.*

Gauge
One motif measures 3½in (9cm) across widest part worked on size F (4.00mm) hook.

Motif
Using size F (4.00mm) hook and white, make 6ch, sl st into first ch to form a ring.
1st round 6ch, 1tr into ring, *2ch, 1tr into ring, rep from * 9 times more, 2ch, sl st into 4th of the 6ch.
2nd round Sl st into next sp, 3ch, 1dc, 2ch and 2dc into same sp as sl st, *3dc into next sp, 2dc, 2ch and 2dc all into next sp, rep from * 4 times more, 3dc into next sp, sl st into top of 3ch. Fasten off.
Make 248 more motifs in white, then make 36 each in dark pink and blue, 32 in orange and 30 each in light pink, yellow, emerald and jade.

To finish
Following diagram, join motifs.
Using white, work a row of sc around edge, working 2sc into each sp at outer corners of each motif and working 2sc tog at inner corners (i.e. at each joining).

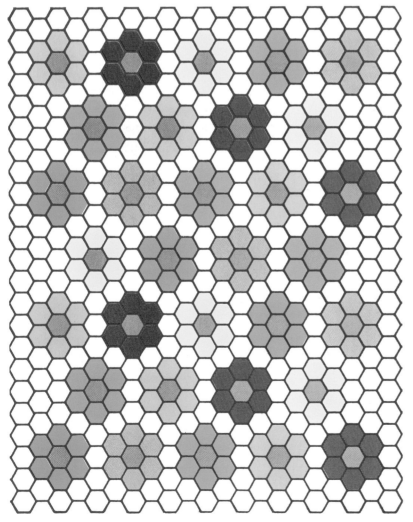

Knitting / COURSE 56

Using bobbins in jacquard knitting

One major problem with multi-colored knitting, where you may be using several balls of yarn across a row, is preventing them from becoming tangled. The yarns have a tendency to twist around each other and you must spend time at the end of each row untangling all the strands.

Cut-out cardboard bobbins are a solution to the tangling problem in jacquard knitting if small, separate balls of yarn are required. Wind the yarn onto the bobbins before you begin to work. As you knit, the bobbins hang at the back of the fabric, are easy to handle and prevent too many tangles.

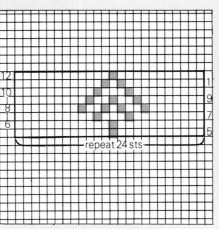

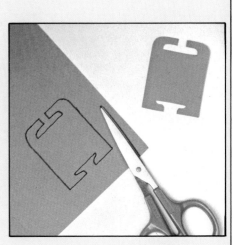

1 When working a jacquard motif or repeating design, first calculate the number of small, separate balls of yarn you need. For example, this section of mosaic pattern needs a separate ball each time it is repeated across a row; If you have 97 stitches in the fabric, you will have 4 repeats of the pattern across the row and correspondingly need 4 bobbins of yarn.

2 Use stiff cardboard to make the bobbins. Draw a shape as shown in the diagram, making it about 1½in (4cm) across and 2in (5cm) deep. Cut out each bobbin with a pair of scissors. Make as many bobbins as there are small, separate balls of yarn.

3 Wind the yarn from the main ball of color evenly around the center of the bobbin until it is as full as necessary. The working end of yarn should flow from the slit at the top.

4 In working this section of mosaic pattern, small amounts of color C are wound around bobbins. The main colors A and B are stranded and woven throughout the rows from the main balls. Keep the working yarn from the bobbin fairly short to prevent it from tangling with an adjacent yarn.

5 At the end of a row on the wrong side of the work, the main color is in position at the side. The bobbins hang neatly down from their respective areas of color without being tangled.

Multi-colored stranding

Working multi-colored jacquard designs sometimes involves stranding the yarns not in use loosely across the back of the work. This is particularly important where there is more than one color in a row but where using bobbins is not practical. You must be constantly aware of your stitch gauge over a patterned section, checking it and using one size larger needles over the jacquard design if it becomes tighter than the rest. Change color carefully, always pulling the stitches equally tightly.

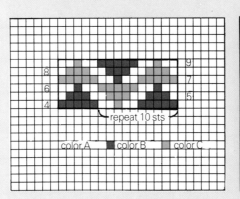

color A color B color C

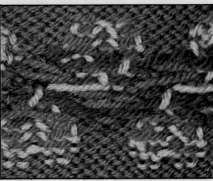

Mike Berend

1 This chart represents rows 4 to 9 of the zig-zag heart motif border in Stitch Wise. In these rows 3 colors are stranded simultaneously across each row.
Join in the main balls of all 3 colors at the beginning of the 5th row and work stranded knitting as usual, remembering to weave in any yarn carried across more than 5 stitches (i.e. color C in 5th row should be woven in with 3rd of 5 stitches in B).

2 Here you can see the wrong side of the complete 12 rows of pattern: it must be neat and tidy to prevent a lumpy mass of strands from bulging through the front of the fabric. Remember to weave all the strands in with the last stitch of every row so that each color spans a complete row.

Stitch Wise

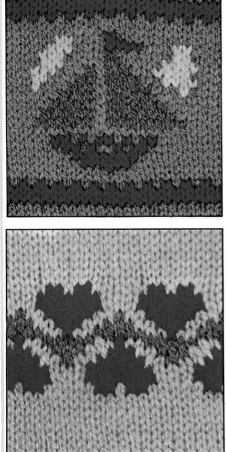

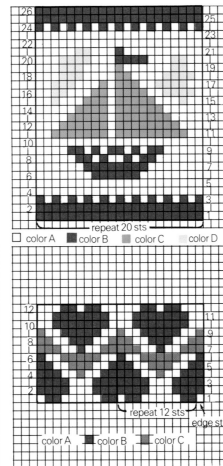

color A color B color C color D

repeat 20 sts

color A color B color C

repeat 12 sts
edge st

Ship motif border

Using B, cast on a multiple of 21 stitches. Note the following points when working the pattern from the chart. Join in color A on the 3rd row; strand A and B across this row, and at the end cut off B.
In rows 6 to 9 the base of each ship needs a small, separate ball of B, as does each area of background (A) between them. Each set of sails requires a separate ball of color C, as do the pairs of clouds in D *between* motifs: strand the yarn between the clouds in the pair. The flag in B on top of each ship must also be worked with a separate ball of yarn.

Zig-zag heart motif border

You need a multiple of 12 stitches to repeat this design, plus one extra to make it balance across a row. There is no need to use separate balls of yarn. See the step-by-step sequence on multi-colored stranding for further details.

Child's hooded sweater

This sweater—suitable for both girls and boys—is really cozy on chilly days.

Sizes
To fit 26[28:30:32]in (66[71:76:83]cm) chest.

Chris Harvey

Length to back neck, 19¼[20¾:22¼:24]in (48[52:56:60]cm).
Sleeve seam, 15½[16:17:17¾]in (39[41:43:45]cm).
Note: Directions for larger sizes are in brackets []; if there is only one set of figures it applies to all sizes.

Materials
16[18:20:22]oz (450[500:550:600]g) of a knitting worsted in main color (A)
4oz (100g) each of contrasting colors (B and C)
1 pair each Nos. 6 and 8 (4½ and 5½mm) knitting needles
2 toggles

Gauge
17 sts and 20 rows to 4in (10cm) in stockinette st on No. 8 (5½mm) needles.

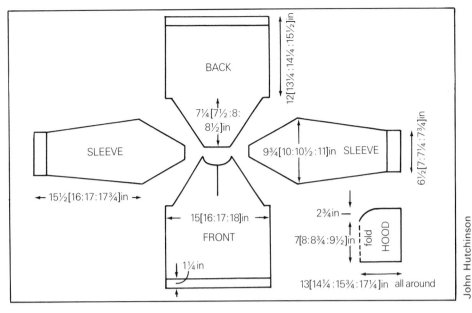

John Hutchinson

Back
Using No. 6 (4½mm) needles and A, cast on 65[69:73:77] sts.
1st row K1, *P1, K1, rep from * to end.
2nd row P1, *K1, P1, rep from * to end.
Rep these 2 rows for 1¼in (3cm); end with a 2nd row. Change to No. 8 (5½mm) needles. Beg with a K row, cont in stockinette st, working 2 rows each in C, B and A. Wind off 3 small balls of C and 2 of B to work motifs; use a separate ball for each motif, but carry A across row.
1st row K8 A, *1 C, 7[8:9:10] A, 2 B, 5 A, 2 B, 7[8:9:10] A, rep from * once more, 1 C, 8 A.
2nd row P7 A, *3 C, 5[6:7:8] A, 4 B, 3 A, 4 B, 5[6:7:8] A, rep from * once more, 3 C, 7 A.
3rd row K6 A, *5 C, 4[5:6:7] A, 5 B, 1 A, 5 B, 4[5:6:7] A, rep from * once more, 5 C, 6 A.
4th row P5 A, *7 C, 3[4:5:6] A, 11 B, 3[4:5:6] A, rep from * once more, 7 C, 5 A.
5th row K4 A, *9 C, 3[4:5:6] A, 9 B, 3[4:5:6] A, rep from * once more, 9 C, 4 A.
6th row As 5th, but P instead of K.
7th row K3 A, *11 C, 3[4:5:6] A, 7 B, 3[4:5:6] A, rep from * once, 11 C, 3 A.
8th row P3 A, *5 C, 1 A, 5 C, 4[5:6:7] A, 5 B, 4[5:6:7] A, rep from * once more, 5 C, 1 A, 5 C, 3 A.
9th row K3 A, *4 C, 3 A, 4 C, 5[6:7:8] A, 3 B, 5[6:7:8] A, rep from * once more, 4 C, 3 A, 4 C, 3 A.
10th row P4 A, *2 C, 5 A, 2 C, 7[8:9:10] A, 1 B, 7[8:9:10] A, rep from * once more, 2 C, 5 A, 2 C, 4 A.
Work 2 more rows each in A, B and C. Cut off contrasting colors. Cont in stockinette st with A only until work measures 9½[10¾:11¾:13]in (24[27:30:33]cm); end with a P row. Work 2 rows each in C, B and A. Work motifs again, reversing patt and colors by starting with 10th row and working back to 1st row, reading P for K and K for P, also B for C and C for B. After completing 10 motif rows, work 1 row with A.

Shape armholes
Next row Using A, bind off 4 sts, P to last 4 sts, bind off 4. Join in B.
Next row Using B, K1, sl 1, K1, psso, K to last 3 sts, K2 tog, K1.
Next row Using B, P to end. Cut off B.
Rep last 2 rows using C. Cut off C. **.
Using A, rep last 2 rows until 23[25:29:31]sts rem; end with a K row.
Next row P1, P2 tog, P to last 3 sts, P2 tog tbl, P1.
Cont to dec at each end of every row until 17[19:19:21] sts rem; end with a P row.
Bind off.

Front
Work as for back to **. 53[57:61:65]sts.
Divide for front opening
Next row Using A, K1, sl 1, K1, psso, K23[25:27:29], K2 tog, K to last 3 sts, K2 tog, K1. 51[55:59:63] sts.
Next row P23[25:27:29], K5, P to end.
Next row K1, sl 1, K1, psso, K22[24:26:28], turn and leave rem sts on a spare needle.
Next row K2, P to end.
Keeping 2 sts at front edge in garter st, cont to dec at armhole edge on every alternate row until 14[15:17:18] sts rem; end with K row.
Shape neck
Bind off 3[4:4:5]sts at beg of next row. 11[11:13:13]sts.
Next row K1, sl 1, K1, psso, K to last 2 sts, sl 1, K1, psso.
Next row P to end.
Rep last 2 rows once, then first again.
Keeping neck edge straight, dec at armhole edge on next 3[3:5:5] rows. Bind off rem 2 sts. Return to sts left at base of front opening. With RS facing, rejoin yarn and bind off center sts. K to last 3 sts, K2 tog, K1.
Next row P to last 2 sts, K2.
Complete to match first side, reversing shaping.

Sleeves
Using No. 6 (4½mm) needles and A, cast on 27[29:31:33]sts. Work 2in (5cm) ribbing as for back; end with a 2nd row. Change to No. 8 (5½mm) needles. Beg with a K row, cont in stockinette st, inc one st at each end of first and every foll 8th row until there are 41[43:45:47]sts. Cont straight until sleeve measures 12[12½:13½:14¼]in (30[32:34:36]cm); end with a P row. Work 2 rows each in C, B and A. Work 10 rows of motif as at beg of front, noting there will be 2 hearts in C and 1 in B. Work 2 rows in A.
Shape top
Working 2 rows each in B and C, then cont with A only, dec as for back armhole shaping at each end of next and every other row until 5 sts rem; end with a P row. Bind off.

Hood
Using No. 8 (5½mm) needles and A, cast on 55[61:67:73]sts.
1st row K to end.
2nd row K2, P to last 2 sts, K2.
Rep these 2 rows until work measures 7[8:8¾:9½]in (18[20:22:24]cm); end with a WS row.
Shape back
Next row K25[28:31:34], sl 1, K1, psso, K1, K2 tog, K to end.
Cont to dec in center of every alternate row 5 times more, then on every row 4 times.
Next row K18[21:24:27], turn, fold work in half and graft top (or bind off and join seam).

To finish
Press or block according to yarn used. Join raglan seams, sewing last part of sleeve seams to bound-off sts at underarm. Join side and sleeve seams. Sew on hood. Press seams. Sew one toggle to each side of neck and make a loop to form a figure 8 to fasten.

Shoestring

Border print apron

This ruffled apron is practical enough for kitchen tasks yet pretty enough for the dining room.

Finished size
34½in (88cm) long.

Materials
2¼yd (2m) of 51in (130cm)-wide border print fabric
Matching thread

1 Avoiding border design, cut a piece of fabric 36×29½in (90×75cm).
2 From border cut one strip 74×6in (188×15cm) for ruffle, one strip 2¼yd × 4¾in (2m×12cm) for waistband/tie and one piece 6×4¾in (15×12cm) for pocket.
3 On long and two shorter edges of apron, turn under, pin and baste a double ¼in (5mm) hem. Stitch hem in place on side edges only.
4 On ruffle, turn under and stitch a single ¼in (5mm) hem on all edges. Run a line of gathering stitches ¾in (2cm) from one long edge. Pull up gathers to fit lower edge of apron. Secure the thread and adjust the gathers evenly.
5 With wrong side of ruffle to right side of apron, place gathering line of ruffle just above the basted lower edge of apron. Pin, baste and stitch to apron, stitching directly over gathering thread.
6 Turn under, pin, baste and stitch a ¼in (5mm) hem on one long edge of pocket. Pin and baste ¼in (5mm) hems on remaining edges. Run a line of gathering stitches ¾in (2cm) from stitched edge to form ruffle at top of pocket. Pull up gathers until top of pocket measures 4in (10cm). Secure the thread and adjust the gathers.
7 Place pocket 4in (10cm) from top of apron and 6in (15cm) in from one side. Topstitch pocket to apron around basted edges, pleating pocket slightly at the bottom.
8 Run a line of gathering stitches ⅜in (1cm) from top edge of apron and pull gathers up until top measures 12in (30cm). Fasten threads and adjust gathers.
9 Placing right sides together, fold waistband/tie in half lengthwise. Cut each end at an angle. Taking ⅝in (1.5cm) seam allowance, pin, baste and stitch ends and baste long edges, leaving a 12in (30cm) gap in the center for apron. Turn each end of tie right side out.
10 Placing right sides and raw edges together, pin, baste and stitch one side of waistband opening to apron. Turn free edge of waistband to inside and turn under seam allowance. Pin, baste and slip stitch in place.
11 Topstitch close to edges of waistband/tie for a firm finish.

Stefano Massimo

Quilting a geometric jacquard pattern

A geometric jacquard design—such as squares, triangles, hexagons (see Stitch Wise, page 36—is ideal for quilting as the blocks of colored shapes provide natural outlines for the quilting to follow. Quilting requires a number of layers of fabric to produce a padded effect between the stitching lines, so the finished fabric is solid, suitable for vests, jackets, tunics, bags and small areas of detail (such as a yoke) which do not need much "give."

You need some simple dressmaking skills for quilting a knitted fabric—not only for the quilting itself, which can be done by machine or hand, but also for assembling the quilted sections of the garment. One of the neatest methods of finishing the outer edges is with a knitted binding.

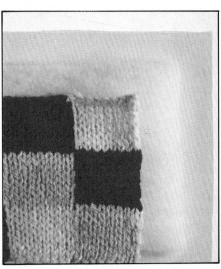

1 Quilting requires 3 layers of fabric—the piece of knitting (here it is one of the geometric designs shown in Stitch Wise), batting (easily available for quilting) and lining material.

2 Cut out batting to same size as the piece of knitting. Use knitting as a guide to cut out the lining, but allow ½in (1cm) seam allowance all around (here it is untrimmed).

3 Pin and baste all 3 layers along the lines to be quilted. Here the colored outlines of the squares form an easy guide. There is no need to baste around the edge; the inner lines of stitching hold the knitting in position.

4 You can sew along the lines of basting using a long machine stitch and ordinary sewing thread. Machine stitching is quick, but you must be accurate. If you prefer to sew by hand, backstitch along the lines.

5 The photograph above shows the finished effect on the right side. Each square is separated by lines of stitching: the batting inside gives each square a cushioned effect. Notice that the stitching goes completely through to the back of the fabric.

Fred Mancini

Joining and finishing a quilted fabric

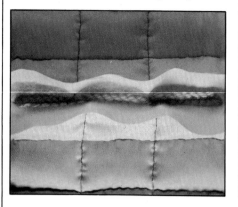

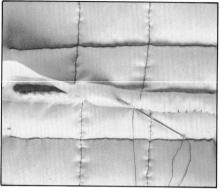

1 To join two sections of quilted fabric, place the pieces together with right sides facing and edges matching. Sew about ½in (1cm) in from the edge either on a machine as shown here or by hand, using backstitch. The sewing thread used here is in a contrasting color for clarity.

2 Trim away all the sections of the hem except one layer of lining as near the stitching line as possible. Turn under a small hem on the lining section and slip stitch the hem flat to the wrong side of the fabric to enclose the trimmed raw edges.

3 Using one of the colors in the jacquard fabric, cast on enough stitches to make a strip of binding about 1½-2in (4-5cm) wide. Work in stockinette stitch until the strip fits along the edge which is to be bound.

Stitc

Gingham

Cast on a multiple of 8 stitches. Each block of color consists of 4 stitches and 4 rows. However, there are only two colors in each row, allowing you to strand the color not in use across the back of the work.

Hexagons

Cast on a multiple of 24 stitches to repeat this design using 3 colors. Use separate balls of yarn for each patch of color across a row. Remember to twist the yarns together when changing color.

Diamonds

Cast on a multiple of 18 stitches. For this moderately large version of the diamond pattern you can either use separate balls of yarn or weave the colors into the back of the work.

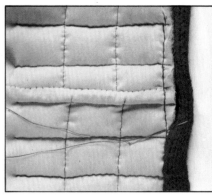

Fred Mancini

4 Place right side of binding to right side of quilting, matching edge to edge. Pin and baste in place. Sew with a backstitch seam about ⅜in (1cm) in from edge.

5 Fold the binding in half to the wrong side of the quilted fabric. Turn under a ⅜in (1cm) hem on the edge of the binding, then pin it in place on top of the line of backstitching. Slip stitch the binding neatly in place.

6 The knitted strip makes a neat binding for the raw edges. The binding is quite thick, so when it is folded double, the edge is rolled instead of sharply creased. It is possible to bind around a curve by easing the knitted strip carefully into position.

Vise

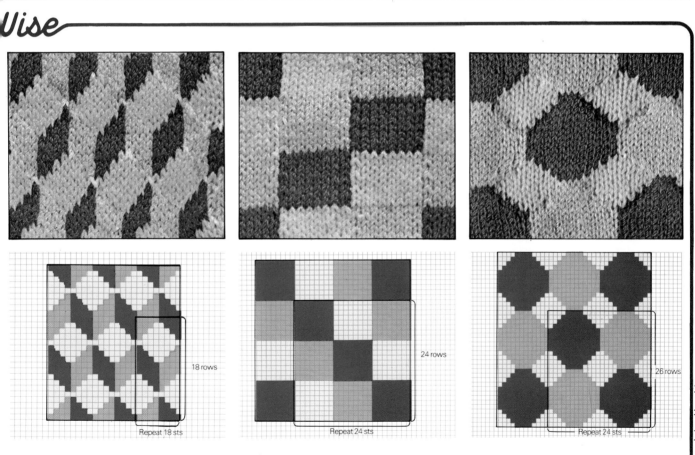

John Hutchinson

Boxes

Cast on a multiple of 8 stitches. You can strand the yarns across the back of the work since each color is used again after only a few stitches. If you use 3 shades of a single color, a 3-dimensional box effect is created.

Squares

Cast on a multiple of 24 stitches. Each block is quite large, consisting of 8 stitches and 8 rows; use a separate small ball of yarn for each block.

Octagons with diamonds

Cast on a multiple of 24 stitches. Ideally use a separate ball of yarn for each octagonal and diamond shape across the pattern to give a neat single thickness fabric.

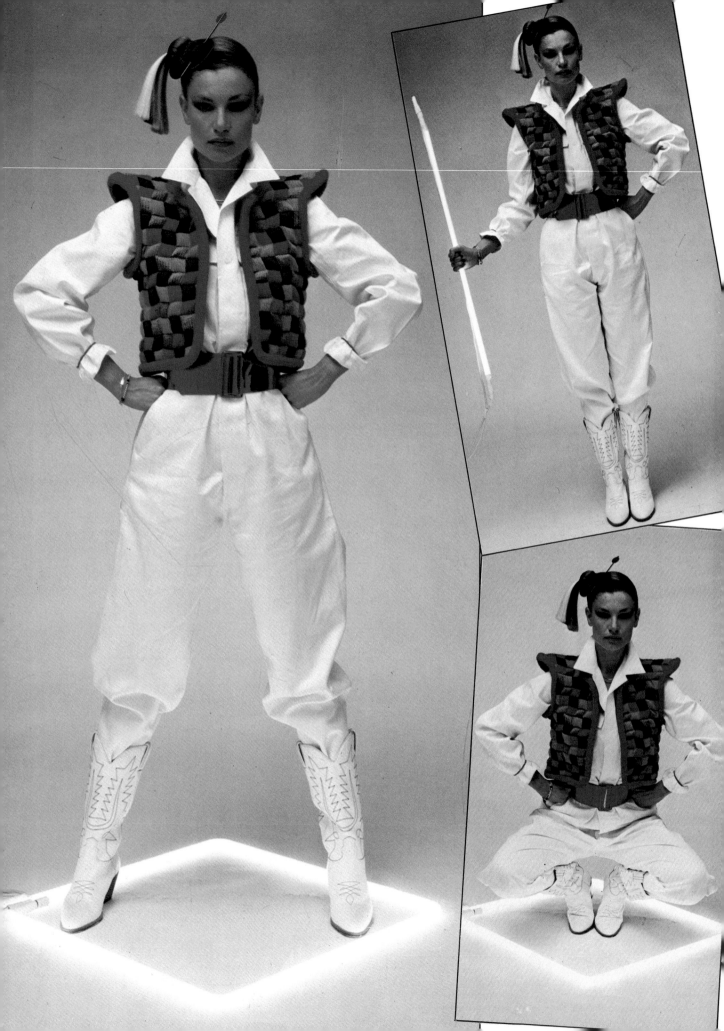

Quilted vest

Countdown to the Space Age in this vest, which is easier to make than you think—the knitting grows quickly and the squares provide guidelines for the quilting.

Sizes
To fit 32-36in (83-92cm) bust.
Length, 17½in (42cm).

Materials
8oz (200g) of red knitting worsted
4oz (100g) each of royal blue, pale blue and pink
⅝yd (.5m) of 39in (90cm)-wide batting for quilting
⅝yd (.5m) of 39in (90cm)-wide fabric for lining
1 pair No. 5 (4mm) knitting needles

Gauge
Each square of 6 sts and 7 rows, worked on No. 5 (4mm) needles, measures 1¼in (3cm).

Note
Before starting, wind the five colors of yarn into separate balls. Twist yarns tog at back when changing color.

Vest
Using No. 5 (4mm) needles and colors as shown on chart, cast on 90 sts for lower edge of back, work 6 sts in each square— 15 squares in all. Beg with a K row, cont in stockinette st and work in squares of 7 rows until 7 lines have been completed.

Shape armholes
Keeping patt correct, bind off 12 sts at beg of next 2 rows. 66 sts. Cont straight until 4 more lines of squares have been completed.

Shape sleeve cap
Keeping patt correct, inc one st at each end of next and foll 8 alternate rows. 84 sts. Cont straight until 7 lines of squares have been completed from beg of armholes; end with a P row.

Shape neck and divide for fronts
Next row Patt 25 sts and leave on holder, bind off next 34 sts for neck, patt rem 25 sts.
Cont on last set of sts for left front.
*Work 4 rows, then dec one st at armhole edge on next and foll 8 alternate rows, **at the same time** work 13 rows straight at neck edge, then inc one st at neck edge on foll 8 rows.*
Next row Cast on 9 sts, patt to end. 33 sts.
Cont without shaping until 7 lines of squares have been completed from shoulder, ending at side edge.
Next row Cast on 12 sts for underarm, patt to end.
Work until 7 more lines of squares have been completed. Bind off.
With WS of work facing, rejoin yarn to sts on holder at shoulder and work as for

left front from * to *. Work 1 row. Complete to match left front, reversing shaping.

Outer binding
Using No. 5 (4mm) needles and red, cast on 10 sts. Beg with a K row, cont in stockinette st for 85in (216cm). Bind off.

Armhole binding
Work 2 pieces each 26in (66cm) long as given for outer binding.

To finish
Cut lining and batting and baste tog with knitted fabric (see step-by-step instructions, page 35). Sew along horizontal lines, changing direction each time, then along vertical lines again changing direction. Sew on armhole binding (see step-by-step instructions, pages 36 and 37). Join side seams and hem lining to cover seams. Sew binding all around edges.

Designed by Sandy Black

Beg knitting here ↗
Rep squares as needed across row
Each square = 6 sts + 7 rows

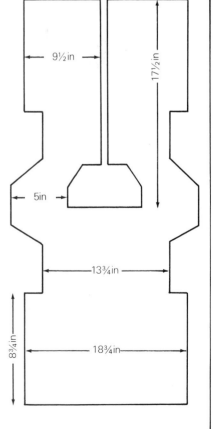

John Hutchinson

Knitting / COURSE 58

*Flat-fabric mittens
*Making mittens with a palm thumb
*Patterns for children's and adults' mittens

Flat-fabric mittens

Flat-fabric mittens are easy for a beginner to make before attempting more complicated gloves, which are knitted in rounds on a set of four needles. These mittens are worked on two needles and have an inconspicuous seam up the side of the hand and around the thumb.

A mitten is made up of sections. First, there is a ribbed cuff worked on smaller needles than the main fabric so that it stretches and then fits neatly. After the ribbing there are usually a few straight rows in the main fabric to fit over the wrist. The thumb shaping takes place between the wrist and joint of the thumb: usually you must increase on each side of a triangular gusset to accommodate the extra width of the thumb. After dividing off the thumb stitches and completing it separately, you work the rest of the mitten straight to within a short distance of the top. Decrease rows form the top shaping with a double decrease in the center of a row and single ones at the sides. When the mitten is folded in half, the shaping

slopes inward at the sides of the fingers toward the bound-off group at the top.

The diagram on the right shows how measurements are taken for a mitten. The widest part of the hand is around the knuckles (1); this measurement indicates the number of cast-on stitches needed. However, a second width measurement must be taken at the joint of the thumb (2). The difference between these two measurements gives the number of stitches in the thumb.

Thumb shaping occurs in the length between wrist and thumb joint (3); frequency of increasing depends on the stitch gauge. The length of the thumb itself (4) should always be generous: in most cases it is equal in length to the line of thumb shaping (3). Adequate length must be allowed to accommodate the middle finger (5) within the bound-off stitches at the top of the mitten. Below the overall length (5) there is also a straight section—up to 1in (2.5cm)—for the wrist and ribbed cuff.

Making mittens with a palm thumb

Conventionally, mittens and gloves are worked in rounds on a set of needles. If you are not proficient at circular knitting, making a pair of gloves can be a daunting task. As a first exercise in glove making, try the basic mitten pattern shown here.

These mittens are ideal for a beginner; they are worked flat on two needles and only the thumb needs to be shaped. The thumb shaping here starts on the palm from the base of the thumb. Other mittens may have a straight thumb which lies at the side of the mitten, dividing equally the palm and back of hand sections. Variations in design on this basic theme are endless: see pages 42 to 45 for some patterns.

Directions here are for a right-hand mitten. To make the left mitten, reverse the position of the thumb by working the first increase row (see step 2) as follows: K19, inc in next st, K1, inc in next st, K22. Also, separate the thumb stitches (see step 5) by working: K34, turn and cast on 2 sts.

1 For an adult-sized mitten, in knitting worsted, cast on 44 stitches. Using No. 2 (3mm) needles work 2in (5cm) in single ribbing. Change to No. 4 (3¾mm) needles for the main fabric and, continuing in stockinette stitch, work 2 rows.

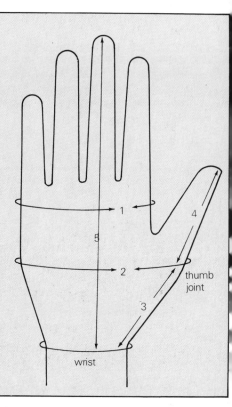

2 Begin the shaping for the thumb. **First inc row** K22, inc in next st, K1, inc in next st, K19. The first 22 stitches (half the total number) represent the back of the mitten, while the thumb shaping is entirely on the second or palm section of the stitches. Here the start of the thumb shaping is marked with pins.

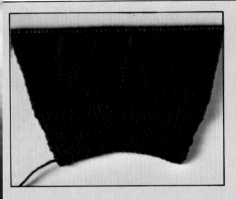

3 Work 3 rows without shaping. **2nd inc row** K22, inc in next st, K3, inc in next st, K19. Continue in this way, working 2 more stitches between increases on every following 4th row, until there are 56 stitches. There are 15 stitches in the thumb shaping, which forms a triangular shape between the back and palm sections.

4 Work a purl row, then begin to work the thumb. **Next row** K37 (22 back and 15 thumb stitches), turn and cast on 2 sts. Here the wrong side of the work is facing and the 2 extra stitches have been cast onto the left-hand needle.

5 Separate the thumb stitches from the rest of the work. **Next row** P16, turn and cast on 2 sts. The work has been turned; extra stitches are on left-hand needle. Measurements are taken from a flat hand; cast-on stitches on each side provide extra width around thumb. (Palm stitches can be slipped onto a stitch holder while you work thumb.)

6 Continue to work on the 18 thumb stitches only until the thumb measures 2in (5cm), ending with a purl row. Shape top by knitting 2 stitches together across next row, purling a row, then knitting first st and knitting 2 stitches together across following row. 5 stitches remain.

7 Cut off the yarn, leaving a long end. Thread the end into a tapestry needle and draw it through the remaining stitches. Fasten the stitches off securely, then use the long end of yarn to join the thumb seam.

8 Now that the thumb is complete, continue knitting the rest of the mitten. You have already worked across the back stitches before working the thumb; with the right side facing, rejoin yarn at base of thumb and pick up 4 stitches from those cast on previously. Knit across the palm stitches to the end of the row.

9 Work a further 3¼in (8cm) across all 46 stitches, ending with a purl row. Start shaping top of mitten. **First dec row** K2, *sl 1, K1, psso, K16, K2 tog, K2, rep from * once more. Purl one row.

10 Continue shaping by working 2 fewer stitches between both sets of decreases on next and following 2 alternate rows. Purl one row, then bind off. The decreasing makes distinctive lines of shaping sloping inward toward the top on both sides of the mitten.

11 Finish the mitten by joining the top and side seams. When the fabric is folded in half the thumb section lies on the palm half, immediately bordering the side edge.

Fred Mancini

Children's and adults' mittens

There are mittens here for the whole family. The patterns are easy to knit, so start now and banish cold hands.

Adult's Fair Isle mittens

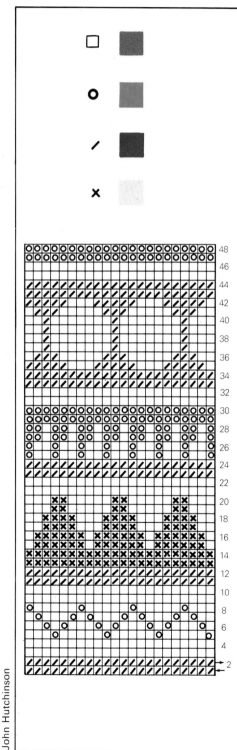

Size
Width around hand above thumb, 7in (18cm).

Materials
- 1 × 2oz (50g) of a sport yarn in each of 4 colors
- 1 pair each Nos. 2 and 4 (3 and 3¾mm) knitting needles

Gauge
26 sts to 4in (10cm) in stockinette st on No. 4 (3¾mm) needles.

Note
Working in stockinette st and reading odd-numbered rows from right to left and even-numbered rows from left to right, work the 22 sts of back of mitten in Fair Isle patt from chart. Where there is only 1 color in a row, work this color across palm; otherwise work the palm in main color. Cut off colors when not in use.

Right-hand mitten
Using No. 2 (3mm) needles and main color, cast on 44 sts. Work 20 rows K1, P1 ribbing. Change to No. 4 (3¾mm) needles. Working first 22 sts from chart, work 2 rows stockinette st.
Shape thumb
1st inc row K22, inc in next st, K1, inc in next st, K19.
Work 3 rows without shaping.
2nd inc row K22, inc in next st, K3, inc in next st, K19.
Work 3 rows straight. Cont to inc in this way on next and every foll 4th row until there are 56 sts. Work 1 row.
Divide for thumb
Next row K22 sts from chart, using main color K15, turn and cast on 2 sts.
Next row P16, turn and cast on 2 sts. Using main color, cont on these 18 sts for 2in (5cm); end with P row.
Shape top
1st row (K2 tog) 9 times.
2nd row P to end.
3rd row K1, (K2 tog) 4 times.
Cut off yarn leaving a long end; thread through rem sts, draw up and fasten off securely. Join thumb seam.
Using right-hand needle and main color, pick up 4 sts from base of thumb, K to end of row. 46 sts. Working 22 sts in Fair Isle from chart, cont straight until 48th row has been completed.
Shape top
Use main color only.
1st row K2, *sl 1, K1, psso, K16, K2 tog, K2, rep from * once more.
2nd and every alt row P to end.
3rd row K2, *sl 1, K1, psso, K14, K2 tog, K2, rep from * once more.
5th row K2, *sl 1, K1, psso, K12, K2 tog, K2, rep from * once more.
7th row K2, *sl 1, K1, psso, K10, K2 tog, K2, rep from * once more.
8th row P to end.
Bind off. Join top and side seams.

Left-hand mitten
Work to match right-hand mitten, working last 22 sts in patt from chart and reversing position of thumb as foll:
1st inc row K19, inc in next st, K1, inc in next st, K22.
Divide for thumb as foll:
Next row Using main color K34, turn and cast on 2 sts.
Next row P16, turn and cast on 2 sts.

Adult's striped mittens

Size Width around hand above thumb, 7in (18cm).

Materials
- 2 × 1oz (25g) balls of a knitting worsted in red
- 1 ball each of yellow, green, blue and white
- 1 pair No. 3 (3¼mm) knitting needles

Gauge
26 sts to 4in (10cm) in garter st on No. 3 (3¼mm) needles.

Right-hand mitten
Using No. 3 (3¼mm) needles and red, cast on 44 sts. Work 20 rows K1, P1 ribbing. Cont in garter st and stripe sequence of 4 rows blue 2 rows white, 4 green, 2 white, 4 yellow, 2 white, 4 red and 2 white. K 6 rows.
Shape thumb
1st inc row K22, inc in next st, K1, inc in next st, K19. K 5 rows.
2nd inc row K22, inc in next st, K3, inc in next st, K19.
Cont in this way, working 2 sts more between increases, on every foll 6th row until there are 56 sts. K 3 rows.
Divide for thumb
Next row K37, turn and cast on 2 sts.
Next row K16, turn and cast on 2 sts. Cont on these 18 sts in garter st and red only for 2½in (6cm).
Shape top
1st row K1, (K2, K2 tog) 4 times, K1.
2nd row K to end.
3rd row K1, (K2 tog) 6 times, K1.
Cut off yarn leaving a long end; thread through rem sts, draw up and fasten off securely. Join thumb seam.
Using right-hand needle and appropriate color, pick up and K 4 sts from base of thumb, K to end of row. Work a further 4in (10cm) in stripes; end with WS row.
Shape top
1st row K2, *sl 1, K1, psso, K16, K2 tog, K2, rep from * once more.
2nd and every alternate row K to end.
3rd row K2, *sl 1, K1, psso, K14, K2 tog, K2, rep from * once more.
5th row K2, *sl 1, K1, psso, K12, K2 tog, K2, rep from * once more.
7th row K2, *sl 1, K1, psso, K10, K2 tog, K2, rep from * once more.
8th row K to end.
Bind off. Join top and side seams.

John Hutchinson

Victor Yuan

Left-hand mitten

Work to match right-hand mitten, reversing position of thumb as foll:

1st inc row K19, inc in next st, K1, inc in next st, K22.

2nd inc row K19, inc in next st, K3, inc in next st, K22.

Divide for thumb as foll:

Next row K34, turn and cast on 2 sts.

Next row K16, turn and cast on 2 sts.

Adult's mittens with snowflake pattern

Size

Width around hand above thumb, 8¾in (22cm).

Materials

2 × 2oz (50g) balls of a sport yarn in main color

Small amount of contrasting color 1 pair each Nos. 3 and 5 (3¼ and 4mm) knitting needles

Gauge

20 sts to 4in (10cm) in stockinette st on No. 5 (4mm) needles.

Right-hand mitten

Using No. 3 (3¼mm) needles and main color (MC), cast on 37 sts.

1st row K1, *P1, K1, rep from * to end.

2nd row P1, *K1, P1, rep from * to end. Rep these 2 rows for 2in (5cm); end with a first row.

Next row (inc row) *Rib 4, inc in next st, rep from * 6 times more, rib 2. 44 sts. Change to No. 5 (4mm) needles.

Shape thumb

1st row K24, pick up loop lying between needles and K tbl—called make 1 (M1)—, K1, M1, K19.

Work 3 rows stockinette st.

5th row K24, M1, K3, M1, K19.

Work 3 rows stockinette st.

9th row K24, M1, K5, M1, K19.

Work 3 rows stockinette st.

13th row K24, M1, K7, M1, K19.

14th row P to end.

Divide for thumb

Next row K34, turn and cast on 3 sts.

Next row P14, turn.

Work 12 rows stockinette st on these 14 sts.

Shape top

1st row *K1, K2 tog, rep from * 3 times more, K2.

2nd row P to end.

3rd row K1, *K2 tog, rep from * 3 times more, K1.

Cut off yarn leaving a long end; thread through rem sts, draw up and fasten off securely. Join thumb seam.

With right-hand needle, pick up and K 3 sts from base of thumb, K to end of row.

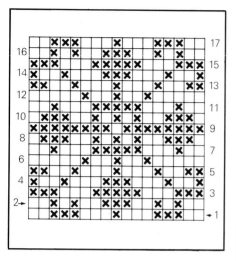

44 sts. P 1 row. Join in contrasting color (C). Beg snowflake patt.

1st row K5 MC, 3 C, 3 MC, 1 C, 3 MC, 3 C, using MC K to end.

2nd row P26 MC, 1 C, 1 MC, 1 C, 2 MC, 3 C, 2 MC, 1 C, 1 MC, 1 C, 5 MC.

Cont in stockinette st and patt as set, beg row 3 of chart work 15 more rows. Using MC only, cont in stockinette st until work measures 4¾in (12cm) from base of thumb; end with a P row.

Shape top

1st row K2, (sl 1, K1, psso, K15, K2 tog, K2) twice.

2nd and alternate rows P to end.

3rd row K2, (sl 1, K1, psso, K13, K2 tog, K2) twice.

5th row K2, (sl 1, K1, psso, K11, K2 tog, K2) twice.

7th row K2, (sl 1, K1, psso, K9, K2 tog, K2) twice.

8th row P to end.

Bind off. Join top and side seams.

Left-hand mitten

Work to match right-hand mitten, reversing position of thumb as foll:

1st row K19, M1, K1, M1, K24.

Divide for thumb as foll:

Next row K29, turn and cast on 3 sts.

Next row P14, turn.

Child's mittens with drawstring

Size

Width around hand above thumb, 7in (18cm).

Materials

1 × 2oz (50g) ball of a sport yarn in main color (A)

1 ball of contrasting color (B) for drawstring and pompom

1 pair each Nos. 3 and 5 (3¼ and 4mm) knitting needles

Gauge

22 sts to 4in (10cm) in patt on No. 5 (4mm) needles.

Right-hand mitten

Using No. 3 (3¼mm) needles and A, cast on 34 sts. Work 15 rows K1, P1 ribbing.

Next row (eyelet-hole row) K1, *yo, K2 tog, rep from * to last st, K1.

Change to No. 5 (4mm) needles. Beg patt.

1st row *K1 tbl, P1, rep from * to end.

2nd row K to end.

These 2 rows form patt and are rep throughout. Work 2 more rows.

Shape thumb

1st inc row Patt 17, (P1, K1, P1) all into next st, K1, (P1, K1, P1) all into next st, patt 14. Patt 3 rows.

2nd inc row Patt 17, (P1, K1, P1) all into next st, patt 5, (P1, K1, P1) all into next st, patt 14. Patt 3 rows.

3rd inc row Patt 17, (P1, K1, P1) all into next st, patt 9, (P1, K1, P1) all into next st, patt 14. Patt 3 rows.

Divide for thumb

Next row Patt 31, turn and cast on 2 sts.

Next row K14, turn and cast on 2 sts.

Cont in patt on these 16 sts for 1¼in (3cm); end with a WS row.

Shape top

Next row K2, (patt 2, work 2 tog) 3 times, patt 2.

Next row K to end.

Next row K1, (K2 tog) 6 times.

Cut off yarn leaving a long end; thread through rem sts, draw up and fasten off securely. Join thumb seam.

Using right-hand needle, pick up and K 4 sts at base of thumb, patt to end of row. Work a further 3½in (9cm) in patt; end with a WS row.

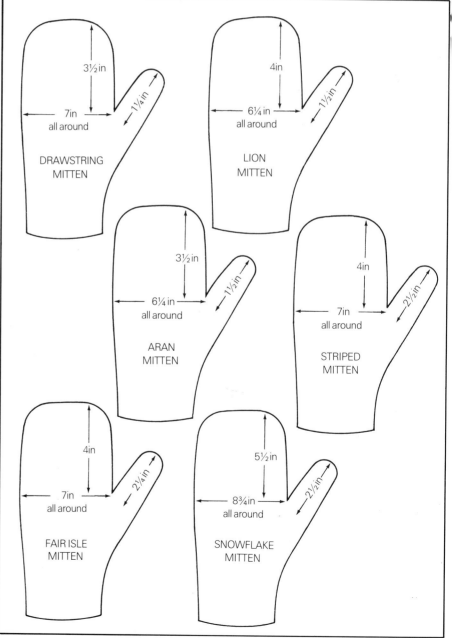

3½in
7in all around
1¼in
DRAWSTRING MITTEN

4in
6¼in all around
1½in
LION MITTEN

3½in
6¼in all around
1½in
ARAN MITTEN

4in
7in all around
2½in
STRIPED MITTEN

4in
7in all around
2¼in
FAIR ISLE MITTEN

5½in
8¾in all around
2½in
SNOWFLAKE MITTEN

Shape top
1st row *K2 tog, rep from * to end.
2nd row K1, *K2 tog, rep from * to end.
Cut off yarn leaving a long end; thread through rem sts, draw up and fasten off securely. Join side seam.

Left-hand mitten
Work to match right-hand mitten, reversing position of thumb as foll:
1st inc row Patt 14, (K1, P1, K1) all into next st, P1, (K1, P1, K1) all into next st, patt 17.
2nd inc row Patt 14, (K1, P1, K1) all into next st, patt 5, (K1, P1, K1) all into next st, patt 17.
3rd inc row Patt 14, (K1, P1, K1) all into next st, patt 9, (K1, P1, K1) all into next st, patt 17.
Divide for thumb as foll:
Next row Patt 28, turn and cast on 2 sts.
Next row K14, turn and cast on 2 sts.

To finish
Ties Using 4 strands of B tog make 2 twisted cords 20in (50cm) long. Thread through eyelet-hole row to tie at center back of mitten. Using remainder of B, make 4 pompoms 2in (5cm) in diameter and attach one to each end of each tie.

Child's Aran mittens

Size
Width around hand above thumb, 6¼in (16cm).

Materials
*1 × 2oz (50g) ball of a knitting worsted
1 pair each Nos. 3 and 5 (3¼ and 4mm) knitting needles*

Gauge
16 sts to 4in (10cm) in stockinette st on No. 5 (4mm) needles.

Cable panel (worked over 12 sts)
1st row P2, K8, P2.
2nd row K2, P8, K2.
3rd and 4th rows As first and 2nd.
5th row P2, sl next 2 sts onto cable needle and leave at back of work, K2, then K2 from cable needle—called C2 B—, sl next 2 sts onto cable needle and leave at front of work, then K2 from cable needle—called C2F—P2.
6th row As 2nd.
7th and 8th rows As first and 2nd.
These 8 rows form patt and are repeated throughout.

Right-hand mitten
*Using No. 3 (3¼mm) needles cast on 29 sts.
1st row K1, *P1, K1, rep from * to end.
2nd row P1, *K1, P1, rep from * to end.
Rep these 2 rows for 2in (5cm); end with a first row.
Next row (inc row) Rib 2, *inc in next st, rib 7, rep from * twice more, inc in next st, rib to end. 33 sts.
Change to No. 5 (4mm) needles.

Shape thumb
1st row K3, work 1st row cable panel, K2, pick up loop lying between needles and K tbl—called make 1 (M1)—, K2, M1, K14.
2nd row P to last 15 sts, work 2nd row cable panel, P3.
3rd row K3, work 3rd row cable panel, K to end.
4th row P to last 15 sts, work 4th row cable panel, P3.
5th row K3, work 5th row cable panel, K2, M1, K4, M1, K14.
These 5 rows set patt. Work a further 9 rows inc as set on 2 foll 4th rows. 41 sts.

Divide for thumb
Next row Patt 27 sts, turn.
Next row P10, turn and cast on 2 sts.
Work 8 rows stockinette st on these 12 sts.

Shape top
Next row *K2 tog, rep from * to end.
Cut off yarn leaving a long end; thread through rem sts, draw up and fasten off. Join thumb seam. Using right-hand needle, pick up and K 2 sts from base of thumb, K to end of row. 33 sts. Work further 3in (8cm) in patt; end with WS row.*

Shape top
1st row K1, K2 tog tbl, K12, K2 tog, K2, K2 tog tbl, K9, K2 tog, K1.
2nd row P to end.
3rd row K1, K2 tog tbl, K10, K2 tog, K2, K2 tog tbl, K7, K2 tog, K1.
4th row P to end.
Bind off. Join top and side seams.

Left-hand mitten
Work to match right-hand mitten from * to *, reversing position of thumb as foll:
1st row K14, M1, K2, M1, K2, work cable panel first row, K3.
Divide for thumb as foll:
Next row K24, turn.
Next row P10, turn and cast on 2 sts.

Shape top
1st row K1, K2 tog tbl, K9, K2 tog, K2, K2 tog tbl, K12, K2 tog, K1.
2nd row P to end.
3rd row K1, K2 tog tbl, K7, K2 tog, K2, K2 tog tbl, K10, K2 tog, K1.
4th row P to end.
Bind off. Join top and side seams.

Child's lion mittens

Size
Width around hand above thumb, 6¼in (16cm).

Materials
*2 × 1oz (25g) balls of a knitting worsted in main color (A)
1 ball of contrasting color (B)
Black yarn for embroidery
4 buttons
1 pair each Nos. 3 and 5mm (3¼ and 4mm) knitting needles*

Gauge
22 sts and 24 rows to 4in (10cm) in stockinette st on No. 5 (4mm) needles.

Right-hand mitten
Using No. 3 (3¼mm) needles and A, cast on 32 sts. Work 16 rows K1, P1 ribbing. Change to No. 5 (4mm) needles. K 1 row and P 1 row.

Shape thumb
1st inc row K16, inc in next st, K1, inc in next st, K13.
Work 3 rows stockinette st.
2nd inc row K16, inc in next st, K3, inc in next st, K13.
Cont to inc in this way, working 2 more sts between increases, on every foll 4th row, until there are 40 sts. Work 3 rows stockinette st.

Divide for thumb
Next row K27, turn and cast on 2 sts.
Next row P12, turn and cast on 2 sts.
Work 1in (2.5cm) stockinette st on these 14 sts; end with a P row.

Shape top
Next row K1, (K2, K2 tog) 3 times, K1.
Next row P to end.
Next row (K2 tog) 5 times, K1.
Cut off yarn leaving a long end; thread through rem sts, draw up and fasten off securely. Join thumb seam. Using right-hand needle, pick up and K 4 sts at base of thumb, K to end of row. Work a further 3¼in (8cm) stockinette st; end with a P row.

Shape top
1st row K2, *sl 1, K1, psso, K10, K2 tog, K2 rep from * once more.
2nd and every alternate row P to end.
3rd row K2, *sl 1, K1, psso, K8, K2 tog, K2, rep from * once more.
5th row K2, *sl 1, K1, psso, K6, K2 tog, K2, rep from * once more.
7th row K2, *sl 1, K1, psso, K4, K2 tog, K2, rep from * once more.
8th row P to end.
Bind off. Join top and side seams.

Left-hand mitten
Work to match right-hand mitten, reversing position of thumb as foll:
1st inc row K13, inc in next st, K1, inc in next st, K16.
2nd inc row K13, inc in next st, K3, inc in next st, K16.
Divide for thumb as foll:
Next row K24, turn and cast on 2 sts.
Next row P12, turn and cast on 2 sts.

To finish
Sew 2 buttons for eyes onto palm of mittens level with beg of top shaping.
Mane Cut 5in (13cm) lengths of color B. Taking 2 strands tog each time, knot a pair of fringes through matching edge sts at back of hand and palm, beg about 8 rows below top shaping and cont all around to similar position on opposite side. Embroider nose and whiskers in black yarn as shown.
Tail Using 4 strands of B tog make 2 twisted cords approx 4¾in (12cm) long. Attach fold end to back of each mitten, then brush out knotted end.

Working single loop stitch

There are a number of loop stitch fabrics which have an unusual "furry" appearance and texture. The loops are worked onto the main background as you are knitting, using your left thumb as a guide. In single-loop stitch, the loops are formed on a right-side row with the loopy fabric facing you.

Producing a loopy fabric is a slow task until you become adept at the technique. Try to keep the loops an even length, but don't worry too much, since the shaggy quality of uneven loops is part of the character of the work.

A loopy fabric is warm but quite soft (unless the yarn is too thick and it becomes solid and distorted); it is most suitable for outdoor wear. Use it as an allover fabric for coats, jackets, rugs, buggy and crib blankets or trimmings such as collars and cuffs.

Cutting the loops after they have been knitted gives a fringed effect. Try experimenting with different types of yarn for a variety of interesting fabrics and textures.

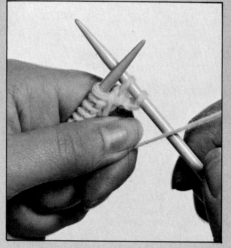

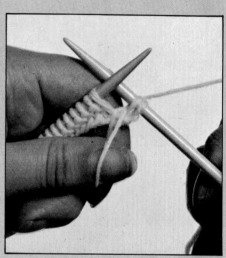

1 Cast on an even number of stitches.
1st row K to end. Start loop row: 2nd row K1, knit the next stitch without allowing the original loop to fall from the left-hand needle, bring the yarn to the front of the work between the needles.

2 Continue with 2nd row. Make a loop by passing yarn in a clockwise direction around tip of left thumb, which is held close to needles. Take yarn to back of work again between the needles.

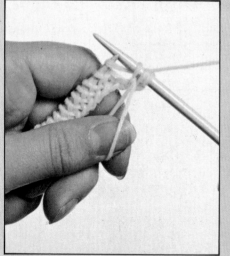

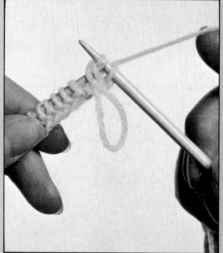

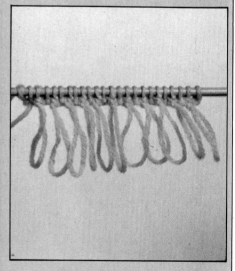

3 With the yarn still wound around your thumb, insert the right-hand needle into the loop remaining on the left-hand needle and knit it in the usual way. This time allow the original stitch to fall from the left-hand needle.

4 There are now 2 stitches on left-hand needle from original loop stitch. Return both these stitches to left-hand needle by inserting it from left to right through them. Complete loop stitch by knitting these stitches together through back of loops; this returns loop to a single stitch and also secures it.

5 Continue to the end of the 2nd row, alternately knitting a stitch then making a loop on the next stitch, until you reach the last 2 stitches. Knit these 2 stitches. Here you can see the 2nd row complete: note that the loops are all an even length.

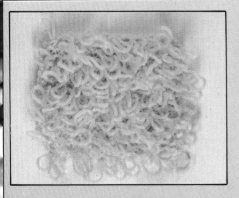

6 To make this loopy fabric, knit one row between each row of loops. Work the next loop row as follows: **4th row** K2, *make a loop on next st, K1, rep from * to end. The loops are on alternate stitches to those in the previous row. These 4 rows form the pattern.

7 If you want cut loops, wait until the fabric is complete. Starting at the lower edge, insert a pair of scissors through a number of loops in a line; pull the loops taut then cut through them.

8 The cut loops have a shaggy appearance rather than the curly look of uncut ones. A few rows of cut loops on the edge of a stockinette stitch fabric make an unusual fringe. Alternatively, combine cut loops with uncut ones in an allover fabric to give an interesting texture.

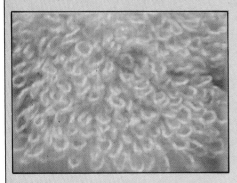

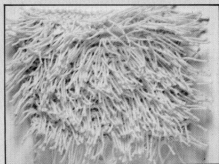

A loopy fabric in a fine mohair yarn has a soft, luxurious appearance. It is ideal for evening boleros or capes, bedjackets and baby clothes.

These loops are worked in a bouclé yarn. The nubbly yarn enhances this type of fabric, giving it a curly, fur finish almost like astrakhan. See the toddler's coat on page 49.

Cotton yarn is ideal for loop stitch, especially for making rugs. This type of cut loop fabric is popular for bath mats, since the shaggy finish is very absorbent.

Varieties of single loop stitch

Once you master the technique of making loop stitches you will find them fascinating to work. Spend time investigating the endless varieties and effects you can create from the basic technique. Altering the density or length of the loops or even making crochet loops are a few of the possibilities.

Remember that a loopy fabric uses more yarn than ordinary knitted textures, especially if it is closely looped; if you decide to alter the density of loops on a pattern, allow more or less yarn accordingly.

Produce lighter, sparsely textured fabrics or more solid, dense, shaggy ones by altering the spacing of the loops. Single loop stitch (as shown in the steps) is worked on alternate stitches in alternate rows. Here a lightly looped version is worked on alternate stitches in every fourth row: background fabric is visible between the loops.

Working a loop on each stitch in alternate rows makes a rich pile of loops with no background showing between them. This fabric is extremely thick and warm enough for outdoor wear and solid enough to make into a small rug.

continued

Frederick Mancini

Use your thumb to make the loops any length you like. Usually the thumb is held slightly down from the needles and the resulting loop is about 1¼in (3cm) long. To make shorter loops—about ½-¾in (1.5-2cm) long as above—place your thumb directly over the right-hand needle and wind the yarn tightly around the tip of the thumb only. Shorter loops give the fabric a close-cropped appearance.

Long loops have a slightly untidy and very shaggy look. The longer a loop, the more likely it is to twist up on itself. You can make loops any length you like. Bring the yarn forward to make a loop, insert your thumb and move it down until the loop is long enough—here they are about 2in (5cm) long. Use your thumb to anchor lower edge of loop against fabric while you complete the stitch.

This curly fabric with crochet chain loops makes an interesting alternative. Every fourth row work loops on alternate stitches as follows: K next st without letting it fall from left-hand needle, transfer loop on left-hand needle to a crochet hook and make 12 ch, keeping ch at front and yarn at back, slip loop onto right-hand needle and remove hook, lift last K st over loop to secure it.

Toddler's loopy coat

Bouclé yarn gives this toddler's coat a snug, warm texture.

Sizes
To fit 18[20]in (46[51]cm) chest.
Length, 16[18]in (41[46]cm).
Sleeve seam, 7½[8¾]in (19[22]cm).

Note: Directions for the larger size are in brackets []; if there is only one set of figures it applies to both sizes.

Materials
16[18]oz (450[500]g) of a medium-weight bouclé yarn
4oz (100g) of a knitting worsted
1 pair each Nos. 3 and 8 (3¼ and 5½mm) knitting needles
4 buttons

Gauge
13 sts and 20 rows to 4in (10cm) in loop st on No. 8 (5½mm) needles.

Back
Using No. 3 (3¼mm) needles and knitting worsted, cast on 93[101] sts.
1st row K1, *P1, K1, rep from * to end.
2nd row P1, *K1, P1, rep from * to end.
Rep these 2 rows for 1½in (4cm); end with a 2nd row. Cut off knitting worsted. Change to No. 8 (5½mm) needles. Join in bouclé.
Next row K1, (K2 tog) to end. **.
47[51] sts.
Beg loop st patt.
1st row (WS) K to end.
2nd row K1, *K next st without letting it drop off needle, yarn to front, pass yarn

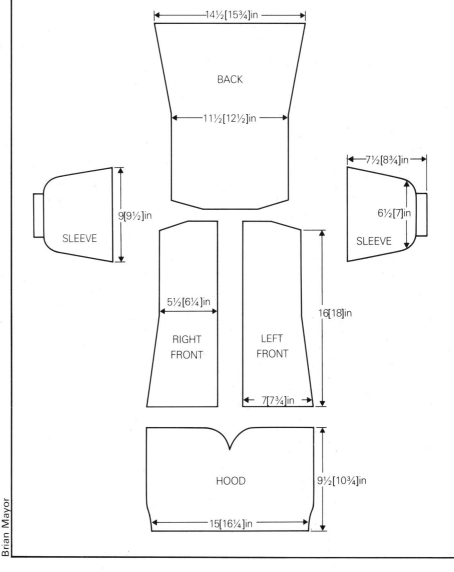

BACK

14½[15¾]in

11½[12½]in

SLEEVE

9[9½]in

7½[8¾]in

6½[7]in

SLEEVE

RIGHT FRONT

LEFT FRONT

5½[6¼]in

16[18]in

7[7¾]in

HOOD

15[16¼]in

9½[10¾]in

Brian Mayor

over left thumb to make a loop about $\frac{3}{4}$in (2cm) long, yarn to back and K st rem on left-hand needle, return 2 sts just made to left-hand needle and K them tog tbl— called loop 1 (L1)—, K1, rep from * to end.
3rd row K to end.
4th row K2, *L1, K1, rep from * to last st, K1.
These 4 rows form patt. Rep them throughout. Cont in patt, dec one st at each end of 9th[11th] and every foll 8th[10th] row until 37[41] sts rem. Cont straight until work measures 16[18]in (41[46]cm); end with a WS row.
Shape shoulders
Bind off 6[7] sts loosely at beg of next 2 rows and 7 sts at beg of foll 2 rows. Bind off rem 11[13] sts.

Left front
Using No. 3 (3¼mm) needles and knitting worsted, cast on 45[49] sts. Work as for back to **. 23[25] sts. Cont in patt as for back, dec one st at end of 9th[11th] and every foll 8th[10th] row until 18[20] sts rem. Cont straight until work is 5[7] rows less than back to shoulders; end at front edge.
Shape neck
Bind off 3 sts at beg of next row. Dec one st at beg of 2[3] foll alternate rows; end at side edge.
Shape shoulder
Bind off 6[7] sts at beg of next row. Work 1 row. Bind off rem 7 sts.

Right front
Work to match left front, reversing shaping.

Sleeves
Using No. 3 (3¼mm) needles and knitting worsted, cast on 41[45] sts. Work as for back to **. 21[23] sts. Cont in patt as for back, inc one st at each end of 5th and every foll 6th row until there are 29[31] sts. Cont straight until sleeve measures 7½[8¾]in (19[22]cm); end with a RS row. Bind off loosely.

Hood
Using No. 3 (3¼mm) needles and knitting worsted, cast on 97[105] sts. Work as for back to **. 49[53] sts. Cont in patt as for back until work measures 7½[8¼]in (19[21]cm); end with a RS row.
Shape back
Next row K24[26], turn and leave rem sts on a holder.
Dec one st at beg of next and foll 2 alternate rows, then at same edge on foll 2[4] rows. Bind off rem 19 sts. Return to sts that were left. With WS facing, rejoin yarn to next st, K2 tog, K to end. Complete to match first side.

Right front band
Using No. 3 (3¼mm) needles and knitting worsted, cast on 93[101] sts. Rib 5 rows as for back.

Next row (buttonhole row) Rib 3, *bind off 2, rib 15[17], rep from * twice more, bind off 2, rib 37[39].
Next row Rib to end, casting on 2 sts over those bound off in previous row. Rib 5 more rows. Bind off in ribbing.

Left front band
Work to match right front band, omitting buttonholes.

To finish
Do not press.
Join shoulder seams.
Sew in sleeves, matching center of bound-off edge to shoulder seams.
Join side and sleeve seams.
Sew on front bands.
Join back seam of hood. Sew on hood, beg and ending in center of front bands.
Sew on buttons.

Marcus Wilson-Smith

Knitting / COURSE 60

Working double loop stitch

In single loop stitch (see page 46) only one loop at a time can be worked on each stitch. The double loop stitch method allows two or more loops—depending on how many times the yarn is wound around your fingers—to be worked on any stitch. Although the finished effect is similar to a single loop fabric, there are a number of differences in technique. Here the wrong side of the work is facing as you make the loops and you wind the yarn around the fingers of your left hand, instead of the thumb.

The remarks on density of loops on a fabric for the single loop stitch also apply here, although by its nature double loop stitch produces a bulkier fabric; therefore the loops must not be placed too close together. You can alter the length of the loops by winding the yarn around more or fewer fingers accordingly.

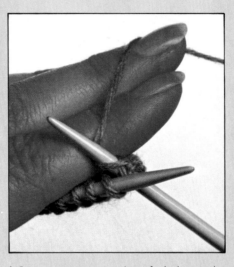

1 Cast on an even number of stitches and knit 3 rows. Start loop row: **4th row** (WS) K1, insert right-hand needle knitwise into next st, wind yarn clockwise over top of right-hand needle and around 2 fingers of left hand held close to needles at back of work.

2 Continue to wind yarn over right-hand needle point and around 2 fingers again to make a double loop. Note that the loops are forming at the back of the work, which is the right side.

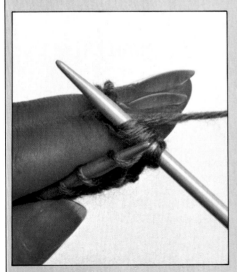

3 Now wind yarn over the top and around the right-hand needle point again in the usual way when knitting a stitch.

4 Draw all 3 loops on right-hand needle through loop on left-hand needle. Use left-hand needle point inserted from left to right to transfer 3 loops to left-hand needle next to original stitch.

5 Complete the loop stitch by knitting the 3 transferred loops together with the original stitch (4 loops in all) through the back of the loops. Although it is quite time-consuming, you must pull the double loop of individual stitches lightly to draw the stitch tight and secure it.

continued

Fred Mancini

6 Continue to the end of the 4th row, alternately knitting a stitch, then making a double loop on the next stitch, until you reach the last 2 stitches. Knit these 2 stitches. Turn the work with the right side facing to see the full effect of the 4th row.

7 To make this loopy fabric, knit 3 rows between each row of loops. Work the next loop row as follows: **8th row** K2, *make a loop on next st, K1, rep from *to end. The loops are on alternate stitches to those in the previous row. Repeat these 8 rows throughout to form the pattern.

8 The reverse side of a loopy fabric has a strong, solid texture. This one consists of garter stitch ridges with a gap, or "loose" row, every time a loop row is worked.

Stitch Wise

Mixed ribs

This fabric is less elastic than true ribbing. It is reversible, even though it is worked differently on both sides. The fabric does not curl up, so it can be used for trimmings such as button bands, pockets or cuffs.
Cast on a multiple of 6 sts.
1st row *K3, P3, rep from * to end.
2nd row *K1, P1, rep from * to end.
These 2 rows form patt. Rep them throughout.

Basketweave rib

A simple rib texture with a distinctive knit ribbing separates sections of basket-weave pattern. Use as an allover fabric or combine in panels with cables.
Cast on a multiple of 5 sts plus 1 extra.
1st row (RS) K1 tbl, *P1, K2, P1, K1 tbl, rep from * to end.
2nd row P1, *K1, P2, K1, P1, rep from * to end.
3rd row K1 tbl, *P4, K1 tbl, rep from * to end.
4th row P1, *K4, P1, rep from * to end.
These 4 rows form patt. Rep them throughout.

Seed knit rib

This is similar in appearance to mixed rib pattern and uses two mixed ribs; it, too, is a reversible fabric.
Cast on a multiple of 4 sts plus 3 extra.
1st row K3, *P1, K3, rep from * to end.
2nd row K1, *P1, K3, rep from * to last 2 sts, P1, K1.
These 2 rows form patt. Rep them throughout.

Making a loopy edge

This is a method of producing a loopy trimming for the side edge of a piece of knitting without incorporating the loops into the fabric as you are working. It is similar to the technique used for knitting a fringe (see Volume 8, page 48).

The side edges only—not cast-on or bound-off edges—of any knitted fabric, whether it is plain or patterned, can be unraveled to give this loopy effect.

Note that if you bind off on a right-side row, the loops are on the left-hand edge; bind off on a wrong-side row to produce loops on the right.

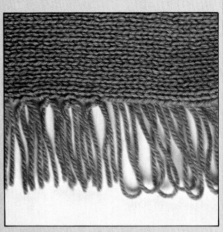

1 Work the fabric in the usual way. Bind off as usual but fasten off 1, 2 or more stitches before the last stitch. Drop these stitches from the left-hand needle and unravel them down the length of the work to create a loopy edge. The length of the loops depends on the number of unraveled stitches.

2 Here you can see the finished effect of the loops on the right of the photograph. You can cut the loops (see left) to make a fringe. Take a number of cut strands and knot them together for a decorative finish and also to prevent the cut ends from unraveling further.

Twisted purl rib

Knit rows alternating with a simple pattern row create this attractive rib texture of single twisted stitches against a purl background. Unlike true ribbing, the fabric is not elastic.

Cast on a multiple of 3 sts plus 2 extra.
1st row (WS) K to end.
2nd row P2, *K1, tbl, P2, rep from * to end.
These 2 rows form patt. Rep them throughout.

Sand stitch

This easy variation of single ribbing produces a fabric that is attractive on both sides. Cast on an even number of stitches.
1st row *K1, P1, rep from * to end.
2nd row K to end.
These 2 rows form patt. Rep them throughout.

Twisted single rib

This version of single ribbing is just as elastic as the original. Knitting stitches through the back of the loop gives them a twisted appearance and looks more decorative than severe lines of vertical knit ribs. Cast on an even number of stitches. **1st row** *K1 tbl, P1, rep from * to end. This row forms patt. Rep it throughout.

Fred Mancini

Woman's sweater and loopy jerkin

Fisherman's rib and loop stitch combine in a classic sweater and jerkin to wear with all your separates. You'll wonder how you managed without them.

Sizes

To fit 32[34:36:38]in (83[87:92:97]cm) bust.

Sweater Length, 21½[22:22½:23]in (54.5[56:57:58.5]cm).

Sleeve seam, 16½[17:17:17½]in (42[43:43:44]cm).

Vest Length, 22[22½:23:23½]in (56[57:58.5:60]cm).

Note: Directions for the larger sizes are in brackets []; if there is only one set of figures it applies to all sizes.

Materials

Sweater 15[16:17:18]oz (400[425:450:500]g) of a sport yarn
1 pair each Nos. 2 and 4 (2¾ and 3½mm) knitting needles
Jerkin 21[22:23:24]oz (575[600:625:650]g), of a knitting worsted
1 pair each Nos. 4 and 6 (3½ and 4½mm) knitting needles

Gauge

Sweater 24 sts and 56 rows to 4in (10cm) in patt on No. 4 (3½mm) needles.
Jerkin 20 sts and 32 rows to 4in (10cm) in patt on No. 6 (4½mm) needles.

Sweater

Back

Using No. 4 (3½mm) needles cast on 96[102:108:114] sts. Work 20 rows K1, P1 ribbing. Beg patt.

1st row (RS) K to end.

2nd row *K1, K1 through center of next st in row below, rep from * to last 2 sts, K2. The 2nd row forms patt: rep it throughout. Cont in patt until work measures 14¾[15:15¼:15½]in (37.5[38:38.5:39.5]cm); end with a WS row.

Shape armholes

Bind off 5 sts at beg of next 2 rows. Dec one st at each end of next and every foll alternate row until 74[78:82:86] sts rem. Cont straight until armholes measure 6¾[7:7¼:7½]in (17[18:18.5:19]cm); end with a WS row.

Shape shoulders

Bind off 5[6:6:6] sts at beg of next 6 rows and 7[5:6:7] sts at beg of foll 2 rows. Bind off rem 30[32:34:36] sts.

Front

Work as given for back to armhole shaping.

Shape armholes and divide for neck

Next row Bind off 5 sts, patt until there are 43[46:49:52] sts on right-hand needle, turn and leave rem sts on a spare needle.

Complete left side of neck first. Work

1 row. Cont in patt, dec one st at neck edge on foll 3rd[3rd:1st:1st] row and every foll 5th row, *at same time* dec one st at armhole edge on next and every foll alternate row until 6[7:8:9] decs have been worked. Keeping armhole edge straight, dec at neck edge only as before until 22[23:24:25] sts rem. Cont straight until front measures same as back to shoulder; end at armhole edge.

Shape shoulder

Bind off 5[6:6:6] sts at beg of next and foll 2 alternate rows. Work 1 row. Bind off rem 7[5:6:7] sts.

Return to sts on spare needle. With RS of work facing, rejoin yarn to next st and work to end of row. Complete to match first side, reversing shapings.

Sleeves

Using No. 4 (3½mm) needles cast on 48[50:52:54] sts. Work 20 rows K1, P1 ribbing. Cont in patt as for back, inc one st at each end of 9th[11th:11th:5th] and every foll 16th[16th:16th:17th] row until there are 72[74:76:78] sts. Cont straight until sleeve measures 16½[17:17:17½]in (42[43:43:44]cm); end with a WS row.

Shape top

Bind off 5 sts at beg of next 2 rows. Dec one st at each end of 5th and every foll 6th row until 56 sts rem, then at each end of every 4th row until 40[42:44:46] sts rem. Dec one st at each end of every foll alternate row until 26 sts rem. Work 1 row. Bind off 3 sts at beg of next 4 rows. Bind off rem 14 sts.

Neckband

Join right shoulder seam. Using No. 2 (2¾mm) needles and with RS facing,

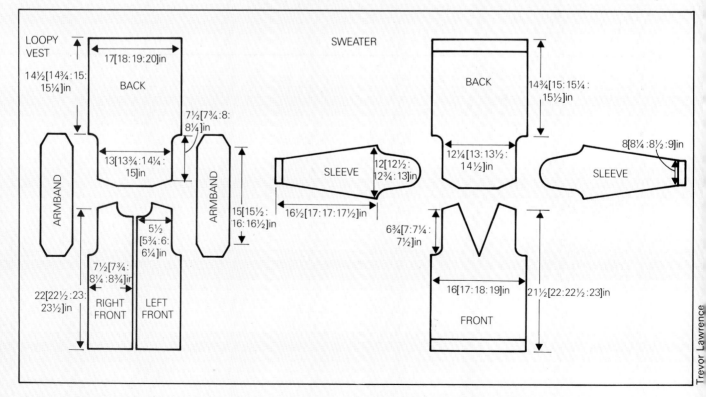

needle, wind yarn over right-hand needle point and around first and second fingers of left hand twice, then over and around right-hand needle point again, draw all 3 loops through st and return to left-hand needle, K loops tog tbl with original st—called loop 1—, K1, rep from * to end.

5th-7th rows K to end.
8th row K1, *K1, loop 1, rep from * to last 3 sts, K2.

These 8 rows form patt. Cont in patt until work measures $14\frac{1}{2}[14\frac{3}{4}:15:15\frac{1}{4}]$in $(37[37.5:38:39]$cm); end with a WS row.

Shape armholes
Keeping patt correct, bind off 5 sts at beg of next 2 rows. Dec one st at each end of next and every foll alternate row until 65[69:71:75] sts rem. Cont straight until armholes measure $7\frac{1}{2}[7\frac{3}{4}:8:8\frac{1}{4}]$in $(19[19.5:20.5:21]$cm); end with a WS row.

Shape shoulders
Bind off 4[4:4:5] sts at beg of next 6 rows and 5[6:7:5] sts at beg of foll 2 rows. Bind off rem 31[33:33:35] sts.

Left front
Using No. 4 ($3\frac{1}{2}$mm) needles cast on 55[57:59:63] sts. Work 21 rows ribbing as for back. **
Next row Rib 15, then leave these sts on a holder, rib 9[10:11:8], (work 2 tog, rib 8) 2[2:2:3] times, work 2 tog, rib to end. 37[39:41:44] sts.
Change to No. 6 ($4\frac{1}{2}$mm) needles. Work in patt as for back until front matches back to underarm; end at side edge.

Shape armhole
Bind off 5 sts at beg of next row. Work 1 row. Dec one st at armhole edge on next and every foll alternate row until 27[28:29:31] sts rem. Cont straight until armhole measures 20[20:20:22] rows less than back to shoulders; end with a WS row.

Shape neck
Dec one st at neck edge on next and every foll alternate row until 17[18:19:20] sts rem. Work 1 row.

Shape shoulder
Bind off 4[4:4:5] sts at beg of next and foll 2 alternate row. Work 1 row. Bind off rem 5[6:7:5] sts.

Right front
Work as given for left front to **.
Next row Rib 9[10:11:8] (work 2 tog, rib 8) 2[2:2:3] times, work 2 tog, rib to end. 52[54:56:59] sts. Cut off yarn.
Change to No. 6 ($4\frac{1}{2}$mm) needles.
Next row Sl first 15 sts onto a holder, rejoin yarn to next st and work first row of patt to end.
Complete to match left front, reversing shapings.

Armbands (make 2)
Join shoulder seams. Using No. 4 ($3\frac{1}{2}$mm)

needles cast on 13 sts.
1st row (RS) K6, sl 1, K6.
2nd row P6, P1 winding yarn twice around needle, P6.
3rd row Inc in first st, K5, sl 1 dropping extra loop, K5, inc in last st.
4th row P7, P1 winding yarn twice around needle, P7.
Cont in this way, keeping center st as above and inc one st at each end of 3rd and every foll 4th row until there are 21 sts. Cont straight, keeping center as before, until band fits from underarm to shoulder; end with a P row. Insert a marker at each end of last row to mark shoulder line. Cont in this way until armband is 16 rows less than first part from shoulder line. Dec one st at each end of next and every foll 4th row until 13 sts rem. Work 3 rows. Bind off.

Left front band
Using No. 4 ($3\frac{1}{2}$mm) needles and with RS facing, K across left front sts on holder, dec 2 sts evenly across row, turn and cast on 12 sts. 25 sts.
Next row P12, P1 winding yarn twice around needle, P12.
Next row K12, sl 1 dropping extra loop, K12.
Cont in this way until band fits up front edge to neck shaping; end with a P row. Cut off yarn and leave sts on holder.

Right front band
Using No. 4 ($3\frac{1}{2}$mm) needles cast on 12 sts, then with RS facing, K across right front sts on holder, dec 2 sts evenly across row. 25 sts. Complete as for left front band; with a P row. Do not cut off yarn.

Neckband
Using No. 4 ($3\frac{1}{2}$mm) needles and with RS facing, bind off 12 sts of right front band, K to end of band, pick up and K 20[20:20:22] sts up right front neck, 31[33:33:35] sts across back neck, 20[20:20:22] sts down left front neck, K across 13 sts of left front band, then bind off rem 12 sts. 97[99:99:105] sts. Beg with a P row work 12 rows stockinette st.
Next row (WS) K each st tbl to mark neckband edge.
Beg with a K row, work 12 rows stockinette st. Bind off.

To finish
Press or block armbands and front bands according to yarn used. Join side seams. Sew armbands in position, matching marker to shoulder seam and slip stitching half of armband to bound-off sts at underarm. Fold in half to WS and slip stitch in place. Sew front bands in position along front edge, turn to WS and slip stitch in place. With RS tog, join ends of neckband. Turn neckband to RS; slip stitch in place on WS of neck. Press bands lightly if appropriate.

pick up and K 64[66:68:70] sts down left front neck, one st from center of V, 64[66:68:70] sts up right front and 38[40:42:44] sts across back neck. 167[173:179:185] sts.
Next row (WS) (K1, P1) 50[52:54:56] times, K2 tog, P1 (center st), K2 tog, (P1, K1) 31[32:33:34] times.
Rib 7 more rows, dec one st at each side of center st on every row. Rib 8 more rows, inc one st at each side of center on every row. Bind off loosely in ribbing.

To finish
Press or block, according to yarn used. Join left shoulder and neckband seams. Set in sleeves. Join side and sleeve seams. Turn neckband in half to WS and slip stitch loosely in place.

Jerkin

Back
Using No. 4 ($3\frac{1}{2}$mm) needles cast on 97[103:109:115] sts.
1st row (RS) K1, *P1, K1, rep from * to end.
2nd row P1, *K1, P1, rep from * to end.
Rep these 2 rows 9 times more, then the first of them again.
Next row (inc row) Rib 4[7:2:5], (work 2 tog, rib 6) 11[11:13:13] times, work 2 tog, rib to end. 85[91:95:101] sts.
Change to No. 6 ($4\frac{1}{2}$mm) needles. Beg patt.
1st-3rd rows K to end.
4th row (WS) K1, *insert right-hand needle knitwise into next st on left-hand

Sewing/COURSE 56

*Selecting fabrics
*Pressing and ironing
*Laundering and removing
  stains
*Working with difficult
  fabrics
*Fabric dictionary

Selecting fabrics

Choosing the right fabric—and then handling and caring for it properly during construction and wear—can make all the difference in producing a successful garment you'll enjoy wearing for years.
Keep the following points in mind:

● Buy enough fabric. Check the pattern specifications and examine fabrics to see if there is a one-way design, nap or pile, or plaids or stripes that must be matched. If so, you may need extra fabric.

● Choose fabric suitable to the garment style; if the garment is gathered or pleated, for example, make sure that the fabric will adapt to the design.

● If two or more fabrics are to be combined in one garment, make sure that they are compatible in weight and fiber content as well as pattern and color, so that they require the same handling and cleaning; for example, avoid trimming a washable garment with collars and cuffs in a fabric that should be dry cleaned.

● Select appropriate thread—cotton or silk for cotton and linen fabrics, silk or synthetic for woolen or stretch fabrics, and synthetic for man-made fabrics. Sewing threads are also graded according to whether they are intended for hand-sewing, machine-sewing or embroidery. The color of thread should be one shade darker than the fabric, as thread appears lighter when stitched on the garment.

● With some types of fabric, you will need a special needle—a fine needle for fine fabrics, a thick needle for heavy fabrics or a ball point needle for knits and synthetic fabrics.

● Keep in mind how you plan to use the garment. Is it for day or evening wear, informal or formal? Do you intend to wear it in summer or winter, or all year round? Does it need to match an existing garment?

● Make sure the fabric suits you. Boldly patterned or strongly colored fabrics can be difficult to wear, and bright prints or emphatic horizontal stripes can make a large person seem larger. Take the bolt of fabric, unroll enough to hold against you, and check the effect in a long mirror. If you are doubtful, try to find a ready-made garment similar to the one you want to make and try it on to see the effect of the color and design.

● Fabrics should always be labeled with their composition. Note this when buying, so that you have a guide to washing, pressing, the type of thread to use and general after care (see the charts that follow). By law your retailer must have care labels available for all uncut fabric. Be sure to ask for a label so you can sew it into the finished garment.

● Last, but by no means least, buy good quality fabric. Make sure that the weave is firm and even, so that the threads do not shift when the fabric is stitched and that there are no unusually thin or thick areas. The dye should look even and fresh, and the fabric should be as wrinkle-resistant as possible: take a corner of the fabric in one hand and crush it; the wrinkles should fall out. Check that printed fabrics follow the grain.

Pressing and ironing

All fabrics need pressing at every stage of a garment's construction (see Volume 11, pages 75-76) and many benefit from ironing after laundering.
Pressing is done with the weight of the iron, in the direction of the grain of the fabric, and, with all fabrics except cotton and linen, requires a pressing cloth: a dry cloth with a steam iron and a damp cloth with a dry iron.
Press on the wrong side to prevent shine, be careful when pressing over bulky areas like zippers and pockets, and do not press over pins. Use a pressing ham for curved areas.
Many fabrics need ironing, either after laundering or to freshen the garment. Ironing differs from pressing in that it is the motion of the iron, not its weight, that affects the fabric. The type of fabric will determine the temperature of the iron and whether the fabric should be damp or dry and ironed from the right or the wrong side (see the table at right).
Permanent press fabrics normally do not need ironing—particularly if the garment is removed from the dryer promptly—but the crispness of shirt collars, cuffs, etc., may be improved with a quick touch-up ironing job.

Ironing instructions

Temperature and conditions	Fabric
Hot iron	
damp fabric/right side	cotton, linen
damp fabric/wrong side	viscose, glazed cotton (polish on right side)
Warm iron	
damp fabric/right side	silk
damp fabric/wrong side	wool/cotton mixtures
press over damp cloth or	wool, including angora,
steam iron/wrong side	mohair, cashmere
steam iron/wrong side	velvet and other pile
over velvet board	fabrics
dry fabric/right side	drip-dry fabrics, nylon, polyester
Cool iron	
damp fabric/wrong side	acetate
Do not iron	corduroy, man-made and rubber stretch fabrics, fiberglass, vinyl

Washing and removing stains

Most of the garments you make will need laundering, and you may have to remove an occasional stain. To avoid the risk of ruining the garment, use the appropriate methods (see charts).
When in doubt about fiber content, wash under mildest conditions, and follow the tips below.

● Hand wash—woolens, fiberglass

● May not be colorfast—corduroy, denim

● Do not soak—flame-resistant fabrics (on some, use detergent, not soap), woolens, silk, leather, non-colorfast articles

● Do not use chlorine bleach—woolens, silk, flame-resistant or easycare fabrics (use hydrogen peroxide on woolens and silk). Always test for colorfastness when using bleach

● Do not wring—permanent-press fabrics

● Drip-dry—fiberglass, water-repellant and Scotchgard® fabrics

● Do not wash—some foam-backed and laminated fabrics

LAUNDERING SUGGESTIONS

WASHING

Water	Hot wash (130°F or more)	Warm wash (approx. 100°F)	Cold wash (below 100°F)
Water temperature guide	Sturdy whites and colorfast pastels	Dark or non-colorfast colors	Extra sensitive colors
	Heavily soiled clothes	Knits, delicate fabrics or fabrics with special finishes (e.g. permanent press), most synthetics	Machine-washable woolens, silks (CHECK fabric care instructions) *Caution:* in water under 50°F, detergents do not dissolve well

DRYING

When to remove clothes from dryer	Damp dry Cottons, linens or other fabrics that need ironing	Slightly damp Corduroys, quilted items, and knits keep shape better if removed when still slightly damp and folded or hung to complete drying	Fully dry Permanent press (remove from dryer as soon as cycle is finished to minimize wrinkling)

Special laundering hints

Wool and silk Unless especially indicated, should be dry cleaned or carefully hand-washed only. Can be damaged by heavy duty detergents, hot water, chlorine bleach, and too-vigorous agitation.

Permanent press Should be washed before they look soiled. Finish makes them tend to look fresh even when they should be washed, and heavy soiling is more difficult to remove. Permanent press fabrics must be "softened" by heat (water or air) to shed wrinkles. While they are soft, fabrics can be re-wrinkled by being crushed, as in spinning. They should be cooled by a cold rinse before any spinning, and have a "cool-off" period of tumbling without heat at end of drying cycle. Remove from dryer promptly.

Knits Turn inside out before laundering to prevent snagging and pilling. Use a cold rinse to prevent wrinkling. Dry lightweight and heavyweight knits in separate loads to eliminate over-drying which may cause shrinkage.

CHECK LABEL INSTRUCTIONS ON ALL FABRICS FOR LAUNDERING. The law requires that all uncut fabrics be accompanied by a care label that can be sewn into the finished garment. Be sure to ask for it when you purchase your fabric.

Hints for removing stains

● Treat all stains as soon as possible—then washing in detergent is often all that is necessary.
● Use the mildest treatment first. When using chemical solvents, test on an inconspicuous place first.
● Place the area to be treated over an absorbent cloth such as an old towel.
● To prevent a ring, treat the area around the stain first and work toward the center.
● If treatment requires using solvent first and then laundering, wash in rich suds immediately afterward, before the fluid has dried on the fabric.
● If a treatment does not work the first time, repeat it. If this fails, have the item dry-cleaned, identifying the stain and what you have used trying to remove it.

● Take care with poisonous and flammable preparations. Work in a well-ventilated room.
Do not smoke.
● Useful stain-removing agents include:
laundry borax—safe on most fabrics
glycerine—safe on any fabric and any color
white vinegar or acetic acid—do not use on acetates and avoid contact with skin
household ammonia—do not add to hydrogen peroxide for use on woolens; test on colored fabrics
painter's thinner, gasoline, lighter fuel—grease solvents
● For specific stains, the following list may be helpful.

Adhesives—clear or contact adhesives: treat from wrong side with amyl acetate (do not use on acetate); latex adhesive: if wet, remove with damp cloth, if dry, loosen with liquid grease solvent.
Alcohol (and fruit juice)
    beer—rinse or soak fresh stains in lukewarm water, then launder in heavy-duty detergent. For dried stains, launder, then bleach in hydrogen peroxide solution (white cottons/linens), sponge with white vinegar solution (colored fabrics), or sponge with borax (acetates).
    whisky, gin, vodka, rum, liqueurs—rinse with warm water, then launder in heavy-duty detergent at highest temperature for fiber.
    wine—throw salt on stain immediately to prevent spreading. Rinse in warm water or soak and sponge in warm detergent solution. Wash at highest temperature for fabric. Treat difficult stains with hydrogen peroxide.
Blood (and proteinaceous stains like egg, gravy, chocolate, ice cream)—soak in cold water and salt or warm detergent. Hot water will set stains. Soak stubborn stains in hydrogen peroxide solution plus a few drops of ammonia. Launder.
Candle wax—pick off as much as possible by hand, then use blotting paper and an iron to lift out

Simple stain treatments

Perspiration stains should be sponged with a weak solution of ammonia while they are fresh.

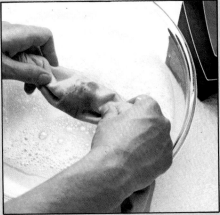

When dipping or soaking a stain, hold cloth by this area and then twist unstained parts to prevent solution from spreading.

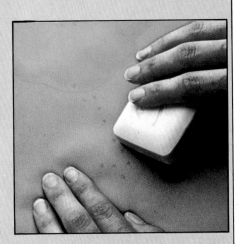

To treat stains caused by mildew on colored fabrics, dampen affected areas and rub them with soap, then dry outdoors in sunshine if possible.

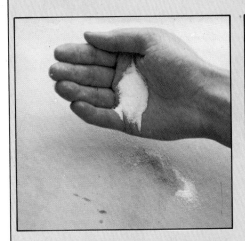

Salt thrown on tablecloths stops wine or beet stains from spreading. Soak in warm water as soon as possible.

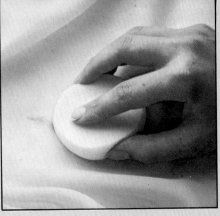

Dried make-up stains should be softened first with glycerine, then washed in hot water with detergent.

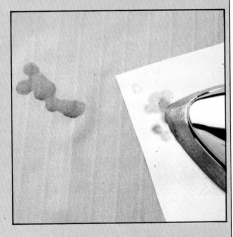

Candle wax should be picked off by hand as thoroughly as possible. Then "sandwich" stained area between clean blotting paper and lift out wax with iron.

Simon Butcher

remaining wax. (See photograph above.)

Chewing gum — harden gum with ice or in re-frigerator, then pick off. Launder in warm water.

Coffee, tea — wash in rich suds as soon as possible. Treat difficult stains with hydrogen peroxide.

Flower, grass, perfume — soak with enzyme pre-soak for at least 30 minutes. Rinse. Pretreat with detergent. Launder, using enzyme detergent and bleach safe for fabric.

Grease, fats, oils (including shoe polish, wax polish, lipstick, creosote, tar) — treat heavy stains with grease solvent or soak in solvent detergent, then wash at maximum temperature. For unwash-able fabric, spread absorbent chalk or powder over small marks and brush off; or press with warm iron over blotting paper. Dry cleaning may be necessary.

Ink

washable — sponge or rub under cold water, then launder in heavy-duty detergent.

permanent — dab with denatured alcohol, then wash in detergent.

ballpoint — dab with non-flammable dry cleaning solvent or use grease solvent, then sponge with warm water or launder.

felt-tip — dab with dry cleaning solvent and treat as ballpoint.

duplicating machine — treat with castor oil, then wash in strong detergent.

Iodine — wash immediately; soak old stains in a solution of sodium thiosulphate.

Jam — fresh stains usually wash out. Soak old stains in borax or heavy-duty detergent. If some stains remain, try hydrogen peroxide. Launder.

Make-up — wipe fresh stains; soak 5 minutes in weak ammonia solution. Rinse well, then launder in solvent detergent at maximum temperature. For dried stains, see illustrations above. For unwashable fabrics, remove surface and apply grease solvent.

Mascara — use aerosol grease solvent followed by diluted ammonia. Or soak in strong solvent detergent, then wash.

Mildew — while growth is fresh, launder in heavy-duty detergent. Chlorine bleach solution plus a little vinegar may be used on whites (not easy-care fabrics); soak other whites (except nylon) in hydrogen peroxide solution. For colored fabrics, see illustrations above.

Nail polish, hair spray — wipe immediately, then use amyl acetate (test first; be careful with acetates). Dab remaining stain with dry cleaning solvent, wash.

Paints — prompt treatment is most important

oil-based — dab fresh stains with painter's thinner

and sponge with cold water, then launder. Dried stains require dry cleaning.

latex — sponge fresh stains with cold water, then launder. If ignored, a plastic film will develop which cannot be removed.

Perspiration — sponge fresh stain with weak sol-ution of ammonia, then rinse. If color is affected, sponge with vinegar, then rinse. Bleach white cotton in solution of hydrogen peroxide or soak in detergent. For unwashable fabrics, dab with weak solution of vinegar to clear stain and deodorize.

Rust — on cotton or linen, soak in lemon juice and press under a piece of damp fabric. Or use weak oxalic acid solution, rinse well and wash. On silk and wool, use weak hydrochloric acid solution, rinse well.

Scorch marks — rub light marks immediately under cold running water, then soak in warm borax solution. Rinse well and launder if possible. On whites, careful bleaching with hydrogen peroxide solution is a last remedy.

Urine — rinse or soak in cold water, then launder.

Vomit — remove surface deposit, then rinse well under cold running water. Soak and launder in heavy-duty detergent. For unwashable fabrics, re-move deposit and sponge with warm water with a few drops of ammonia added.

Working with difficult fabrics

Eight exciting looks from one basic blouse pattern. Note how the different fabrics produce different effects.

Fabrics vary tremendously in weight, thickness and texture. Some are more difficult than others to work with; some ravel during cutting or are thick and therefore hard to cut; some slide or stick and are awkward to stitch or blunt the needle. If you take certain precautions and test stitches and pressing on fabric scraps first, however, you will find it is easy to work successfully with so-called difficult fabrics. Here is a list of fabrics, with the problems they present and the best ways to overcome them.

Knits

Any machine-knitted fabric; varying degrees of stretchiness.
Styles to choose Simple, soft-fitting, clinging designs.
Cutting Avoid placing patterns on central crease in synthetic fabrics; it may be difficult to press out.
Stitching Use fine synthetic thread and ballpoint machine needle with zig-zag or multiple machine stitch. Stitch any strain-bearing seams twice or reinforce with tape. Hang garment overnight before hemming.
Pressing Press lightly with steam or dry iron and damp pressing cloth.

Place brown paper under seams to prevent seam allowances from marking fabric.

Beaded or sequined fabrics

Beads or sequins can be applied to knitted or woven base fabric; fabrics may be lightly or heavily encrusted.
Styles to choose Fabrics are difficult to work, so choose styles with a minimum of seams and darts.
Cutting Lay pattern pieces in one direction, matching motifs if necessary. Pin within seam allowance and try to avoid cutting sequins; cut through single thickness only. If the beads are close together remove the appropriate amount with small scissors before cutting fabric; fasten threads to stop the rest from unraveling. Re-apply beads or sequins if necessary after seaming.
Stitching Slip-baste seams and darts on right side. When you are sure of the fit, remove beads from final seam allowances and dart area. Use zipper foot for all stitching. Remove beads from hem allowance, and from seam allowance if using a zipper. Use small snaps instead of buttonholes.
Pressing Use a cool dry iron only and

cover fabric with a dry cloth. Press on wrong side on a padded board.

Sheer fabrics

Transparent fabrics classified as crisp or soft. Crisp sheers include voile, organdy and net; soft are batiste, chiffon, China silk, cheese-cloth, georgette and gauze.
Styles to choose Airy, floating, full.
Cutting To prevent fabric from sliding, pin to thick blanket or sheet fastened to cutting surface. Allow large seam allowances if fabric ravels easily.
Stitching Place pins within seam allowance to avoid marking fabric. Use fine needle and silk or synthetic thread. Stitch between layers of tissue paper, using French seams and narrow hand-sewn or machine-stitched hems; make a normal hem on an underlining. Bind edges of net.
Pressing Press lightly with a steam or dry iron; press embroidered sheers face down on a towel.

Satin

Cotton satin is easy to work with but synthetics fray and are slippery.
Styles to choose Anything from overalls to an evening dress.
Cutting and stitching Handle as little as possible. Leave large seam allowances. Prevent seams from puckering by using polyester thread.
Pressing Your iron must be smooth and

Jean-Claude Volpelière

not discolored; use a pressing cloth or tissue paper and always press on wrong side. On delicate satins, finger-press seams; otherwise, press seams over brown paper.

Lace

Machine-made lace comes in light, medium and heavy weights.
Styles to choose Simple styles with few seams and darts, which break up fabric design. Lace cannot bear much strain, so avoid close-fitting waists or armholes. Collars are difficult to work: instead of buttonholes, use loops.
Linings and underlinings Use underlining to support fragile lace and to prevent scratching. Suitable underlinings are silk organza, fine net or chiffon; match fiber with that of lace. For a more sculptured style, use taffeta or satin.
Cutting Make sure pattern motifs run in the same direction and are not broken up by seams. Make use of any scalloped edges by positioning pattern pieces so they fall on hemlines.
Stitching Stitch fragile laces as sheers and underlined lace in the normal way. Some heavy laces must be hand-sewn. Reduce seam allowances to $\frac{1}{4}$in (5mm) and overcast raw edges to finish. Face hems with fine organza. On delicate laces use a placket fastening instead of a zipper.
Pressing Use steam or dry iron with slightly damp muslin pressing cloth

on top and pressing pad or towel underneath to prevent flattening.

Metallics

Any fabric that has metal threads knitted or woven into it—from sheer silks to lamés and brocades.
Styles to choose Draped or tailored, depending on fabric.
Cutting Place pattern pieces in the same direction. Leave large seam allowances if fabric ravels
Stitching See Brocade. Use synthetic thread and fine needle; metallic threads make needles blunt, so change them when necessary.
Pressing Iron only if absolutely necessary, with dry iron on wrong side over a dry cloth. Finger-press seams.

Brocade

Woven or jacquard knits; if they contain metallic threads handle as metallics (see above).
Styles to choose Evening coats, tunics or simple dresses.
Cutting Brocade ravels, so leave large seam allowances. Make sure fabric runs in the same direction if it has a sheen and match pattern motifs.
Stitching Finish seams with overcasting or zig-zag stitching. Avoid bound buttonholes. Do not use a zipper on metallic brocades.
Pressing Press lightly with a cool iron, with towel underneath fabric.

Velvet and corduroy

Silk or rayon velvets are difficult to use; corduroy, pinwale, velveteen and panne velvets are easier.
Styles to choose Heavy velvets are most suitable for suits and evening skirts. Choose simple styles and handle velvet as little as possible; avoid gathers, darts and pleats.
Cutting Lay pattern pieces so pile runs upward on finished garment for a richer look.
If possible, use fine pins or needles to prevent permanent marks.
Stitching To prevent velvet from slipping, baste with silk thread, using small stitches and back-stitching at 2-3in (5-8cm) intervals. Machine-stitch in direction of pile with tissue paper strips between fabric layers to prevent wrinkling; finish seams with overcasting or zig-zag if necessary. Insert zipper by hand and substitute loops for buttonholes. Use straight or bias seam binding for hems, or overcast raw edge and hem in place, picking up one thread at a time.
Pressing Remove basting and hang garment in steamy bathroom to remove slight wrinkles.
Press pile-side down on a needleboard. (Use an ordinary board for velveteen and corduroy; press flat but lightly and with damp cloth.)
For seams, use pressing cloth made from a velvet scrap placed pile-side down on seam.

More difficult fabrics

Coated fabrics

These include vinyl-coated, bonded or laminated fabrics.

Styles to choose Vinyl-coated fabrics can be made into raincoats, ponchos, aprons and general-purpose bags. Bonded and laminated fabrics make simple, casual coats.

Cutting If the finish is slippery, lay fabric wrong side down. Attach pattern pieces with steel pins placed within seam allowance to avoid making holes.

Stitching To prevent fabric from slipping, use a roller foot or insert tracing paper between seam foot and fabric. Seams on vinyl fabrics can be top-stitched. Prevent foam-backed fabrics from sticking to machine by basting straight seam binding or a strip of cotton over foam.

Pressing Do not press vinyl- or polyurethane-coated fabrics. If they crease, roll them around a cardboard tube and leave overnight

Fur fabrics

Various types and depths of pile, with knitted, woven or foam backing.

Styles to choose Aim for simple lines; intricate seaming is lost in pile of fabric.

Cutting As with leather, check the fit before cutting your fabric. Make a muslin shell first. Lay out pattern pieces so that pile runs downward. Cut fabric pile-side down on single thickness only.

Depending on backing fabric, pin pattern pieces or attach them with transparent tape. With soft pencil or chalk, mark outline of pattern pieces and draw arrows in direction of pile. Cut through backing only and ease pile apart.

Stitching This also depends on the backing fabric. Stitch firm-backed fur by hand. Trim seam allowance to ¼in (5mm), hold edges together with clothes pins and overcast with fine, sharp needle and silk or synthetic thread. On knit-backed fabrics use small zig-zag machine stitch, or blanket-stitch by hand. Use a roller foot for vinyl-coated backings. On foam-backed furs, place strips of cotton over seamline or stitch between layers of paper. After stitching, shave pile from seam allowances. Tease out pile along seams on right side with a pin.

Finishing touches Cut darts open and grade enclosed seams, such as collars, to reduce bulk. For hems, shave 2in (5cm) of pile along hem edge and stitch a 2in (5cm)-wide grosgrain ribbon onto it; turn up hem and slip stitch ribbon to backing. On heavier fabrics turn up hem and glue in place. Buttonholes are difficult, so use hook or frog fastenings or fake buttons by stitching buttons on top and snaps underneath.

Pressing Finger-press seams and with a cool, dry iron, carefully press garment pile-side down on needleboard or towel to prevent flattening.

Leather and suede

Fine, smooth leather, suede and chamois are most suitable; usually sold in specialist shops.

Styles to choose Simple skirts, tunics and vests are easiest; on first attempt avoid facings, set-in sleeves, buttonholes. Size of pattern pieces must fit into size of skin. Discuss requirements with retailer and take pattern along if in doubt. If necessary, join pieces so that the maximum amount of skin is used.

Cutting Needles and pins leave permanent holes, so make a muslin shell and make adjustments on that. Always lay pattern pieces on flat skin, with nap running down. Note any blemishes on right side of skin and mark position on wrong side. Cut left and right pattern pieces separately. Attach pattern to skin with transparent tape and mark outlines of edges and darts lightly with ballpoint pen.

Stitching Do not baste. Use transparent tape, paper clips or clothes pins to hold seam allowances together; use pure silk or synthetic thread. On plain seams or darts a few dabs of glue under the seam allowances produce a neat, flat effect. For hand sewing use a glover's needle, and for machine stitching a wedge-point needle; replace when blunt. A roller foot will prevent material from sliding. Use plain or lapped seams; leave hems raw or glue down. Tie off thread ends (back-stitching can tear fabric).

Finishing touches If darts are bulky, cut them open and pare away undersides of seam allowances with razor blade; practice this technique first. If using bound buttonholes, sew small reinforcing buttons on wrong side of buttons; otherwise insert metal eyelets. Instead of facings turn under back edges and topstitch. If lining, stitch tape to seam allowance and slip stitch lining to this.

Pressing Finger-press seams on fine skins; on heavier skins use a mallet or rolling pin to flatten seams. Press carefully on wrong side with medium-hot dry iron and dry cloth.

Fabric dictionary

T = Thread appropriate

I = Special ironing

P = Pins mark fabric

S = Special seams

C = Care when cutting

F = Fabric likely to ravel

A

Acetate Lustrous man-made cellulose fiber which can be woven to produce a satin, taffeta, brocade or raw silk effect; also used for knit fabrics and linings **C, T, I**

Acrilan (trade name) An acrylic fiber

Acrylic A fiber derived from oil with a wool-like appearance. Soft and bulky, it is used for knitted, woven, permanently pleated or pile fabrics **T, I**

Antron (trade name) A nylon fiber **T, I, C**

Arnel (trade name) Triacetate fiber

Avisco (trade name) An acetate fiber **C, T, I**

B

Batiste Fine light-weight fabric in plain weave cotton or man-made fibers; heavier when made in wool **T**

Brocade Heavy fabric with rich complex jacquard weave in silk or man-made fibers. Different weight for evening wear and home decorating fabrics **C, F, I**

Buckram Cotton or linen fabric stiffened with paste, glue or clay for interfacings

Burlap Coarse openly-woven fabric made from jute yarns. For upholstery and wall coverings **F**

Butcher linen Stiff, heavy, plainly woven cotton fabric, used for aprons and coats

C

Cambric Plain weave fabric of medium-weight cotton or linen fabric. Now used for summer dresses

Canvas (duck) Heavy plain weave fabric, closely woven. Cotton or man-made fibers in various weights. For interlinings, upholstery and accessories

Cashmere An expensive soft fine fabric of wool of the cashmere (or Kashmir) goat, blended with sheep's wool to improve its wearing ability

Celanese (trade name) A nylon fiber **T**

Cheesecloth Loose plain weave cotton fabric; the texture is uneven due to highly twisted yarns **F, I**

Chenille Fabric with closely spaced tufts in continuous lines, of cotton or cotton and man-made fiber blends, used for bedspreads and loungewear **C, T, I**

Chiffon Sheer, delicate, plain weave fabric from silk or man-made fibers; can have a rough handle, drapes well. For evening dresses, scarves and blouses **C, F, P, T**

Chintz Closely woven glazed cotton with multi-colored, often floral, print. For home decorating

Ciré An extremely shiny glossy fabric finish; often used to mean nylon or acetate fabrics with ciré finish used for windbreakers and other outerwear

Corduroy Hard-wearing fabric with lengthwise cords of pile in various widths and weights. Cotton or man-made fibers. For coats, dresses and trousers

Cotton Fabric made from cotton-plant fiber; woven or knitted. Listed here under generic names

Crash Loose plain weave coarse cotton or linen fabrics for home decorating

Crepe Slightly crinkled puckered surface made from highly twisted natural yarn or man-made fibers. Various weights; hangs and drapes well; for blouses, dresses and evening wear **T, I**

Crepe de Chine Traditionally a soft silk fabric; now often in man-made fibers **T, I**

Creslan (trade name) An acrylic fiber **I**

Cretonne Cotton fabric similar to an unglazed chintz

D

Dacron (trade name) Polyester fiber **T**

Damask Jacquard weave fabric for home decorating, similar to brocade but flatter and reversible; usually linen, or viscose rayon fiber

Denim Tough cotton fabric with twill weave giving color and white effect; can be brushed

Double knit Knit fabric with firm body and limited stretch capacity, providing body and stability similar to a woven fabric

Dralon (trade name) Acrylic fiber used widely for home decorating **C, T, I**

Drill Hard-wearing twill weave fabric in cotton, linen or man-made fibers

Dynel (trade name) Modacrylic flame-retardant fiber **T**

E

Encron (trade name) A polyester fiber **T**

Eyelet lace Open embroidery on linen and cotton fabrics. Design consists of holes edged in embroidery

F

Faille Soft silk or man-made fiber fabric with narrow horizontal ribs. For evening wear **C, T, F, I**

Felt Dense fabric of wool or hair fibers compressed with heat and moisture For toys, accessories and appliqué

Flannel Plain or twill weave fabric with soft napped surface in wool

Flannelette Cotton or man-made fiber fabric with brushed surface for warm shirts and nightwear

Fleece Heavy, compact, long-napped fabric usually of man-made fibers used for overcoating **I**

Fortrel (trade name) A polyester fiber **T**

G

Gabardine Closely woven twill weave fabric in wool, cotton or blends. Used for rainwear, skirts, suits

Gauze Sheer openly-woven fabric; made in many fibers **T, I, P, S**

Georgette Like chiffon with a more pronounced crepe appearance. Fine but crisp wool, silk or man-made fibers **C, T**

Gingham A firmly woven fabric of cotton, blended or man-made fibers with vertical and horizontal colored yarns forming checks and stripes

Grosgrain A plain weave fabric with a pronounced horizontal rib in silk or rayon for suits, ribbons and trimming

H

Herculon (trade name) An olefin fiber mainly used for outerwear and home decorating fabrics **I**

Hopsack Double plain weave, loosely structured fabric in wool or linen

Huck toweling Fabric with a woven raised pattern, using linen, cotton or man-made fibers. Absorbent; used for towels and dishcloths

J

Jacquard Type of loom producing complex woven structures. Jacquard knits have complex color patterns

Jersey knit Machine weft knit fabric. Has more widthwise than lengthwise stretch, so may sag in stress areas unless garment is lined **C, F, T, I**

K

Knit Any weft or warp knitted fabric in various weights and fibers which drapes well, stretches and is crease resistant. Double knit is more stable than single **C, F, T, I**

Kodel (trade name) A polyester fiber **T**

L

Lace Decorative open structure. Traditionally hand-made, now woven or knitted using cotton yarn or man-made fibers. For evening and wedding dresses, home decorating and trimmings **T, I, S, C**

Lamé Woven or knitted fabric with metallic threads; covered with acetate or polyester film **P, F, I**

Lawn Lightweight sheer plain weave fabric in cotton, cotton/man-made fiber blends or linen. For blouses, summer clothes and interfacings in fine fabrics

Linen From stem of flax plant in various weights, often with a rough slub texture. Tough, absorbent, cool; crease resistant when blended with man-made fibers **F**

Lycra (trade name) A spandex fiber with great elasticity; used in lingerie, swim wear, ski clothes **T, I, C**

M

Madras Fine hand-woven Indian cotton with stripes and plaid patterns

Melton Wool fabric with a dull, non-lustrous surface, used for overcoating, uniforms

Milium (trade name) Lining fabric with heat-retaining finish obtained by application of aluminum

Modacrylic Modified acrylic fibers with flame-retardant properties

Mohair Hair fiber from the Angora goat, often blended with other fibers in knitted and woven fabrics

Moiré A watermark pattern usually applied to silk, acetate/viscose, rayon or grosgrain. Used for evening wear **T, P**

Muslin Fine, loosely woven cotton fabric. For baby clothes, lightweight interfacings **S**

N

Net Fairly crisp woven mesh fabric with geometric holes. For dresses, trimmings or interfacings. Cotton net is highly flammable, so try to buy flame-retardant brands **S**

Ninon Sheer soft lightweight fabric in silk or synthetic yarns **S**

Nun's veiling Fine soft plain weave fabric in wool or synthetic fibers

Nylon (polyamide) Man-made petro-chemical fiber; fine, strong and elastic. Knitted and woven nylon fabrics shed creases and dry quickly; non-absorbency is difficult in hot weather and gives problems with static electricity **T, I, C**

O

Organdy Sheer plain weave fabric in cotton or synthetic fibers. Can be treated to retain crispness, for dresses, children's clothes and interfacings **T, P**
Organza Plain openly-woven fabric from silk or man-made fibers
Orlon (trade name) An acrylic fiber
Ottoman Similar to faille but with wider ribs, in wool, silk or synthetics

P

Peau de soie Heavy, satin weave fabric with a lustrous sheen, in silk, rayon or synthetics. For formal wear **T, I, P**
Pinwale corduroy Corduroy woven with thin vertical cords of pile **I, C**
Piqué Firm cotton fabric with raised, dotted, ribbed or honeycomb surface
Plissé Puckered texture on cotton or man-made fiber fabrics **I**
Polyester Versatile man-made fiber, petroleum-derived. Woven or knitted into many textures and finishes **T, I**
Poplin Crisp hard-wearing plain weave fabric with a soft sheen and fine ribs; cotton or cotton and man-made fiber blends

Q

Qiana (trade name) Nylon silk-like fabric used primarily for easy-care blouses and dresses **T, I, C**

R

Rayon Man-made fiber (viscose rayon) derived from cellulose. Fabrics can resemble silk, cotton, linen or wool **T, I, F**

S

Sailcloth Plain weave strong canvas type fabric in cotton or man-made fibers
Satin Weave which gives a smooth, shiny surface in silk, cotton or man-made fibers. Types include crepe-backed, double-faced and slipper (light, tightly woven) **T, I, P, C, F**
Seersucker Texture of puckered stripes on cotton and cotton blends **I**
Serge Hard-wearing twill weave fabric in wool or man-made fibers. For uniforms, tailored suits and coats
Shantung Plain weave in raw silk or man-made fibers, spun for slub effect **T, F**
Sharkskin Fine worsted quality fabric of wool or wool/man-made blends, with small color-effect weaves or fancy designs
Silk Natural continuous filament produced by the silkworm. Types include China and Japan (linings), Honan or pongee (slight slub), shantung, surah, Thai (heavy, slubbed, vivid colors) and tussore (raw silk with uneven texture, natural color) **T, I, P, C**

T

Taffeta Crisp silk or rayon plain weave fabric. Types include faille, shot (iridescent), moiré and paper (lightweight) **T, P, C**
Terrycloth Woven in cotton or cotton blends with uncut loops on one or both sides. (For toweling often has velour on one side.) Can be knitted to make stretch toweling. Hard-wearing and absorbent **S**
Ticking Strong cotton with woven vertical stripes; with waxed surface for covering mattresses and making pillows
Trevira (trade name) A polyester fiber often blended with natural fibers to make woven or knitted fabrics such as silky knits or gabardine **T, I**
Triacetate Modification of acetate. Man-made cellulose-based fiber with a crisp, silk-like feel **I, S**
Tricot Drapable warp knit fabric of fine cotton or man-made fibers. Used for lingerie **T, I, C**

Tulle Fine net in silk or nylon **T, I**
Tweed Rough-textured woven (sometimes knitted) wool or wool blend often with multicolored yarns. Identified by place names or patterns, such as Harris or hound's-tooth **I, S**

U

Unbleached muslin Plain weave cotton fabric in various weights and widths for muslin shells, interfacings and linings

V

Velour Knitted or woven fabric with thick short pile. Use wool velour for coats, terrycloth velour for bath towels **I, S**
Velvet Woven warp pile fabric from silk, cotton or man-made fiber yarns. Types include faconne (cut), Lyons (for home decorating) and panne (pronounced one-way silky pile). **T, P, C, F**
Velveteen Woven weft pile fabric, often cotton; less thick nap than velvet **I, P, C, F**
Vinyl Non-porous synthetic coating for wovens or knits. For raincoats, upholstery **P, S**
Viyella (trade name) Lightweight woven fabric, 55% wool/45% cotton
Voile Lightweight sheer openly-woven cotton or cotton blends, wool or silk **C**

W

Whipcord Like gabardine but heavier, with a pronounced cord in cotton, wool, man-made fibers or blends. For uniforms and riding gear
Wool Fiber from fleece of sheep. Fabrics may be woven or knitted and are warm, absorbent; often blended with man-made fibers for thrift and washability **I, S**
Worsted Finest quality wool fiber with smooth hard yarns. Can be woven or knitted; hard-wearing with a smooth non-fibrous surface

---

Fabric weaves

Close-ups of weaves show how fabrics are formed.

Hound's-tooth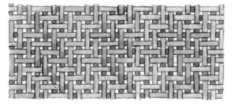

Plain weave

Hopsack

Twill

Satin

Types of velvet weave

Herringbone

Runaway engine

Scraps of bright-colored felt, stuffing, vinyl and a little embroidery thread are all you need to make this toy engine, which a toddler will enjoy "driving."

Finished size
$17\frac{1}{2} \times 12\frac{1}{2}$in (45×32cm).
A seam allowance of $\frac{3}{8}$in (1cm) is included throughout.

Materials
Piece of yellow felt 42×12in (107× 30cm)
Piece of green felt 33×23in (84× 58cm)
Piece of red felt 35×21in (89×53cm)
Piece of black felt 11×7in (28×18cm)
Scraps of pink and orange felt
12in (30cm) square of vinyl
Black and red embroidery floss
Small piece of brown yarn
Paper for pattern
Matching thread
Fabric glue
Suitable stuffing

1 For chassis cut out two pieces from yellow felt, each $11\frac{3}{4} \times 8\frac{1}{4}$in (30×21cm), two pieces $12\frac{1}{2} \times 3\frac{1}{4}$in (32×8cm) and two pieces $9 \times 3\frac{1}{4}$in (23×8cm).
2 Place one short chassis strip on one long chassis strip with one short end matching; pin and stitch.
3 Repeat step 2 to join the other two strips, then join the two pairs to form a ring.
4 Place one large chassis piece on one side of ring, with its corners matching the four seams; pin and stitch.
5 Repeat step 4 to join other large chassis piece to other side of ring, leaving an opening in one long side.
6 Trim seams and turn chassis right side out. Stuff firmly. Turn in opening edges and slip stitch them together.
7 For boiler cut out one piece from red felt $21 \times 11\frac{1}{2}$in (53×29cm) and two circles each $7\frac{1}{2}$in (19cm) in diameter.
8 Fold boiler in half lengthwise; pin and stitch long edges.

9 Place a circle at one end of boiler, matching edges; pin and stitch.
10 Repeat step 9 to join other circle to other end, leaving an opening.
11 Turn boiler right side out. Stuff firmly. Turn in opening edges and slip stitch them together.
12 Glue the boiler to the middle of one side of the chassis with fabric glue.
13 For wheels cut out eight circles from red felt, each 4in (10cm) in diameter, and four strips each $12 \times 1\frac{1}{4}$in (30×3cm).
14 Place one strip around one circle, matching edges; pin and stitch. Leave short ends unstitched. Join another circle to other side of strip.
15 Turn wheel right side out. Stuff firmly. Slip stitch short ends of strip.
16 Cut out four circles from black felt, each $1\frac{1}{4}$in (3cm) in diameter, for hub caps. Glue one hub cap to one side of wheel.
17 Repeat steps 14 to 16 to make three more wheels.
18 Glue wheels on each side of the chassis $\frac{3}{4}$in (2cm) from each end.
19 For chimney cut out two circles from black felt, each $2\frac{1}{2}$in (6.5cm) in diameter, and one strip $9 \times 2\frac{1}{4}$in (23×6cm).

Spike Powell

20 Make the chimney the same way as the wheels. Glue the chimney to the top of the boiler.
21 Make a paper pattern for the cab. On paper draw a rectangle $13\frac{1}{2} \times 8\frac{1}{4}$in (34× 21cm). Cut out and fold it in half lengthwise. Mark a point $2\frac{1}{4}$in (5.5cm) from the corner on one short edge; mark a point $1\frac{3}{4}$in (4.5cm) from same corner on long edge. Join these two points with a curved line. With the paper still folded, cut along line. Cut out the pattern.
22 From green felt cut two cab pieces and two strips: one $32\frac{1}{2} \times 3\frac{1}{4}$in (83×8cm) and one $8\frac{1}{4} \times 3\frac{1}{4}$in (21×8cm).
23 Place long strip on one cab piece, matching one long edge to the long and curved edges of the cab piece. Pin, baste and stitch.
24 Sew other cab piece to free edge of strip in the same way.
25 Place short strip on cab base, matching edges. Pin, baste and stitch, leaving an opening in one long side.
26 Trim seams and turn cab right side out. Slip stitch opening edges together.
27 Glue cab to back end of chassis and boiler, matching base edges.
28 For buffers and running boards, cut two circles from black felt, each 2in (5cm) in diameter, and two strips, each $11 \times \frac{3}{4}$in (28×2cm). Glue these in place as shown in the photograph.
29 From black felt cut out two small headlamps as shown and one $\frac{3}{8}$in (1cm)-diameter circle. Glue all three pieces to the front of the boiler for "eyes" and "nose."
30 Using six strands of black embroidery floss work a curved "mouth" in stem stitch on boiler front.
31 Continuing in stem stitch, work two windows on cab front and back. Work a window on one side of cab and a window and door on the other. Add a line for cab back and a door handle.
32 Cut a $1\frac{1}{2}$in (4cm) circle of pink felt for engineer's head. Cut a small square of orange felt for the jacket.
Pin both head and jacket in window above door and blanket stitch in place.
33 Embroider features, collar and buttons on the engineer.
34 Sew brown yarn all around the head. Cut the yarn short and fluff it out.
35 Cut a base for the chassis and one for the cab from vinyl. Glue them in place on the base of each piece.

Sewing / COURSE 57

*Cutting and joining a
  continuous bias strip
*Flat corded seam
*Making an uncorded
  tubing tie
*Pattern for a corded blouse:
  adapting the pattern;
  directions for making

Cutting and joining a continuous bias strip

Making a continuous bias strip is a useful technique when you need several strips to make a piece long enough for your pattern. It saves matching and joining individual pieces, and the width of the strips can be varied. To make a finished cording $\frac{1}{4}$in (5mm) wide (as on the blouse on page 68), cut the strip $1\frac{3}{4}$in (4cm) wide, which is twice the width of the finished strip plus $\frac{5}{8}$in (1.5cm) seam allowances. To make a $\frac{3}{8}$in (1cm)-wide tube as shown on page 67), cut the strip 2in (5cm) wide. Seam allowances can be trimmed after assembling. If you are using a cord inside the bias strip or tubing, make the strip three times the width of the cord, plus seam allowances.

1 Lay the fabric flat. Using a right triangle aligned with one selvage or with the straight grain, draw a series of parallel lines on the fabric following the angle of the triangle. These lines will be on the true bias.

2 Within the marked area, draw a square, using two parallel lines for two sides of the square as shown. Cut out the square and mark the first two parallel lines with different colored threads on one edge.

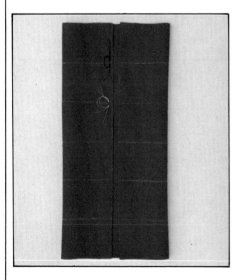

3 Bring together the two sides which are perpendicular to the parallel lines to form a tube.

4 Before basting, pin the tube so that the lines are stepped. This means matching the cut corner to the first colored thread and the first marked parallel line to the second colored thread. This will leave an extra strip at the end. Pin, baste and stitch on seamline.

5 Starting at one end, cut around the strip, following the parallel lines and cutting a continuous strip. If the strip is not going to be used immediately, it is advisable to seal the stitched ends of each seam with a dab of clear nail polish or glue (test it on the fabric first).

Flat piped seam

This simple technique gives a decorative finish to a garment. It can be used on collars, cuffs, pockets, or ruffles, or in a flat seam. It is made with a bias strip in self-fabric or contrasting fabric, as on the blouse on page 68. Piped seams can be fine or bold, depending on the width of the strip. Allow 1¼in (3cm) seam allowance.

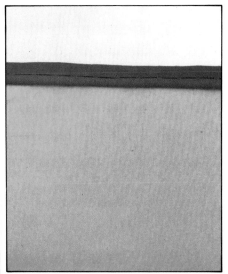

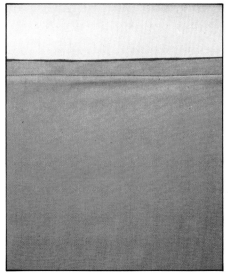

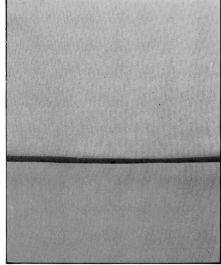

1 With wrong sides together, fold the strip in half lengthwise and pin it to the right side of the garment edge, matching the seamlines and raw edges. Baste firmly in place along the seamline.

2 With right sides together and seamlines and raw edges matching, pin and baste the other garment piece over the piping. Stitch the seam, taking a ⅝in (1.5cm) seam allowance. Although cord is not used here, it is best to use a zipper foot to stitch the seam to prevent the piping from being flattened. Remove basting.

3 Press the seamline only, from the wrong side. If the cording has been inserted into a seam, press the seam allowance to one side on the right side of the garment, (or, in the case of an armhole cording, press the cording toward the sleeve). Do not press the cording itself.

Making an uncorded tubing tie

This method makes a neat, even tube that is easy to turn right side out. The filler cord should be narrower than the finished width of the tube; that is ¼in (5mm) or less for a ⅜in (1cm)-wide tube.

A corded tube can be made using the same method, but you will need twice as much cord and it will be stitched in the middle, so that when the tube is turned right side out, it will cover the cord. The excess cord is cut off.

To measure the length of the tie, use filler cord tied around the neck in a bow or knot. Mark the length and measure it against the bias strip.

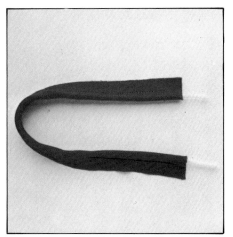

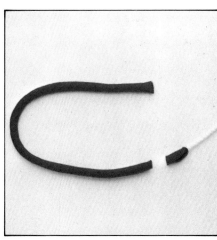

1 Cut a bias strip the length and width required, joining if necessary to make it the right length. Cut filler cord to the same length as the tie plus 2in (5cm). With right sides together, fold the strip in half lengthwise with the cord inside and sticking out about 1in (2.5cm) at each end. Pin, baste and stitch to enclose the cord, using a zipper foot.

2 Stitch across one end, catching in the cord. Trim seam allowance and excess cord at the stitched end before turning right side out. To turn, pull the free end of the cord until the whole tube is right side out. Cut off excess cord and finish both ends by turning in and slip stitching together.
Tie a knot at each end of the tie for a decorative finish.

Simon Butcher

Piped blouse

This tailored blouse and the co-ordinating pants on page 77 make a stylish twosome.

Adapting the pattern

The blouse is made by adapting the pattern for the basic shirt from the Pattern Pack, available in sizes 10 to 20, corresponding to sizes 8-18 in ready-made clothes.

Materials
Two sheets of tracing paper 36 × 40in (90 × 100cm approx)
Flexible curve
Yardstick; right triangle

Note: The fronts are cut the same except for the neck cutting line adjustment, where the foldline and pattern line markings are different.

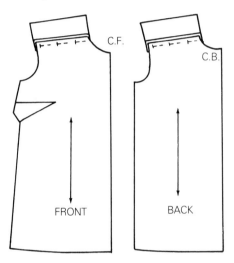

1 Pin the shirt front yoke to the shirt front and the back yoke to the shirt back, overlapping the seam allowances so that the seams are aligned. Trace both complete pieces, front and back, leaving an extra 4in (10cm) at center front edge for extension. Mark grainlines.

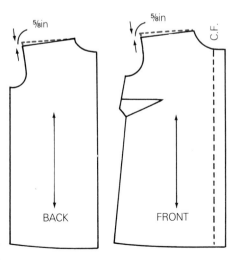

2 To allow for the shoulder pad, raise the shoulder cutting line edge by ⅝in (1.5cm) on front and back sections. Re-draw the shoulder cutting line, tapering into the neck cutting line.

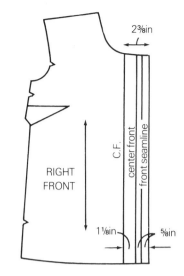

3 To adapt the right front pattern, extend center front by 2⅜in (6cm), for all sizes. Mark the center front line and a line 1⅛in (3cm) from this line and parallel to it. This will also be the center front. Mark a line ⅝in (1.5cm) out from the new center front line. This will be the front seamline. Now add another ⅝in (1.5cm) for seam allowances. All the lines should be parallel to the straight grain.

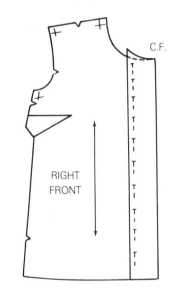

4 Fold the pattern so that the center front lines are aligned and a small pleat forms on the right side. Draw the neck cutting line before cutting the pattern. Do not forget to open out the pleat. Mark notches and seamlines. Mark button and buttonhole positions, starting 1in (2.5cm) from neck cutting line and spaced at approximately 3½in (9cm) intervals (for ⅜in [1cm]-diameter buttons). Adjust these positions for larger sizes or different-size buttons.
5 To make the contrast facing pattern, cut out a rectangle 2⅜in (6cm) wide by length of pattern at center front line. Mark ⅝in (1.5cm) seam allowances all around; the straight grain will be parallel to the front cutting line.

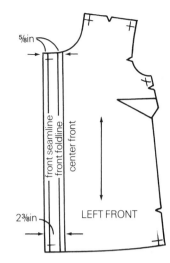

6 To adapt the left front pattern, extend the center front by 2⅜in (6cm) as before, for all sizes. Mark the center front line and a line ⅝in (1.5cm) from it which will be the front foldline. Mark another parallel line ⅝in (1.5cm) from the cutting line at the front edge. This will be the seamline. Both lines should follow the straight grain.

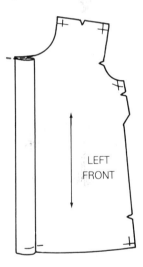

7 Fold the pattern back on the front foldline and turn in the seam allowance. Re-draw the neck cutting line before cutting out the pattern. Mark notches and seamlines.

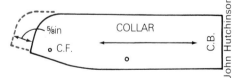

8 Trace the basic mandarin collar pattern, extending the front neck cutting line by ⅝in (1.5cm). Using a flexible curve, re-draw the front cutting line, keeping the front parallel to the original front line and tapering into the top cutting line. Mark center front and the fold on the center back. Grain line is on center back line or perpendicular to it.

John Hutchinson

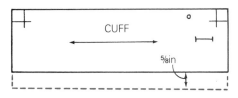

9 Trace the basic cuff pattern. Add ⅝in (1.5cm) to the lower edge foldline and cut out. Mark all seamlines, notches, button and buttonhole positions. Mark the grain line.

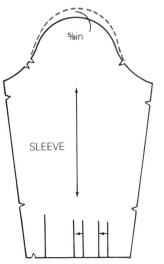

10 To adapt the sleeve pattern, trace the basic sleeve and raise the cutting line at the shoulder point by ⅝in (1.5cm). Re-draw the sleeve cap, tapering it into the notches on each side. Mark the grain line, slash point and pleat lines.

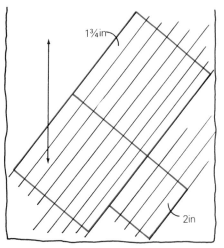

11 The bias strips for the cording should be 1¾in (4cm) wide. This measurement will give a finished width of ¼in (6mm) and allow ⅝in (1.5cm) seams. The width for the bias strips for the tubing tie will be 2in (5cm). This will give a finished width of ⅜in (1cm), with ⅝in (1.5cm) seam allowances. Cut enough to make continuous bias strips, following directions on page 66.

Directions for making

Suggested fabrics
Fine, soft fabrics such as crepe, satin, foulard; medium-weight, crisp fabrics such as gingham, poplin or seersucker.

Materials
- *36 or 45in (90 or 115cm)-wide fabric without nap:*
  - *For sizes 10-16: 2⅝yd (2.3m)*
  - *For sizes 18, 20: 2¾yd (2.5m)*
- *36 or 45in (90 or 115cm)-wide contrasting fabric without nap (for coordinated pants in next course, add 1⅛yd [1m])*
  - *Sizes 10, 12: ⅞yd (.7m)*
  - *Sizes 14, 16: 1yd (.9m)*
  - *Sizes 18, 20: 1¼yd (1.1m)*
- *36in (90cm)-wide non-woven interfacing:*
  - *For all sizes: ⅜yd (.3m)*
- *Matching thread*
- *1⅛yd (1m) each of ¼in (6mm) and ⅜in (1cm) diameter filler cord*
- *10 buttons ⅜in (1cm) in diameter for sizes 10 to 14; 10 buttons ⅝in (1.5cm) diameter for sizes 16 to 20. If you use a different size button, adjust buttonholes to fit*
- *Pair of shoulder pads (optional) or ¼yd (.2m) polyester fiberfill*

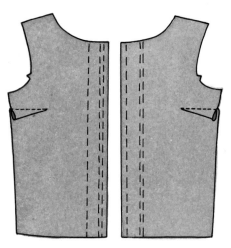

1 Prepare the fabric and lay out the adapted pattern pieces as shown in the cutting diagram, noting any pieces which have to be laid on a fold.
Cut out and transfer all pattern lines and notches to the fabric before removing the pattern.

2 With right sides together, fold, baste and stitch the bust darts. Press them downward. Mark the pattern lines on the right and left center fronts with tailor's tacks or tailor's chalk.
Be sure to mark all the lines on the right side of the fabric.

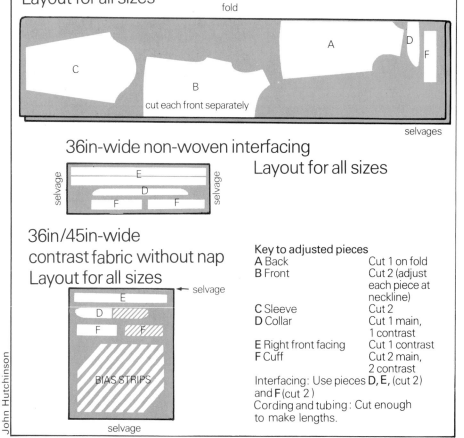

Cutting layout: 36in/45in-wide fabric without nap
Layout for all sizes

fold

C

A   D   F

B

cut each front separately

selvages

36in-wide non-woven interfacing
Layout for all sizes

selvage   E   D   F   F   selvage

36in/45in-wide contrast fabric without nap
Layout for all sizes

selvage

E
D
F   F

BIAS STRIPS

selvage

John Hutchinson

Key to adjusted pieces
A Back	Cut 1 on fold
B Front	Cut 2 (adjust each piece at neckline)
C Sleeve	Cut 2
D Collar	Cut 1 main, 1 contrast
E Right front facing	Cut 1 contrast
F Cuff	Cut 2 main, 2 contrast

Interfacing: Use pieces **D, E,** (cut 2) and **F** (cut 2)
Cording and tubing: Cut enough to make lengths.

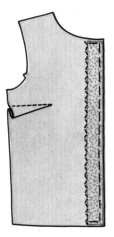

3 Pin and baste the interfacing to the wrong side of the left front section, matching neck, hem and front cutting lines. Catch-stitch the interfacing to the foldline just outside the center front line.

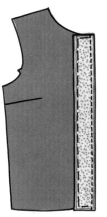

4 Baste the interfacing to the wrong side of the contrast facing sections, matching all edges. With right sides together, pin, baste and stitch the facing to the right front section, matching neck, hem and front cutting lines, taking a $\frac{5}{8}$in (1.5cm) seam. Grade the seam and press.

5 With right sides together, join the left and right front sections to the back at the shoulders and underarm, taking $\frac{5}{8}$in (1.5cm) seam allowances. Finish the raw edges and press the seams open. Turn up a narrow double hem around the lower edge with a finished width of $\frac{1}{4}$in (6mm). Baste and stitch all around. Press.

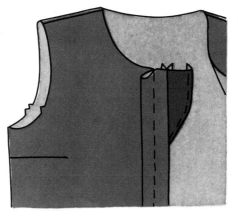

6 Make a $\frac{5}{8}$in (1.5cm)-wide pleat on the right side of the right front section by bringing the center front lines together. Baste along this line and press the fold of the pleat away from the center front. Press the facing seam flat. Turn under a $\frac{5}{8}$in (1.5cm) seam allowance on the contrast facing, baste and press.

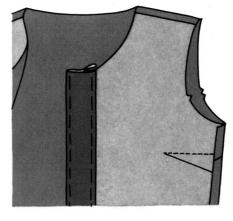

7 Working from the wrong side of the right front section, fold in the contrast facing and baste close to the seam. Pin and baste the facing through all thicknesses close to the other folded edge. This will catch down the pleat on the right side of the garment.

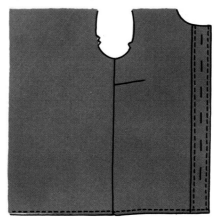

8 Working from the right side of the right front section, topstitch close to the seam and the pleat line on each side of the band. Mark the buttonhole positions and make vertical buttonholes evenly

spaced from the neck edge on the center front line. Remove all basting. Press. Check that raw edges on contrast facing are fully enclosed in the stitching.

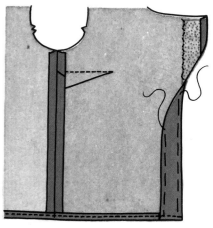

9 Working from the wrong side of the left front, turn in facing on foldline nearest to center front line where interfacing ends. Baste and press folded edge only. Turn in remaining raw edge, taking a $\frac{5}{8}$in (1.5cm) seam allowance. Baste through all thicknesses close to fold.

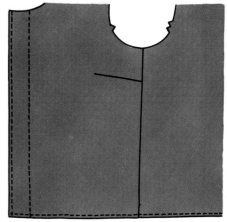

10 Working from the right side of the left front section, topstitch each side of the band, following the basting lines. Make sure the facing is caught in the stitching on the wrong side.

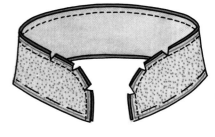

11 Baste the interfacing to the wrong side of the main color collar section. With right sides together, pin, baste and stitch the collar pieces together around the outer edges, taking a $\frac{5}{8}$in (1.5cm) seam and matching all edges. Remove basting and press.

Terry Evans

71

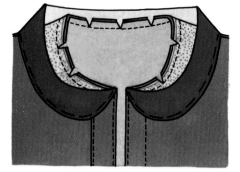

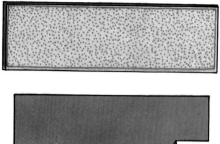

raw edges and starting and finishing at the underarm seams. Overlap the ends as shown in the diagram. The finished cording should not be more than $\frac{1}{4}$in (6mm) wide.

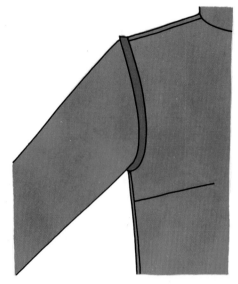

12 Clip curves on outer edge and turn the collar right side out. Baste close to the seamed edge all around and press. With right side of the main fabric facing right side of the garment and keeping the contrast fabric clear, pin, baste and stitch collar to neck edge, matching center back, center fronts, notches and raw edges.

15 Make the cuff sections in the same way as the collar, placing the interfacing on the wrong side of the main color sections before stitching it to the contrast pieces. Stitch around the outer edge as for the collar but continue the seam along the lower edge as far as the pattern mark for the lap. Grade seams and clip corners. Press before turning right side out.

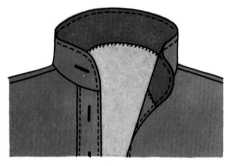

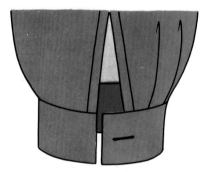

13 Grade the seam and clip curves. Remove basting. Press the seam up into the collar. Turn in the remaining raw edge taking a $\frac{5}{8}$in (1.5cm) seam and clipping curves as you work. Slip stitch the collar to the neck edge just inside the seam. Topstitch the collar close to the outer edge all around. Remove basting and press. Make a buttonhole on the right center front.

16 Pin, baste and stitch the underarm seams of the sleeves. Remove basting, finish raw edges and press seam open. Finish the sleeve opening and attach the lapped cuff to the sleeve as shown in Volume 5, page 64. Remove all basting, press and make buttonhole on each cuff.

18 Ease the sleeve cap, pulling up the gathering threads so that the sleeve fits the armhole. With right sides together and matching underarm seams, shoulder points and notches, pin, baste and stitch the sleeve to the armhole. Overcast the raw edges of the seam together with the raw edges of the cording. Remove basting and press seam into sleeve. From the right side of the garment, gently press the cording toward the sleeve all around.

19 Make shoulder pads and attach to inside of garment as shown in Volume 9, page 60 or cover ready-made shoulder pads with self-fabric and attach in the same way.

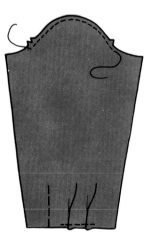

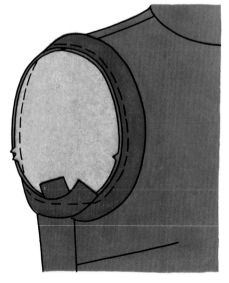

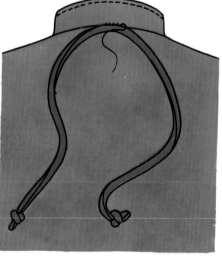

Terry Evans

14 Run a row of gathering stitches at the sleeve cap between the notches for easing the sleeve into the armhole. Fold the pleats at the lower edge of the sleeve in the direction shown on the pattern. Baste and stitch to hold in place.

17 Make a continuous bias strip from contrasting fabric as shown on page 66. Fold in half lengthwise to make a cording. Apply the cording to the armhole edges, as shown on page 67, matching

20 Make the tubing tie as shown on page 67 and slip stitch the center of the tie to the center back of the blouse on the neck seam. Sew buttons on the left front and cuff underlaps to match the buttonholes.

Shoestring

Handy holder

Make this attractive, useful holder for wooden spoons, whisks, spatulas and other kitchen utensils.

Belinda

Finished size
$15\frac{3}{4} \times 9\frac{1}{2}$in (40×24cm).

Materials
$\frac{5}{8}$yd (.5m) of 36in (90cm)-wide cotton print fabric
Piece of iron-on interfacing $17\frac{1}{4} \times 11$in (44×28cm)
Piece of red poplin 24×5in (60×12cm)
Piece of blue poplin 18×8in (44× 20cm)
Two 1in (2.5cm) D rings
Matching thread

1 For main piece cut two pieces of printed fabric, $17\frac{1}{4} \times 11$in (44×28cm).
2 Place interfacing, shiny side down, on wrong side of one main piece, matching all edges. Iron interfacing firmly in place.
3 Place one main piece on top of the other, matching all edges. Fold in half lengthwise. Then fold in half widthwise. Gently round off the corners.
4 From red fabric cut out two pieces, each 8×5in (20×12cm), for lower pocket and two pieces, each 4in (10cm) square, for small top pocket. From blue fabric cut out two pieces, each 5×8in (12×20cm) for long pocket and two pieces, each 4×5in (10×12cm), for middle-sized pocket.
5 Curve the two bottom corners of each pair of pockets. Fold each pocket in half lengthwise. Place pockets together, matching lower edges. Gently round off lower corners.
6 Place first pair of red pockets together with right sides facing. Pin, baste and stitch around edges, taking $\frac{5}{8}$in (1.5cm) seam allowance and leaving an opening in the top edge.
7 Trim and turn pocket right side out. Turn in opening at top edge. Pin, baste and topstitch close to upper edge of pocket.
8 Repeat steps 6 and 7 to make the remaining three pockets in the same way as the first one.
9 Arrange the four pockets on the interfaced main piece as shown, with the bottom edge of the lower pocket $1\frac{1}{2}$in (4cm) up from lower edge of main piece. Pin, baste and topstitch pockets in place, close to side and bottom edges.
10 For hangers cut two pieces of printed fabric, each 3in (7.5cm) square.
11 Fold one hanger piece in half with right sides together. Pin, baste and stitch down length, taking $\frac{3}{4}$in (2cm) seam allowance. Trim and turn right side out.

12 Fold hanger in half through D ring, matching short edges. Pin the hanger to the right side of the interfaced main piece, $1\frac{1}{4}$in (3cm) in from one side along the top edge, with raw edges matching.
13 Repeat steps 11 and 12 to make the second hanger in the same way.
14 Place backing pieces together with right sides facing. Pin, baste and stitch together, catching in the two hangers, taking a $\frac{3}{4}$in (2cm) seam allowance and leaving a 4in (10cm) opening in the lower edge.
15 Trim and turn holder right side out. Turn in opening edges and slip stitch them together. Topstitch all around holder close to edge, matching topstitching on pockets.

*Conspicuous fly front
*Bound slit pockets
*Cummerbund
*Pattern for corded
 pants:
 adapting the pattern;
 directions for making

Conspicuous fly front

This type of fly fastening can be used on center front or center back seams on pants, shirts, dresses and pullover jackets. It is very strong and can be adapted to suit a variety of fastenings: snaps, buttons, toggles or Velcro® (sewn to facing and underlap section before assembling). The facing on the overlap can be made of self fabric or a contrasting fabric as on the pants on page 77.

1 Baste interfacing to the left front facing and catch-stitch to the foldline. Mark the center front lines and the foldline on the left front pants piece with tailor's tacks or chalk. Mark the crotch on the seamline with a tailor's tack for the bottom of the opening. Finish the outer edges of the facing with overcasting.

2 Fold the facing to the wrong side on the left front section, matching center lines. Baste along the center front line as far as the tailor-tacked point. Baste and stitch around the facing close to the finished edge and the folded edge.

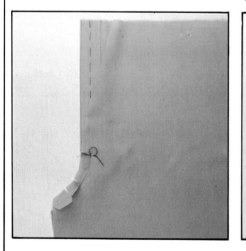

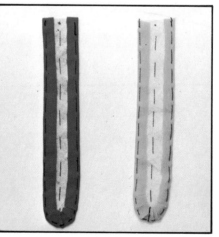

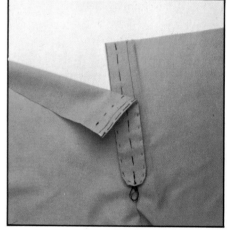

3 With right sides together and center front lines and seamlines matching, baste and stitch front sections together along the crotch seam, taking ⅝in (1.5cm) seam allowance. Stitch as far as the marked point. Clip the curves, slash the right front at this point almost to the stitching just above the crotch seamline, and press the seam open.

4 Baste trimmed interfacing to the wrong side of the main fly section. Turn in a ⅝in (1.5cm) seam allowance to the wrong side of the fly front and the contrasting facing sections. Baste close to the fold, clipping curves where necessary. Mark the center front lines with tailor's tacks or chalk. Press.

5 Working from the right side and keeping the right front pants piece flat, lay the main color fly piece over the right front pants section, matching the wrong side of the fly to the right side of the garment. Match the center front lines, top edges and the center point of the curved end to the slash point of the crotch seam. Baste through both thicknesses on the center front line. Trim seam beneath fly to ⅜in (1cm).

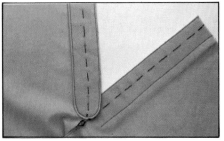

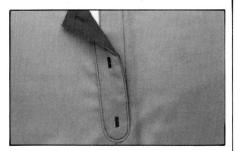

6 Working from the wrong side and with wrong sides together, lay the contrasting fly over the right pants front, matching center front lines and outer edges of both fly pieces. Baste through all thicknesses all around the outer edge.

7 Working from the right side of the garment and keeping the left pants front clear, machine-stitch all around the fly sections close to the outer edges and through all thicknesses. Mark the vertical buttonhole positions, placing the first 1in (2.5cm) from the top edge. Space the remaining buttonholes evenly. There will be three, each $\frac{3}{8}$in (1cm) long for sizes 10-14; $\frac{5}{8}$in (1.5cm) long for sizes 16-20. Press.

8 Make machine-stitched buttonholes on overlap fly, remove basting and press carefully from right side. Remove basting from the underlap and press. Pin the fly fronts together on the center front line. Run a short row of machine stitching over previous stitching on the curved edge only, stitching through all thicknesses. Remove basting. Press well. Sew buttons on underlap of fly to match with buttonholes on overlap.

Bound slit pockets

Bound pockets are strong and decorative. They are versatile too—a bound pocket can be placed at any angle in a garment: the pockets on the pants on page 77 have been placed on the bias and reinforced with non-woven interfacing to prevent stretching. Here they are made in a contrasting fabric, but a more subtle effect can be achieved by making the cording in self-fabric. For a really crisp finish, the pocket should be pressed very hard from the right side using a damp cloth.

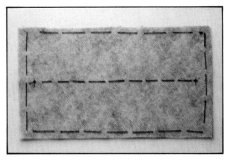

1 Transfer the pocket markings from the pattern to the garment and pocket pieces. To reinforce the pocket opening, baste a piece of non-woven interfacing to the wrong side of the pocket binding, re-marking the pocket position. Cut the interfacing to match the binding piece.

2 With right sides together, baste and stitch the shorter side of one pocket bag section to the long edge of the corded piece taking $\frac{3}{8}$in (1cm) seams. Finish the seam allowances by overcasting together and press toward the pocket bag. Repeat with the other pocket bag.

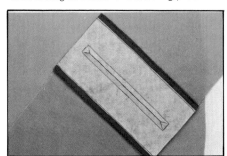

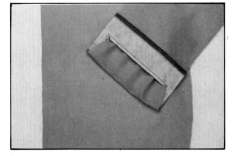

3 With right sides together, position the pocket pieces over the pocket line, matching the pocket position on the binding to the pocket line of the garment. Baste along the pocket position.

4 Using a very small stitch, machine stitch $\frac{1}{4}$in (6mm) away from pocket line all around. Begin stitching at center of one side and return to same place. Leave needle in fabric when turning corners. Remove basting and carefully cut through pocket line to within $\frac{3}{8}$in (1cm) of each end. Cut diagonally into corners. Do not cut stitching.

5 Pull both pocket bag sections through the opening to the wrong side of the garment. Pull out the triangular ends to square the corners.

Simon Butcher

continued

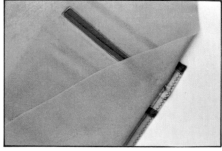

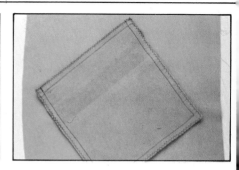

6 Press the seam allowances away from the pocket opening and fold each side of the binding over them to form pleats that meet in the center of the opening. Catch-stitch these together and slip stitch together the small pleats that are formed at each end on the inside. Remove basting and press.

7 With the right side of the pocket facing up and using a small stitch, machine stitch all around the pocket lines following the seams. Press.

8 Working from the wrong side, bring the top pocket section down over the binding and the lower pocket. Matching side edges, baste the two pocket sections together. Trim the lower section to match the upper and stitch around the entire bag close to the ends of pocket opening. Finish outer edge of pocket bag with overcasting. Remove all basting and press.

Cummerbund

A cummerbund is easily made from about a yard of any firm, finely woven fabric, preferably without nap. A remnant of furnishing brocade is particularly effective used in this way. Cummerbunds can be worn with pants and narrow or full skirts. They are perfect to link up separates or to dress up a daytime outfit for the evening.

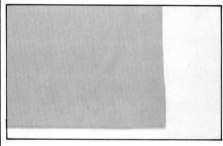

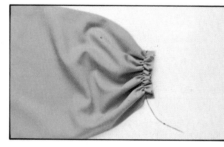

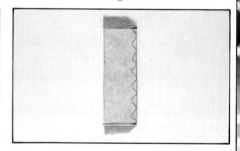

1 Fold cummerbund in half lengthwise with right sides together and raw edges matching. Baste and stitch the long edge, taking a $\frac{5}{8}$in (1.5cm) seam. Remove basting, press and turn right side out.

2 Run a row of machine gathering stitches at each short end on the seamline. Pull up threads to gather each end of the cummerbund to 3in (7.5cm) deep.

3 Baste and catch-stitch interfacing to each half of the lap sections. Fold the lap pieces in half lengthwise with right sides together. Pin, baste and stitch across short ends. Clip corners and grade seams.

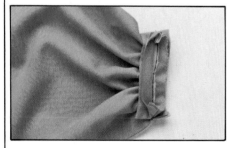

4 Turn right side out and press. Working from the right side of the cummerbund, pin the overlap piece to one end, with right sides together and raw edges matching. Keeping the top layer clear, baste and stitch through all thicknesses, taking a $\frac{5}{8}$in (1.5cm) seam. Grade seams and press.

5 Turn wrong side out. Pull overlap piece over the edges to enclose all raw ends. Turn in the remaining edge of the overlap and slip stitch in place. Repeat with the underlap piece at the other end of the cummerbund.

6 Sew hooks and eyes or snaps to the underlap and overlap sections. Press the cummerbund lightly after removing all basting stitches. Or, make button holes by hand on the overlap and attach buttons to the underlap.

Piped pants

These pants, with their coordinating cummerbund, team up perfectly with the blouse on page 68. They look stylish in a sophisticated silk print, but are fun and practical in cotton.

Adapting the pattern

Measurements
The pattern for the pants is adapted from the basic pants in the Stitch by Stitch Pattern Pack.

Materials
4 sheets of tracing paper
approximately 36×52in (90×130cm)
Yardstick, right triangle
Flexible curve

1 Trace the front and back basic trouser patterns to the **hemline** only. Mark the straight grain on each leg and extend it at each end to cross the hem and waistline. At the lower hem edge, measure out from the grainline toward the inner leg seam 3⅛in (7.8cm) for a size 10, adding an extra ¼in (6mm) for each larger size. Join this point to the notches on inner leg cutting line.

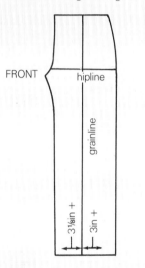

2 Measure out from the grain line toward the outside leg seam at the hem edge 3in (7.5cm) for a size 10, adding an extra ⅜in (1cm) for each larger size. Join this point to the hip line.

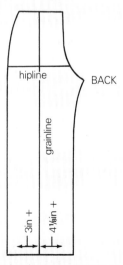

3 For the pants back pattern, measure out from the grain line toward the inner

leg seam at the hem edge 4⅛in (10.5cm) for a size 10, adding an extra ¼in (6mm) for each larger size. Join this point to the notches as before.

4 Measure out from the grain line toward the outside leg seam at the hem edge 3in (7.5cm) for a size 10, adding an extra ⅜in (1cm) for each larger size. Join this point to hipline as on front pattern.

5 At the hemline, divide each of the pants patterns into four parts: measure the distance between the grain line and the new inner leg cutting line, divide by two and mark. Repeat this step from the grain line to the outside leg cutting line.

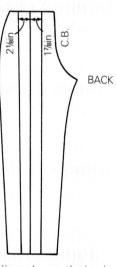

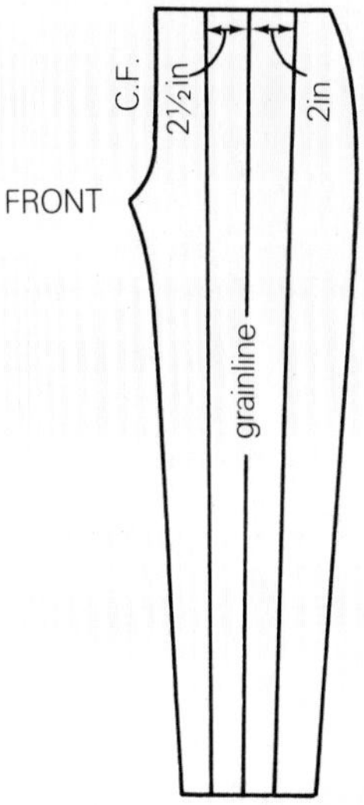

6 At the waistline edge on the front pattern, measure out from the grainline toward center front 2½in (6.5cm) for sizes 10 to 14; 2⅛in (5.5cm) for sizes 16 to 20. Join this point to corresponding point at hem edge with a straight line.

7 At the waistline edge, measure out from the straight grain toward the side seam 2in (5cm) for sizes 10 to 14; 2½in (6.5cm) for sizes 16 to 20. Join this point to the corresponding point at hem edge with a straight line.

8 At the waistline edge on the back pattern, measure out from the straight

grain toward the center back 1⅞in (4.5cm) for sizes 10 to 14; 2¼in (5.7cm) for sizes 16 to 20, joining this point to the mark at the hem as before.

9 At the waistline edge, measure out from the straight grain toward the side seam 2⅛in (5.5cm) for sizes 10 to 14; 2½in (6.5cm) for sizes 16 to 20. Join this point to the mark at the hem.

10 Cut out the front and back patterns and cut along all the dividing lines from waist almost to the hemline. Lay extra paper under the four pieces of each pants section so that they can be taped in place immediately. Before spreading the patterns, draw the straight grain lines on the extra paper.

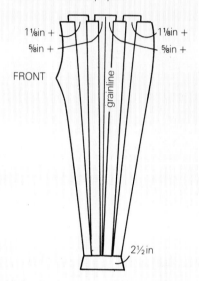

11 On the front pattern keep the hem together and spread pattern by ⅝in (1.5cm) at the waist edge on each side of the new straight grain line for sizes 10 to 14, and by ¾in (2cm) for sizes 16 to 20. Spread remaining sections 1⅛in (3cm) at waist for sizes 10 to 14; 1⅝in (4cm) for sizes 16 to 20. Tape in place.

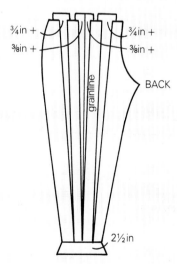

12 On back pattern, keep hem together and spread pattern at waist edge by ⅜in (1cm) at each side of grain line for sizes 10 to 14; ⅝in (1.5cm) for sizes 16

to 20. Spread remaining sections $\frac{3}{4}$in (2cm) for sizes 10 to 14; 1$\frac{1}{8}$in (3cm) for sizes 16 to 20. Tape in place.

13 Trace each completed piece and cut out. Adjust the hem allowance to new shape as shown in Volume 10, page 61. Allow 2$\frac{1}{2}$in (6.5cm) for hem. Cut front section twice. Mark grain lines, pattern markings and seamlines.

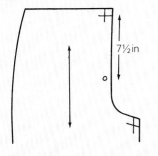

14 On the right front pants pattern, measure 7$\frac{1}{2}$in (19cm) down center front seamline from the waist seamline and mark with a circle. This will be the matching point for the end of the fly.

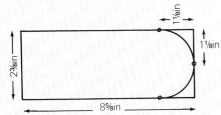

15 On a piece of paper, draw a rectangle 8$\frac{5}{8}$in (22cm) long by 2$\frac{3}{8}$in (6cm) wide. Measure up 1$\frac{1}{8}$in (3cm) from lower edge on each side of rectangle and mark. Divide width in half at lower edge and mark. Using a flexible curve join these three points.

16 Mark $\frac{5}{8}$in (1.5cm) seam allowances all around. Divide the strip in half at the top edge and mark. Using a ruler, join this point to the point at the lower edge. This line is the grain line and center fold line.

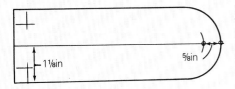

17 Mark a point $\frac{5}{8}$in (1.5cm) up from lower cutting line on center front line. This point will match the circle on the center front. The fly piece will be cut twice in fabric and once in interfacing.

18 Lay extra paper at the center front of the left front pants pattern and tape in place. Measure 7$\frac{1}{2}$in (19cm) down center front seamline from the waist seamline and mark with a circle. This point will be matched to the circle on the right front pattern.

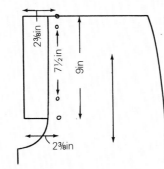

19 Measure 9in (23cm) down center front seamline from waist cutting line and mark. Using a triangle aligned with center front seamline, measure out 2$\frac{3}{8}$in (6cm) from this point and mark. Measure out 2$\frac{3}{8}$in (6cm) from center front seamline at top edge and mark. Join these two points with a straight line.

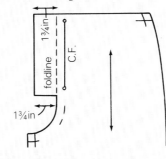

20 Trace left front pattern, marking grain line, $\frac{5}{8}$in (1.5cm) seam allowances, center front line and circles. From cutting line of fly, measure in 1$\frac{3}{4}$in (4.5cm) at top and lower edges. Join these two points for foldline. The interfacing will be matched to this line: make it 9in (23cm) long by 1$\frac{3}{4}$in (4.5cm) wide.

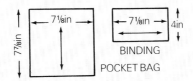

21 To make the waistband pattern measure your waist, add $\frac{3}{4}$in (2cm) for ease, and 2$\frac{3}{8}$in (6cm) for seam allowances and laps. Draw a rectangle this length by 4$\frac{3}{8}$in (11cm) wide. The grain line will be parallel to a straight edge. Center fronts will be 1$\frac{1}{8}$in (3cm) in from each end.

22 To make the pocket bag pattern, draw a rectangle 7$\frac{1}{8}$ by 7$\frac{7}{8}$in (18×20cm). This piece will be cut four times, twice for each pocket. The grain line will be parallel to the long side of the rectangle.

POCKET BAG / BINDING

23 To make the pocket binding pattern, draw a rectangle 7$\frac{1}{8}$ by 4in (18 by 10cm). This will be cut twice in fabric and twice in interfacing. The grain line will be parallel to a straight edge; $\frac{3}{8}$in (1cm) seams are allowed on all pocket pieces.

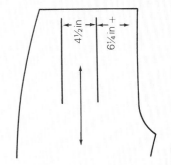

24 On each pattern front measure along the waist seamline from the center front line as follows: 6$\frac{1}{4}$in (16cm) for sizes 10 to 14; 7$\frac{1}{2}$in (19cm) for sizes 16 to 20. Mark this point. Mark another point on the waist seamline 4$\frac{1}{2}$in (11.5cm) from first mark. Draw a line from each of these points parallel to the straight grain.

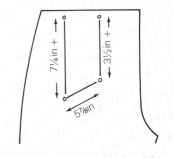

25 On line nearest to center front line measure down 3$\frac{1}{2}$in (9cm) for sizes 10 to 14; 3$\frac{3}{4}$in (9.5cm) for sizes 16 to 20. Mark. On other line measure down 7$\frac{1}{4}$in (18.5cm) for sizes 10 to 14; 7$\frac{1}{2}$in (19cm) for sizes 16 to 20; mark. Join these points with straight line for pocket position; it should be about 6in (15cm) long.

26 To make the cummerbund pattern, draw a rectangle 21in (53cm) wide by your waist measurement plus $\frac{3}{4}$in (2cm). Add $\frac{5}{8}$in (1.5cm) seam allowances all around. Cut one in contrasting fabric. Draw another rectangle 3$\frac{1}{8}$ by 1$\frac{5}{8}$in (8 by 4cm) for the lap pieces, adding $\frac{5}{8}$in (1.5cm) seam allowances all around. Cut two. Grain line is parallel to short side of each rectangle.

Directions for making

Materials

36in (90cm)-wide fabric with or without nap:
    Sizes 10 to 14: 5$\frac{1}{4}$yd (4.8m)
    Sizes 16 to 20: 5$\frac{1}{2}$yd (5m)
48in (120cm)-wide fabric with or without nap:
    Sizes 10 to 14: 2$\frac{7}{8}$yd (2.6m)
    Sizes 16 to 20: 3yd (2.7m)
36/48in (90/120cm)-wide contrasting fabric without nap: for all sizes: 1$\frac{1}{8}$yd (1m)
36in (90cm)-wide non-woven interfacing: for all sizes: $\frac{1}{4}$yd (.2m)
Four $\frac{3}{8}$in (1cm) or $\frac{5}{8}$in (1.5cm) diameter buttons (optional)
Matching thread
$\frac{1}{4}$in (6mm) filler cord

John Hutchinson

Key to adapted pattern pieces

A Pants back	Cut 2
B Pants front	Cut 2 (separately)
C Waistband	Cut 1
D Pocket bag	Cut 4
E Pocket binding	Cut 2 contrast
F Pants fly	Cut 2 (one of contrast)
G Cummerbund	Cut 1 contrast
H Cummerbund lap	Cut 2 contrast

Interfacing: Use pieces C—cut 1 to half width only, F—cut 1, E—cut 2, B—cut 1 to fly underlap only.

Suggested fabrics

Silk crepe de chine, rayon, seersucker, taffeta, moiré, poplin.

1 Prepare the fabric and lay out the pattern as shown in the cutting diagram, noting any pieces to be placed on a fold. Cut out and mark pattern markings before removing pattern pieces.
2 Make the bound slit pockets as shown on page 75. Make the conspicuous fly front and stitch the front crotch seam as shown on page 74.

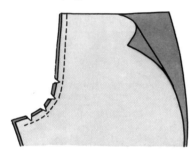

3 With the right sides together and notches and seamlines matching, pin, baste and stitch the back crotch seam, taking a ⅝in (1.5cm) allowance. Clip curves, press seam open.

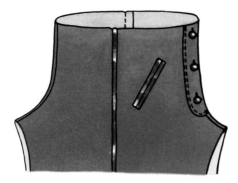

4 Cut out and make a continuous bias piping strip in contrasting fabric as shown on page 66. Apply the piping all along the pants seams at the sides from waist to hem as shown for flat piped seam (see page 67). Join pants fronts to backs at side seams, taking ⅝in (1.5cm) seam allowances. Remove basting, press seams open.

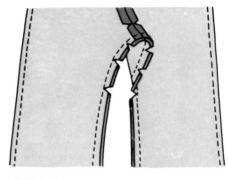

5 With right sides together and notches and front and back crotch seams matching, pin, baste and stitch inner leg seam. Begin the stitching from the crotch and work to the hem; repeat with other leg. A short row of machine stitching across crotch seam on original inner leg seamline will reinforce this point. Remove basting, clip and press seams open.

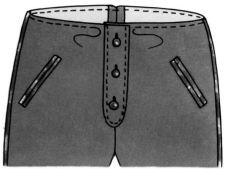

6 Run a row of machine gathering all around the pants on the waist seamline, avoiding the fly pieces. Pull up the threads evenly so that the pants top will fit the waistband (excluding seam allowances). Catch-stitch the interfacing to the waistband along the foldline.
7 Make and apply the waistband as shown in Volume 2, page 64, matching center fronts. Make a horizontal buttonhole on the front waistband overlap, ⅝in (1.5cm) from the outer edge. Topstitch the waistband all around close to the edges. Remove basting and press. Sew button to waistband underlap to match buttonhole.

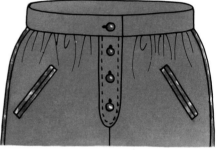

8 Try on pants and mark hemline. Turn up and complete the pants hems as shown in Volume 2, page 65. Press well.

Terry Evans

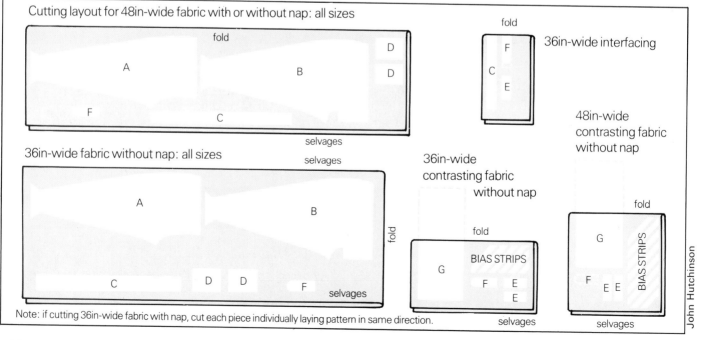

Cutting layout for 48in-wide fabric with or without nap: all sizes

fold

A   B   D D

F   C

selvages

36in-wide interfacing

F
C
E

48in-wide contrasting fabric without nap

36in-wide fabric without nap: all sizes

selvages

A   B

fold

C   D D   F

selvages

36in-wide contrasting fabric without nap

fold

G

BIAS STRIPS

F E
E

fold

G

BIAS STRIPS

F
E E

selvages   selvages

Note: if cutting 36in-wide fabric with nap, cut each piece individually laying pattern in same direction.

John Hutchinson

Floral frame

Pretty printed fabric and a bunch of flowers make a frame befitting a photo of a special friend.

Finished size

Frame size: $8\frac{1}{2} \times 6\frac{1}{4}$in (22×16cm); Window size: $6\frac{1}{4} \times 4$in (16×10cm).

Materials

Two pieces of stiff cardboard $8\frac{1}{2} \times$
$6\frac{1}{4}$in (22×16cm)
Strip of stiff cardboard about $7 \times 1\frac{1}{2}$in
(17×4cm)
Piece of printed fabric, $14\frac{1}{2} \times 9\frac{1}{2}$in
(36×24cm)
Clear glue; sharp craft knife
Fabric flowers; matching thread
8in (20cm) of narrow satin ribbon

1 On one piece of cardboard, measure and mark a rectangle $6\frac{1}{4} \times 4$in (16×10cm), leaving a $1\frac{1}{8}$in (3cm) border all around. Using the craft knife, carefully cut out center and discard.

2 Trim the other piece of cardboard to $8\frac{1}{4} \times 6$in (21.5×15.5cm). In the center of one long side, cut away a small curve. Make the curve $2\frac{1}{4}$in (6cm) long and about $\frac{3}{8}$in (1cm) deep at the center.
3 Cut the fabric in half to make two pieces, each $9\frac{1}{2} \times 7\frac{1}{4}$in (24×18cm).
4 Cover the front of the frame with one piece of fabric. Glue the frame to the wrong side of the fabric, leaving an even margin on all sides. Cut away the fabric from inside the window, leaving a $\frac{1}{2}$in (1cm) margin all around for turning under.
5 Cut across the fabric at the outer corners. Snip into the fabric on the inner corners. Fold the fabric on inner and outer edges over cardboard to wrong side. Glue the fabric edges in place.
6 Cover the back of the frame with the other piece of fabric. Glue the cardboard

to the wrong side of the fabric, leaving an even margin on all sides. Cut across the fabric at the corners. Fold fabric over the cardboard to wrong side and glue edges in place, clipping fabric at indentation.
7 Apply a thin layer of glue to the wrong side of the frame back, along the three straight sides only, to a depth of $\frac{3}{4}$in (2cm). Glue it to the frame front, leaving a small, even margin on all sides. Slip stitch the two pieces together around the three glued sides.
8 Score the strip of cardboard $\frac{3}{4}$in (2cm) down from one short end. Place this end on the center of frame back, $1\frac{1}{4}$in (3cm) down from top; glue it in place.
9 Arrange the flowers neatly in a small bunch. Tie the ribbon around the flowers, into a bow. Snip the ends of ribbon into V shapes. Sew flowers to frame.

Appliqué perse

This is the technique of cutting a printed motif from fabric and applying it to another fabric background. In this way color, tone and visual depth can be incorporated into the design without a lot of effort. Appliqué perse can be used to decorate any plain garment and is a good way to make use of cherished scraps of fabric. The easiest patterns to apply are those with a definite motif and a solid outline; they look best applied to a background matching or co-ordinating with one of the colors in the motif. The stitches used to apply the motif can be made by hand or machine, but machine stitching is much quicker.

For added decorative effect, the motif can be overlapped on an edge with part of the motif left free. This is the technique used for the appliqué on the blouse collar on page 85. In this case the collar was interfaced and faced, with all layers extended along the outline of the motif to make it easier to apply the motif. The satin stitch is continued all around the collar on the seamline for added effect, and the excess fabric is trimmed away when the stitching completed.

Appliqué perse can be carried out by the following method, or a more delicate effect can be obtained if the raw edges of the motif are turned in and slip stitched down. When stitching by machine it is advisable to mount the background fabric in an embroidery hoop, placing it over the larger hoop and pressing the smaller hoop inside, over the right side of the fabric. Your sewing machine manual may include instructions for machine embroidery.

1 Interface the section to be applied and mark all pattern lines on the piece with basting stitches. Cut out the motifs, leaving a margin about $\frac{3}{8}$in (1cm) wide all around the edge of the design.

2 Place the motif right side up on the right side of the interfaced background fabric matching grain lines as much as possible. Pin the motif in place and baste it down just outside the final stitching line.

3 Sew around the motif outline with a firm backstitch or machine straight stitch. Remove basting and trim raw edges to about $\frac{1}{8}$in (3mm) from the stitching line all around. Extra hand-worked stitches can be placed in the center of the motif.

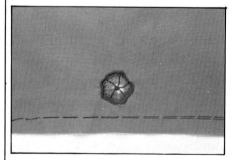

4 Stitch all around the motif, covering the raw edges and the original stitching line with hand-worked blanket or buttonhole stitch or machine satin stitch. Press carefully on the wrong side after removing basting.

5 Build up the design, overlaying parts as necessary. Where the motif is to overlap an edge (as on the blouse on page 85), do not satin stitch the edge which overlaps the pattern line of the garment piece until the section is ready to be completed.

6 Baste the facing section to the main pieces, wrong sides together. Complete stitching of the overlap of the motif, continuing all around the outer edge of the section, following the pattern line. Using very sharp scissors and without cutting the stitches, trim away all the excess fabric from the outer edge of the section and the motif. Remove basting and press on the wrong side.

French seam

This seam is strong because it is made with two rows of stitching. It is therefore suitable for garments that will be laundered frequently. It is neat because no raw edges show on the wrong side, so it is useful for lightweight or sheer fabrics or those which ravel easily. The raw edges are enclosed in the seam "fell", which is the width of the finished seam—in this case on the wrong side of the garment. The fell can be made to any width but a $\frac{5}{8}$in (1.5cm) seam allowance will give a finished width of about $\frac{1}{4}$in (6mm).

To show the technique more clearly, we have used a darker fabric to represent the right side, a lighter one for the wrong side.

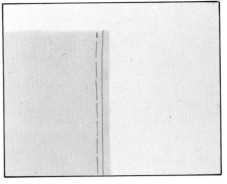

1 Put the two garment pieces to be joined together with their **wrong** sides facing. Baste along the **seamline**. Machine stitch a line halfway between the basting line and the cutting line along the whole length of the seam.

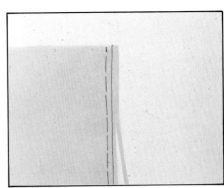

2 Trim the raw edges slightly so that the seam allowance will be narrower than the finished fell. For $\frac{1}{4}$in (6mm) fell width trim to less than $\frac{1}{4}$in (6mm). Remove basting and press on the stitching line.

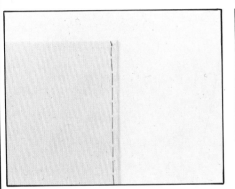

3 Clip seam allowances on any curved seams almost to the stitching. Turn the pieces to the wrong side and press the seam together. Pin and baste on seamline.

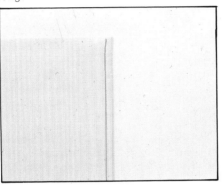

4 Check that no raw edges are showing on the right side of the garment; stitch along the seamline. Remove basting.

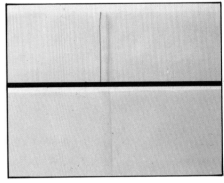

5 From the wrong side, press the fell to one side. Press again from the right side, using the point of the iron along the seamline only.

Working with sheer fabrics

Sheer fabrics, such as voile, organza, organdy, net and chiffon, call for special sewing techniques. It is advisable to use seams in which the raw edges do not show, such as French or double-stitched seams. On underwear or lingerie this is not so important for neatness, but these seams give the extra strength needed. Shell hem edging also makes a pretty finish on the edge of sheer fabrics (see Volume 7, page 59).

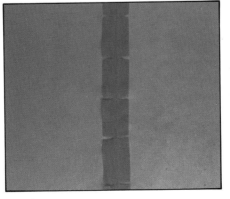

1 If using a selvage in a seam, clip this edge every 2in (5cm) or so after stitching to prevent puckering. If the material is very likely to ravel, avoid using selvages in a seam unless the seam is enclosed, as on a cuff, faced edge, or French seam.

2 If possible, use bindings or full linings for finishing edges, because facings give a stronger color over part of the garment. It may be necessary to cut a double layer of fabric to cover an interfacing to keep the color of the finished garment uniform.

continued

Simon Butcher

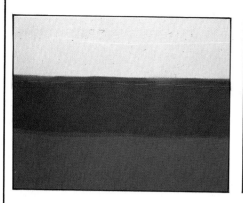

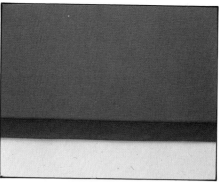

3 Use the correct interfacing for the main fabric. It should be as lightweight as possible, and in a color similar to the main fabric.

4 Cut hems to **exactly** double the width of the finished hem. For example a finished hem of $\frac{3}{4}$in (2cm) will need a hem allowance of $1\frac{1}{2}$in (4cm). The hem will look neater made this way.

5 Be very careful when stitching the seams or sewing by hand. Use small, even stitches; stitches may show on the right side of the work.

"Gigi" blouse

This enchanting blouse with its square collar is perfect for a dress-up occasion. Here it is made in a plain, sheer fabric appliquéd with birds and flowers.

Adapting the pattern

Measurements
The pattern for the blouse is adapted from the basic shirt in the Stitch by Stitch Pattern Pack, available in sizes 10 to 20, corresponding to sizes 8 to 18 in ready-made clothes.

Materials
3 sheets of tracing paper 36×40in 90×100cm approx)
Yardstick; flexible curve
Right triangle

the seams. Trace both complete pieces, marking bust darts, seamlines, grain lines, and notches and leaving $\frac{3}{4}$in (2cm) extra all along center back for the seam. Measure down $8\frac{1}{2}$in (21.5cm) from neck cutting line and mark the point for the zipper. Note that the center front is to be placed on a fold.

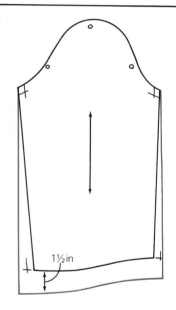

4 Using the triangle and yardstick, straighten the side edges by drawing from armhole to meet extended hemline on each side. Mark the notches, seamlines, grain line and shoulder point.

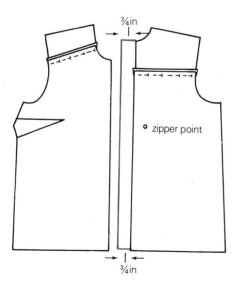

1 Pin the front yoke to the shirt front and the back yoke to the shirt back, aligning

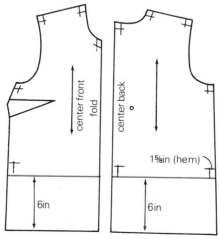

2 From the hem cutting line, measure up 6in (15cm) all around and redraw the hemline on both pieces. $1\frac{5}{8}$in (4cm) is allowed for turning up the hem.

3 Trace the basic sleeve pattern, adding an extra $1\frac{5}{8}$in (4cm) all along the hem edge for the elastic casing. Using a flexible curve, draw in the new hemline and extend this slightly at each side.

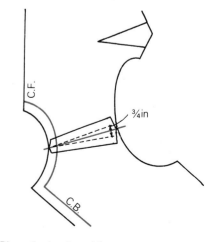

5 Place the back and front patterns together at the shoulder line with the

Marcus Wilson-Smith

seams aligned. Keeping seamlines together at neck edge, swivel pattern so that the back pattern seamline overlaps the front pattern seamline by $\frac{3}{4}$in (2cm). Pin in place. Mark the halfway point of the overlap, joining it to the neck point.

6 Trace the neck seamline, center front, center back and the new shoulder line from the neck edge to the armhole halfway between the overlap.

10-14; $5\frac{1}{8}$in (13cm) for sizes 16-20. Using the triangle, draw a line across bodice front perpendicular to center front.

8 Starting from the shoulder point on the seamline, draw a line to meet the first line, making a right angle where the two lines meet.

9 From the center back neck seamline, measure down $7\frac{1}{8}$in (18cm) for sizes 10-14; $7\frac{1}{2}$in (19cm) for sizes 16-20. Using the triangle, draw a line across the perpendicular to the center back. Square a line to meet this from the shoulder point seamline as before.

Trace the collar pattern, following the center front line, center back seamline, neck seamline and new pattern lines. Mark neck and shoulder points.

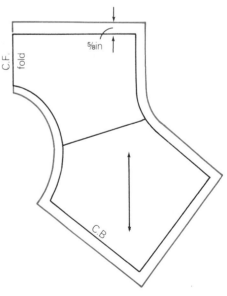

John Hutchinson

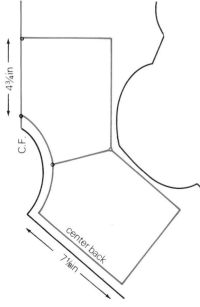

7 From the center front neck seamline, measure down $4\frac{3}{4}$in (12cm) on sizes

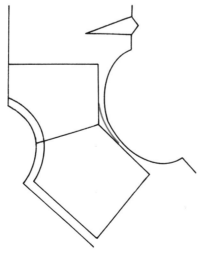

10 Using a flexible curve, smooth out the angle where the lines meet the shoulder.

11 Add a $\frac{5}{8}$in (1.5cm) seam allowance to the neck edge, center back and collar pattern lines. Do not add allowances to the center front line. Mark the grain line parallel to the center front, indicating that this line is to be placed on a fold. Note that extra length or width should be added to this pattern if using long overlapped motifs (see page 82).

Directions for making

Materials

36in (90cm)-wide fabric with/
   without nap:
   Sizes 10, 12, 14: $3\frac{1}{4}$yd (2.9m)
   Sizes 16, 18, 20: $3\frac{1}{2}$yd (3.1m)
48in (120cm)-wide fabric with or
   without nap:
   Sizes 10, 12, 14: $2\frac{5}{8}$yd (2.3m)
   Sizes 16, 18, 20: $2\frac{3}{4}$yd (2.5m)
36in (90cm)-wide interfacing:
   For all sizes: $\frac{3}{4}$yd (.6m)
Matching thread, 8in (20cm) zipper
$\frac{5}{8}$in (1.5cm)-wide elastic:
   Sizes 10 to 14: $1\frac{3}{8}$yd (1.2m)
   Sizes 16 to 20: $1\frac{1}{2}$yd (1.3m)

Motifs cut from chintz or other
   fabric suitable for appliqué perse
Hook and eye
Note: Measurement for fabric does
   not include extra fabric needed for
   collar if using overlap motifs.
   Extra fabric will be needed,
   depending on size and shape of
   motif used.

Key to adjusted pattern pieces

A Blouse back   Cut 2
B Blouse front   Cut 1 (on fold)
C Sleeve   Cut 2
D Collar   Cut 2 (on fold)
Interfacing- Use piece D (Cut 2 on fold)
F Cut 2 (for zipper)

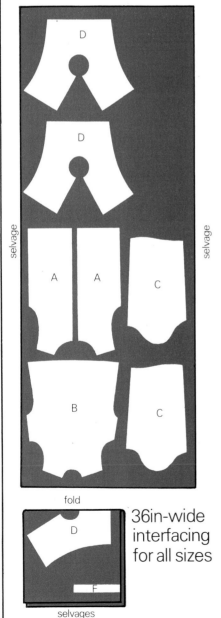

Cutting layout for 48in-wide fabric
with or without nap

D

D

A   A   C

B   C

fold

D

36in-wide
interfacing
for all sizes

F

selvages

selvage

selvage

D

D

C

A

B

fold

selvages

36in-wide fabric
with or without nap

Suggested fabrics
Voile, organdy, organza, lawn, poplin, crepe or crepe-de-chine; for the motif, any printed fabric or chintz that is a suitable weight and texture for background fabric.

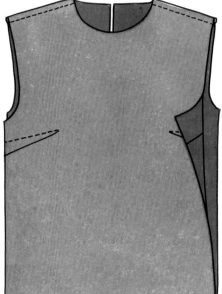

1 Prepare the fabric and cut out the pattern pieces, noting any that are placed on the fold. Transfer all pattern markings before removing the pattern pieces.
2 Join blouse front to blouse backs at the shoulders, using French seams (see page 83). Remove all basting: press.
Pin, baste and stitch bust darts.
Remove basting. Press down.

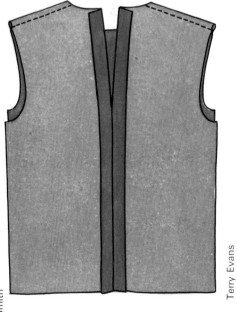

3 With right sides together and making a plain seam, pin, baste and stitch the center back seam from hem edge to zipper point. Take ¾in (2cm) seam allowance. Press the seam open up to the neck edge.

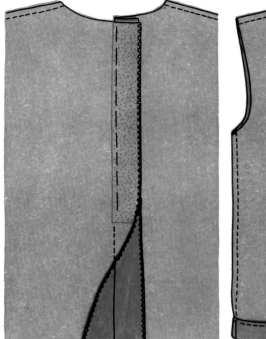

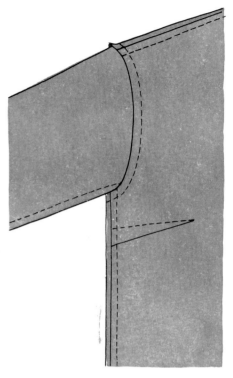

(2cm) leaving an opening near the seam for inserting elastic. Repeat with the other sleeve.

4 Cut a piece of interfacing $\frac{3}{4}$in (2cm) wide by 8in (20cm) long and slide it beneath the seam allowance along the area from neck to zipper point. Overcast raw edges together; repeat other side of seam. The interfacing is to strengthen the zipper. Press seam open.

6 Join the side seams of the blouse using French seams as directed. Press. Pin, baste and stitch a double hem with a finished width of $\frac{3}{4}$in (2cm), leaving an opening for elastic at center back.

9 Insert the sleeves into the armholes, matching underarm seams and shoulder points, using the French seam method. Press.

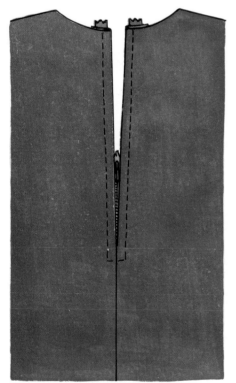

7 Run a row of gathering stitches over the sleeve cap between gathering points. Join the sleeve seam using the French seam method as before. Press.

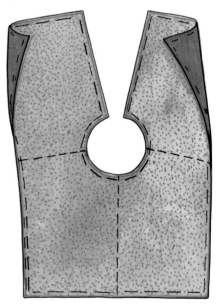

5 Insert the zipper at neckline by the slot seam method (see Volume 4, page 68) making sure the zipper teeth do not show from the right side. Press carefully. This zipper application has a line of stitching on each side of the zipper.

8 Pin, baste and stitch a double hem on the sleeve with a finished width of $\frac{3}{4}$in

10 Put the interfacing on the top layer of the collar with **wrong** sides together to make two layers. Pin and baste around all outer edges, and along center front and shoulder lines, keeping the collar as flat as possible.
11 If an adjustment has been made for the overlap of the motifs, baste around the pattern lines of the collar. Do not remove basting until all stitching is completed.

14 Lay the collar on the blouse, putting wrong side of collar to the right side of the blouse and matching center backs, center fronts and shoulder points. Pin and baste around neck edge, taking a ⅝in (1.5cm) seam.

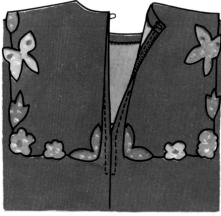

15 Complete the neck edge of the collar with bias binding or self-fabric bias strip as explained in Volume 10, page 64. Remove all basting and press.
16 Sew hook and eye to the neck edge of the blouse beneath the collar and above the zipper.

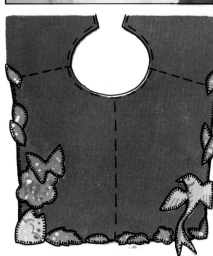

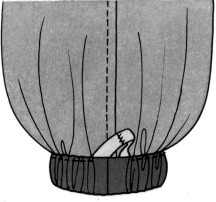

12 Position and apply the motifs as explained on page 82. Pin and baste the undercollar to the top collar with **wrong** sides together and matching neck, center fronts, center backs and pattern lines. Sew the satin stitch edge all around the collar edge from center backs to front, following pattern lines and omitting neck edge. Carefully trim away all excess fabric from outer edges and press.

13 Remove all basting from outer edge of collar, retaining center front and shoulder line basting for matching blouse to neck and neck edge basting. Press carefully on the wrong side.

17 Cut elastic to fit waist and wrists plus an inch or so of overlap for each piece. Insert elastic into sleeve and blouse hem casings, overlapping ends and stitching together. Slip stitch openings closed.

Marcus Wilson-Smith

Terry Evans

*Velvet stitch
*A velvet stitch mirror decoration

Velvet stitch

Of all the varied textures possible in needlepoint, the most luxurious is that formed by velvet stitch. As its name suggests, this stitch produces a pile fabric. It can be used on its own—as in the mirror decoration shown here—or combined with flatter stitches, such as tent stitch, to produce relief effects. By using different colored threads in the needle you can create subtle color effects similar to those in an Impressionist painting.

Velvet stitch takes a bit of time to work but is not difficult. It is advisable to work it in a frame, as you need to use both hands; an artists' stretcher frame or an old picture frame will serve the purpose. You will also need a knitting needle for forming the loops—preferably one with points at both ends. The size of the needle determines the length of the loop. When you're planning a piece of work, experiment with different knitting needles to

find the best size for your purpose.
All of the various kinds of embroidery thread—Persian yarn, crewel, tapestry, stranded floss, and so on—can be used for velvet stitch. For the mirror decoration we have used pearl cotton, which has a lovely sheen as well as a firm twist. For the samples below we have used tapestry yarn. Make some samples of velvet stitch in different threads to compare the different effects.

Working the velvet stitch

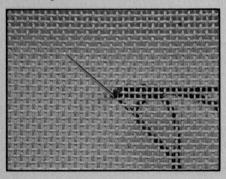

1 Begin with a diagonal stitch, as for a tent stitch, but bring the needle up in the same hole from which it first emerged.

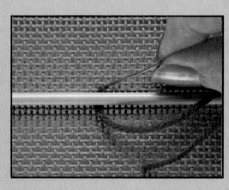

2 Place a knitting needle along the lower edge of the stitch and make another diagonal stitch over the needle and into the same hole as for the first stitch. ·

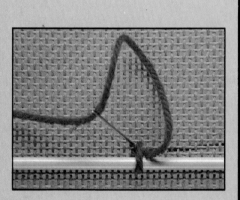

3 Bring the needle up in the hole directly below the second hole, then take it diagonally back to the one above the first hole, as if completing a cross stitch. This anchors the loop and completes the velvet stitch.

4 Move to the right and repeat steps 1-3, using the two right-hand holes of the first stitch and the next two free holes. Continue in this way to the end of the row. If you are working with more than one color, leave the thread on the top of the work; then you can pick it up when it is needed in the next row.

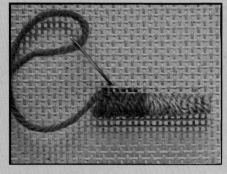

5 Begin the next row above the first, at the left, leaving one canvas thread unworked. When you reach the point of changing color, bring the new thread under the canvas and up through the correct hole for the next stitch.

6 Work from bottom to top throughout, so that all of the pile slants downward. When the work is complete, cut the loops carefully with embroidery scissors.

Frederick Mancini

Soft petals

Inspired by the colors of sweet peas, this velvet stitch mirror decoration would be equally effective on the top of a jewel box or—reduced in size—on a compact.

Size The finished decoration measures 4½in (11.5cm) in diameter. You can vary the size to suit your purpose by using smaller or larger gauge canvas. If you use No. 18 canvas, for example, the work will measure 3in (7.5cm) in diameter.

Materials

A hand mirror, or other round object with a flat surface
Piece of best-quality No. 12 canvas 8in (20.5cm) square—or to fit frame
1 skein each of No. 5 pearl cotton in 8 colors: terra cotta (A), flesh pink (B), scarlet (C), lilac (D), cerise (E), purple (F), khaki (G) and leaf green (H). The shades used were DMC 3328, 754, 606, 316, 601, 327, 640 and 469 respectively
No. 18 tapestry needle
No. 6 (4½mm) knitting needle
Small rectangular frame
Masking tape; compass
Thumbtacks or staples
Thick cardboard (see step 7)
Cotton lining fabric 6in (15cm) square
Matching sewing thread; strong thread
Strong all-purpose glue

Michael Joseph/Designed by Diana Springall

1 Bind the canvas edges with masking tape and tack or staple canvas to frame.
2 Find and mark the vertical center of the canvas. Begin the first row about 1¾in (4.5cm) up from the edge, 6 threads to the left of the center. Using two strands of shade F in the needle, work 6 velvet stitches. Continue with 6 velvet stitches in A and F (one strand of each in the needle).
3 Continue working velvet stitch in rows, following the chart; the darkened lines represent the threads worked over.
4 When the entire circle has been worked, carefully cut the loops with scissors.
5 Remove the work from the frame. If it has become distorted, block it, following the instructions in Needlework course 2, Volume 1, page 72.
6 Cut away the excess canvas, leaving a ⅝in (1.5cm) margin around the work.
7 To support the embroidery you will need a thick cardboard disk with a diameter of 4in (10cm), which can be drawn with a compass. If you are skilled at using a craft knife you can cut out the disk yourself. Otherwise, get someone (such as a picture-framer) to do it for you. Or cut two circles with scissors from thin cardboard and glue them together.
8 Fold the canvas edges over the cardboard disk. Using strong thread, lace the edges together, sewing from one side to the other, all around the circle. Fasten off securely.
9 Cut a circle with a diameter of about 5½in (14cm) from the cotton fabric. Baste and slipstitch this to the underside of the embroidery, turning in the raw edges so that the fabric just hides the unworked canvas.
10 Glue the embroidery in place on the back of the mirror.

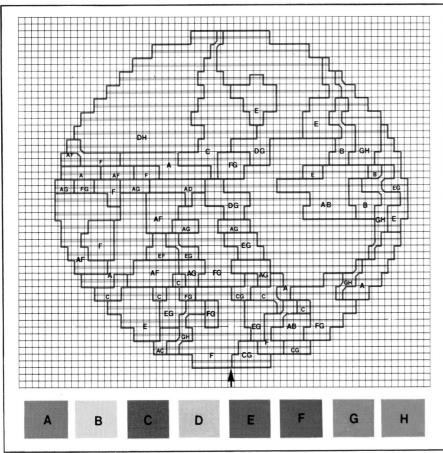

John Hutchinson

| A | B | C | D | E | F | G | H |

EXTRA SPECIAL CROCHET

Tunisian stripes

Stripes of Tunisian crochet make a stylish and comfortable vest guaranteed to appeal.

Sizes
To fit 36[38:40]in (92[97:102]cm) chest.
Length, 20[20½:21½]in (52.5[54:56]cm).

Note: Directions for larger sizes are in brackets []; if there is only one set of figures it applies to all sizes.

Materials
4×2oz (50g) balls of a knitting worsted in main color (A)
3[3:4] balls in each of 2 contrasting colors (B and C)
Size H (5.00mm) Tunisian crochet hook
Size H (5.00mm) crochet hook
5 buttons

Gauge
17 sts and 34 rows to 4in (10cm) worked on size H (5.00mm) Tunisian hook.

Back
Using size H (5.00mm) Tunisian hook and B, make 78[82:88]ch.
Base row Insert hook into one loop only of 2nd ch from hook, yo and draw a loop through, *insert hook into one loop only of next ch, yo and draw a loop through, rep from * to end. 78[82:88] loops on hook. Do not turn the work.
Next row Using C, yo and draw a loop through, first loop on hook, *yo and draw through 2 loops on hook, rep from * to end. 1 loop rem on hook.
Cont in stripe sequence of 1 row B, 2 rows C, 2 rows B, 2 rows A, 2 rows C, 2 rows A and 1 row B, working in patt as foll:
1st row Insert hook from right to left under 2nd vertical bar, yo and draw a loop through, *insert hook from right to left under next vertical bar, yo and draw a loop through, rep from * to end. Do not turn work. 78[82:88] loops on hook.
2nd row Yo and draw a loop through first loop on hook, *yo and draw through next 2 loops on hook, rep from * to end. 1 loop rem on hook. These 2 rows form patt. Cont in patt until work measures 12½(12½:13)in (32[32:33]cm); end with 2nd row.

Shape armholes
Next 2 rows Sl st across first 8[9:10] sts, patt to within last 8[9:10] sts, then work

back.
Dec one st (by working under 2 vertical loops tog) at each end of next and foll 3 alternate rows. 54[56:60] sts. Cont straight until armhole measures 7½[8:8½]in (19[20.5:21.5]cm); end with 2nd row.
Shape shoulders
Next 2 rows Sl st across first 9 sts, patt to within last 8[9:10] sts, then work back. Rep last 2 rows once more. Fasten off.
Right front
Using size H (5.00mm) Tunisian hook and B, make 39[41:44]ch. Cut off yarn. Working in patt and stripe sequence to match back, shape as foll:
Rejoin yarn to 11th ch, (insert hook into one loop only of next ch, yo and draw a loop through) twice, so having 3 loops on hook, then work back.
Next row Remove hook from loop, insert hook into one loop only of the ch to the right of the loop, place loop back on hook and patt to end, then (insert hook into one loop only of next ch, yo and draw a loop through) twice, then work back. Cont to pick up 1 loop at short side and 2 loops at long side on every other row until all ch are being worked on short side (front edge), pick up rem ch at long side and cont in patt on these 39[41:44] sts until front from end of shaping is same

length as back to armholes, ending at front side.
Shape armhole and front edge
Next 2 rows Patt to within last 9 sts, then work back. Dec one st at beg of next and every foll 4th row and at the same time dec one st at armhole edge on next and foll 3 alternate rows. 18 sts. Cont without shaping until armhole is same depth as back armholes to shoulders, ending with a 2nd row.
Shape shoulder
Next 2 rows Patt across 8[9:10] sts, then work back. Fasten off.

Left front
Work as for right front, reversing all shaping and rejoin B to 27th[29th: 32nd] ch for lower shaping.

Armhole edgings (alike)
Join shoulder seams.
Using size H (5.00mm) crochet hook and A, work 3 rows of sc evenly along armhole edge. Fasten off.

The edging
Join side seams.
Using size H (5.00mm) crochet hook join A to right side seam and work a row of sc all around outer edge, sl st into first sc. Work 2 more rounds of sc, working 2sc into each of the 2sc at points on the fronts.
1st buttonhole round Work in sc to beg of 11th stripe in A at lower edge of left front, (2ch, skip next 2sc, 1sc into each of next 10sc) 4 times, then work another buttonhole, work in sc to end, sl st into first sc.
2nd buttonhole round Work 1sc into each sc and 2sc into each buttonhole and point, sl st into first sc.
Work 1 more round, working 2 sc at points. Fasten off.

To finish
Press or block, according to yarn used. Sew on buttons.

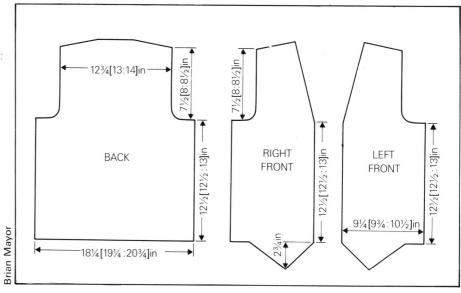

Brian Mayor

BACK — 12¾[13:14]in — 7½[8:8½]in — 12½[12½:13]in — 18¼[19¼:20¾]in

RIGHT FRONT — 7½[8:8½]in — 12½[12½:13]in — 2¾in

LEFT FRONT — 12½[12½:13]in — 9¼[9¾:10½]in

Technique tip
Tunisian crochet

Tunisian crochet is worked with a long hook which resembles both a knitting needle and a crochet hook. The reason for the hook being long is that all the loops are kept on the hook for the first row and worked off on the second row.

First, make a length of chain. Now insert the hook into one loop only of the second chain from the hook, yarn over hook and draw a loop through — this leaves 2 loops on hook.
Work into each chain in this way, keeping each loop on the hook. Do not turn the work.

On the next row the loops are worked off the hook until 1 loop only remains. Yarn over hook and draw a loop through first loop on hook, *yarn over hook and draw a loop through next 2 loops on hook, repeat from * until 1 loop remains on hook.

On the next row the loops are picked up again by inserting the hook from right to left under the vertical loop, placing yarn over hook and drawing a loop through again; do not turn the work at the end of the row.

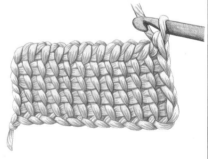

Work loops off hook again until only 1 loop remains on hook. The last 2 rows are repeated throughout.

EXTRA SPECIAL CROCHET

Flash of inspiration

Make this attractive sweater in two lengths.

Sizes
To fit 32[34:36:38]in (83[87:92:97]cm) bust.
Short version Length, 27in (68cm).
Long version Length, 35in (88cm).
Sleeve seam, 17[17¼:17¾:18]in (43[44:45:46]cm).
Note: Directions for larger sizes are in brackets []; if there is only one set of figures it applies to all sizes.

Materials
Short version 23[25:27:29]oz (650[700:750:800]g) of a knitting worsted in main color (A)
6oz (150g) in contrasting color (B)
Long version 29[31:32:34]g (800[850:900:950]g) of a knitting worsted in main color (A)
6oz (150g) in contrasting color (B)
Sizes H and I (5.50 and 6.00mm) crochet hooks

Gauge
13hdc and 10 rows to 4in (10cm) worked on size I (6.00mm) hook.

Back
Using size I (6.00mm) hook and A, make 49[53:57:61]ch.
Base row (RS) 1 hdc into 3rd ch from hook, 1 hdc into each ch to end. Turn.
Patt row 2ch to count as first hdc, 1 hdc into each hdc to end. Turn. 48[52:56:60] hdc. Rep the patt row 14 times more. Using a separate length of A, make 5ch and leave aside.
Next row 6ch, 1hdc into 3rd ch from hook, 1 hdc into each of next 3ch, 1hdc into each hdc to end, then work 1hdc into each of the 5ch. Turn. 58[62:66:70] hdc.
Cont in patt until work measures 25in (63cm) for short version and 33in (83cm) for long version; end with a RS row.
Shape neck
Next row Patt 15[17:17:19], turn and work 2 more rows on these sts. Fasten off. Skip center 28[28:32:32] sts, rejoin yarn to next st and patt to end of row. Turn. Work 2 more rows on these sts. Fasten off.

Front
Work as for back until 27[27:31:31] rows less have been worked to shoulder so ending with a RS row.

Divide for neck
Next row 2ch, 1hdc into each of next 14[16:16:18] hdc, turn.
Cont on these 15[17:17:19] sts, work 26[26:30:30] rows. Fasten off.
Skip next 2 hdc, rejoin yarn to next hdc and work to end of row. 41[43:47:49] hdc. Turn.
Dec one hdc at neck edge, by working 2 hdc tog, on next 4 rows. 37[39:43:45] hdc.
Next row 2ch, 1hdc into each of next 22[24:26:28] hdc joining in B on last of these hdc, work 2hdc in B changing to A on 2nd of these 2hdc, work in A to within last 2hdc, work last 2hdc tog. Turn. This sets position of motif. Cont to work motif from chart, at the same time dec one hdc at neck edge on every row until 15[17:17:19] hdc rem. Fasten off.

Sleeves
Using size H (5.50mm) hook and B, make 27[29:31:33]ch.
Base row 1sc into 3rd ch from hook, 1sc into each ch to end. Turn.
Work 5 more rows in sc, inc 6 sc evenly in last row. 32[34:36:38] sts.
Cut off B, join in A. Change to Size I (6.00mm) hook and work in hdc, inc one

hdc at each end of every 4th row, by working 2hdc into first and last sts, until there are 50[52:54:56] sts, then cont straight until work measures 17[17¼:17¾:18]in (43[44:45:46]cm). Fasten off.

Lower borders (make 2)
Using size H (5.50mm) hook and B, make 64[68:72:76]ch.
Base row 1sc into 3rd ch from hook, 1sc into each ch to end. Turn.
Work 5 more rows in sc.
Next row 1ch, 1sc into each of next 4sc, turn.
Cont on these 5 sts for 6½in (16cm). Fasten off. Skip center 53[57:61:65] sc, rejoin yarn to next sc and work to end. Turn.
Cont on these 5 sts for 6½in (16cm). Fasten off.

Neck border
Using size H (5.50mm) hook and B, make 30[30:34:34]ch.
Base row 1sc into 3rd ch from hook, 1sc into each ch to end. Turn.

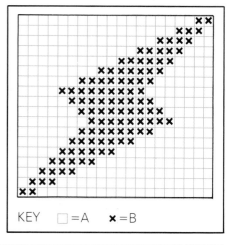

KEY □ =A ✕ =B

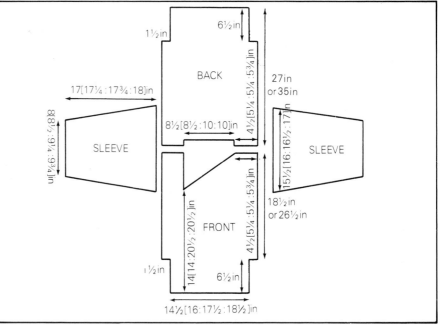

Work 5 more rows in sc.
Next row 1 ch, 1 sc into each of next 6 sc, turn.
Cont on these 7 sts for 8¾[10¾:10¾]in (22[22:27:27]cm); end at inner edge.
**Dec one sc at inside edge on next and foll 4 alternate rows. 2 sts. Fasten off.
Skip next 20[20:24:24] sts, rejoin yarn to next st, 1 ch, 1 sc into turning ch. Turn.
2nd row 1 ch, 1 sc into next ch, 1 sc into next sc, sl st into next sc, turn.
3rd row 1 ch, skip next sl st, 1 sc into each of next 2 sc, 1 sc into turning ch. Turn.
4th row 1 ch, 1 sc, into each of next 2 sc, 1 sc into 1 ch, 1 sc into next sc, sl st into next 4 sc, turn.

5th row 1 ch, skip sl st, 1 sc into each of next sc, 1 sc into turning ch, turn.
6th row 1 ch, 1 sc into each of next 4 sc, 1 sc into 1 ch, 1 sc into next sc, turn.
7th row 1 ch, 1 sc, into each of next 5 sc, 1 sc into turning ch. Turn.
Rep last row until work measures approx 9[9:11:11]in (23[23:28:28]cm); end at inner edge.
Work as first side from ** to end.

To finish
Join shoulder seams. Mark armhole depth 7¾[8:8¼:8½]in (19.5[20:21:21.5]cm) from shoulders. Set in sleeves; join seams. Sew on borders. Press seams.

Town and country

Smart for town, yet comfortable for the country, this go-anywhere sweater will be a firm favorite.

Sizes

To fit 36[38:40]in (92[97:102]cm) chest. Length, 26¼[26½:27]in (67[68:69]cm). Sleeve seam, 19¼ (49cm).

Note Directions for larger sizes are in brackets []; if there is only one set of figures it applies to all sizes.

Materials

10[11:12] x 18[20:22]oz (500 [550:600]g) of a knitting worsted 1 pair each Nos. 2, 4 and 5 (3,3¾ and 4mm) needles.

Gauge

19 sts and 44 rows to 4in (10cm) in ribbing patt on No. 4 (3¾mm) needles.

Back

** Using No. 2 needles cast on 102[112:112] sts and work in K1, P1 ribbing for 2½in (6cm).
Dec row Rib 7[8:6], K2 tog, *rib 7[6:6], K2 tog, rep from * to last 3[6:2] sts, rib to end. 91[99:107] sts. Change to No. 4 (3¾mm) needles. Beg ribbing patt.
1st row K.
2nd row (RS) K1, *K1, K next st inserting needle into st one row below— called knit one below or K1 b—, rep from * to last 2 sts, K2.
3rd row K1, *K1b, rep from * to end. The last 2 rows form patt. Cont in patt until work measures 18in (46cm) from beg; end with WS row.

Shape armholes

Bind of 3 sts at beg of next 2 rows and 2 sts at beg of foll 2 rows. 81[89:97] sts. ** Cont straight until armhole measures 8¼[8½:9]in (21[22:23]cm); end with WS row.

Shape shoulders

Bind off 3 sts at beg of next 12 rows and 4 sts at beg of foll 0[2:4] rows.

Shape neck

Next row Bind off 4, work until there are 12 sts on RH needle, turn and leave rem 29 sts on a spare needle.

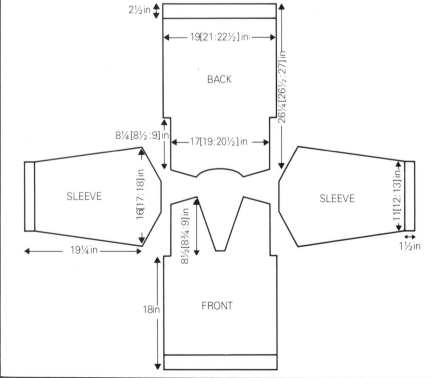

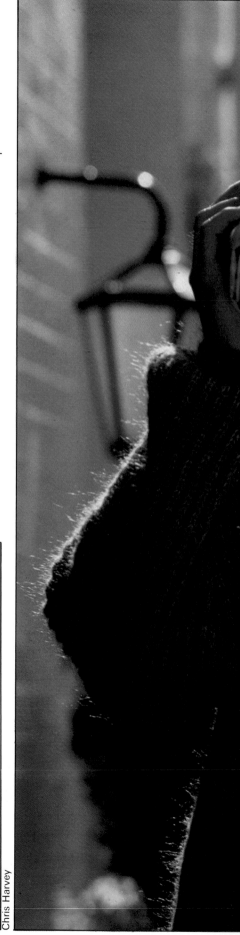

Next row Bind off 8, work to end. Bind off. Rejoin yarn to inner end of sts on spare needle, bind off 13, work to end. Complete to match first side.

Front
Work as for back from ** to ** Cont straight until armhole measures $\frac{3}{4}[1\frac{1}{4}: 1\frac{1}{2}]$in (2[3:4]cm); end with WS row.

Divide neck
Next row Patt 37[41:45], turn and leave rem sts on a spare needle. Cont on first set of sts until armhole measures $4[4\frac{1}{2}: 4\frac{3}{4}]$in (10[11:12]cm); end at armhole edge.

Shape neck
Dec one st at neck edge on next and every foll 4th row 8 times in all. Place a marker at neck edge on last row. Dec one st at neck edge on foll 6th row 3 times in all. Cont straight until armhole measures $8\frac{1}{4}[8\frac{1}{2}:9]$in (21[22:23]cm); end at armhole edge.

Shape shoulder
Bind off 3 sts at beg of next and foll 6 alternate rows and 4 sts at beg of foll 1[2:3] alternate rows. Work 1 row. Bind off. Rejoin yarn to inner end of sts on spare needle, bind off 7, patt to end. Complete to match first side reversing shaping.

Sleeves
Using No. 2 (3mm) needles cast on 52 [56:60] sts and work in K1, P1 ribbing for $1\frac{1}{2}$ (4cm), but inc one st at beg of last row. 53[57:61] sts.
Change to No. 4 ($3\frac{3}{4}$mm) needles. Cont in ribbing patt as for back, but inc one st at each end of every foll 12th row until there are 77[81:85] sts. Cont straight until work measures $19\frac{1}{4}$in (49cm) from beg; end with WS row.

Shape top
Bind off 5 sts at beg of next 2 rows, 4 sts at beg of foll 2 rows, 3 sts at beg of foll 4 rows, 2 sts at beg of foll 0[2:4] rows, one st at beg of foll 20 rows, 2 sts at beg of foll 2 rows and 3 sts at beg of foll 2 rows. Bind off.

Collar
Using No. 2 (3mm) needles cast on 105 sts.
Next row K2, inc in next st to form P1, K1, *P1, K1, rep from * to last 4 sts, P1, inc in next st to form K1, P1, K2.
Next row P2, rib to last 2 sts, P2.
Cont in ribbing inc at each end of next and every foll alternate row 3 times more. Work 1 row.
Change to No. 4 ($3\frac{3}{4}$mm) needles and cont to inc on next and every foll alternate row 4 times in all. Work 1 row. Change to No. 5 (4mm) needles and cont to inc on next and every foll alternate row 4 times in all. 129 sts. Work 9 rows straight.
Next row Rib 1, sl 1, rib 1, psso, rib to last 3 sts, work 2 tog, rib 1.
Next row P2, rib to last 2 sts, P2.

Cont in rib dec at each end of next and every foll alternate row 3 times more. Change to No. 4 (3¾mm) needles and cont to dec on every alternate row 4 times. Change to No. 2 (3mm) needles and cont to dec on every alternate row 4 times. 105 sts. Work 1 row. Bind off.

Front bands
Using No. 2 (3mm) needles cast on 41 sts.
1st row K2, *K1, P1, rep from * to last 3 sts, K1, K2 tog.
2nd row Bind off 1, rib to last 3 sts, P3. Rep these 2 rows 11 times more. 17 sts. Work 15 rows ribbing as set. Bind off. Work another band to match, reversing shaping.

To finish
Join shoulder seams. Set in sleeves, then join side and sleeve seams. Sew front bands to opening up to markers. Sew collar around neck edge and to top of bands. Fold collar in half to WS and slip stitch in place.

Technique tip

Knitting into stitch below

This method is used in ribbing patterns to produce a highly textured fabric.

Insert right-hand needle into center of next stitch on left-hand needle *but* one row below. Knit the stitch in the usual way, drawing right-hand needle point through center of same stitch. Drop the loop from the left-hand needle.

The finished fabric here is a simple knit one, knit one below repeat, known as "fisherman's ribbing".

EXTRA SPECIAL KNITTING

On the right track

Knit these kids' tracksuits in a machine-washable yarn—they'll be their favorite outfits.

Victor Yuan

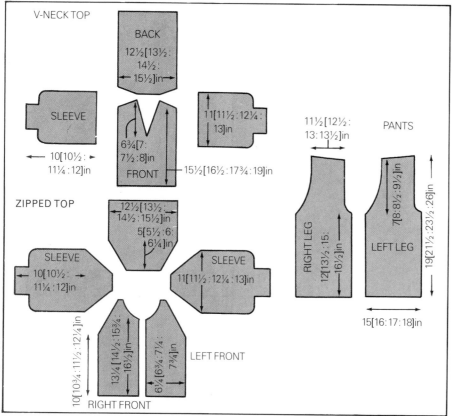

V-NECK TOP

BACK
12½[13½: 14½: 15½]in

SLEEVE
10[10½: 11¼: 12]in

FRONT
6¾[7: 7½: 8]in

11[11½: 12¼: 13]in

15½[16½: 17¾: 19]in

ZIPPED TOP

12½[13½: 14½: 15½]in
5[5½: 6: 6¼]in

SLEEVE
10[10½: 11¼: 12]in

SLEEVE
11[11½: 12¼: 13]in

RIGHT FRONT
10[10¾: 11½: 12¼]in
13¼[14¼: 15¾: 16½]in

LEFT FRONT
6¼[6¾: 7¼: 7¾]in

PANTS

11½[12½: 13: 13½]in

RIGHT LEG
12[13½: 15: 16½]in

LEFT LEG
7[8: 8½: 9½]in
19[21½: 23½: 26]in

15[16: 17: 18]in

Sizes

Tops To fit 22[24:26:28]in (55[61:66: 71]cm) chest.
Length, 15½[16½:17¾:19]in (39[42:45: 48]cm).
Sleeve seam, 10[10½:11¼:12]in (25[27: 29:31]cm).
Pants Waist to crotch (front), 7[8:8½:9½]in (18[20:22:24]cm).
Inside leg, 12[13½:15:16½]in (30[34: 38:42]cm).
Note: Directions for larger sizes are in brackets []; if there is only one set of figures it applies to all sizes.

Materials

A lightweight bouclé or a sport yarn
V-neck top *6[7:7:8] × 1oz (20g) balls in main color (A)*
1[1:2:2] × 1oz (20g) balls in contrasting color (B)
Zipped top *6[7:7:8] × 1oz (20g) balls in main color (A)*
1[1:2:2] × 1oz (20g) balls in contrasting color (B)
Pants *6[7:7:8] × 1oz (20g) balls in main color (A)*
1 pair each Nos. 2 and 4 (3 and 3¾mm) knitting needles
1 set of four No. 2 (3mm) double-pointed knitting needles
12[14:16:16]in (30[35:40:40]cm) open-ended zipper
1yd (1m) narrow elastic for pants

Gauge

24 sts and 36 rows to 4in (10cm) in stockinette st on No. 4 (3¾mm) needles.

V-neck top

Back

Using No. 2 (3mm) needles and A, cast on 75[81:87:93]sts and beg with a K row work 8 rows stockinette st. Place a marker at each end of last row to mark hemline. Change to No. 4 (3¾mm) needles and cont in stockinette st for 15½[16½:17¾:19]in (39[42:45:48]cm) from markers; end with a P row.
Shape shoulders
Bind off 6[6:7:7]sts at beg of next 4 rows, then 6[7:7:8]sts at beg of next 4 rows. Cut off yarn and leave rem 27[29: 31:33] sts on a holder for neck.

Front

Work as for back until work measures 8¾[9½:10¼:11]in (22[24:26:28]cm) from markers; end with a P row.
Divide for neck
1st row K37[40:43:46], turn and leave rem sts on a spare needle.
2nd row P to end.
3rd row K to last 3 sts, sl 1, K1, psso, K1. Cont to dec at neck edge on every 4th row until 24[26:28:30]sts rem, then cont straight until work measures same as back to shoulders; end with a P row.
Shape shoulder
Bind off 6[6:7:7]sts at beg of next and foll alternate row, then 6[7:7:8]sts at beg of foll 2 alternate rows. Return to sts on spare needle; sl first st onto safety pin for front neck, rejoin yarn to next st and K to end of row.
Next row P to end.

Next row K1, K2 tog, K to end.
Cont to match left side, reversing shaping.

Sleeves
Using No. 2 (3mm) needles and B, cast on 33[35:37:39]sts.
1st row K1, *P1, K1, rep from * to end.
2nd row P1, *K1, P1, rep from * to end.
Rep these 2 rows for 1½in (4cm); end with 2nd row. Cut off B. Change to No. 4 (3¾mm) needles and join in A.
Next row K twice into each st to end. 66[70:74:78]sts.
Beg with a P row, cont in stockinette st until work measures 9[9½:10¼:11]in (22[24:26:28]cm); end with a P row. Cut off A, join in B and cont in stockinette st for 1¼in (3cm). Bind off.

Neckband
Join shoulder seams. Using set of four No. 2 (3mm) needles, B and with RS facing, K back neck sts, pick up and K 51[53:55:57]sts down left front neck, K center front st from safety pin, pick up and K 51[53:55:57]sts up right front neck. 130[136:142:148]sts.
Next round Work in K1, P1 ribbing to within 2 sts of center front, sl 1, K1, psso, K1, K2 tog, rib to end.
Rep this round 6 times more. Bind off in ribbing, dec at center front as before.

To finish
Set in sleeves, placing center of sleeves to shoulder seams. Join side and sleeve seams. Fold up hem at lower edge and sl st in position. Make twisted or crochet cord in B and thread through hem.

Zipped top

Back

Work as for V-neck top until work measures 10[10¾:11½:12¼]in (25[27: 29:31]cm) from markers; end with a P row.
Shape armholes
Bind off 3 sts at beg of next 2 rows, then work 2 rows without shaping.
Next row K1, K2 tog, K to last 3 sts, sl 1, K1, psso, K1.
Next row P to end.
Rep the last 2 rows until 25[27:29:31] sts rem; end with a P row. Bind off.

Left front

Using No. 2 (3mm) needles and A, cast on 37[40:43:46]sts and work as for back to armholes; end with a P row.
Shape armhole
Bind off 3 sts at beg of next row, then work 3 rows without shaping.
Next row K1, K2 tog, K to end.
Rep the last 2 rows until 20[21:23:24] sts rem; end with a K row.
Shape neck
Bind off 4[5:5:6]sts at beg of next row.
Next row K1, K2 tog, K to last 3 sts, sl 1, K1, psso, K1.

John Hutchinson

Next row P to end.
Rep the last 2 rows 5[5:6:6] times more.
4 sts.
Cont to dec at armhole edge on alternate rows twice more, then bind off rem sts.

Right front
Work to match left front, reversing shaping.

Sleeves
Work as for sleeves of V neck top until work measures 9[9½:10¼:11]in (22[24: 26:28]cm; then cont in A until work measures 10[10½:11¼:12]in (25[27:29: 31]cm); end with a P row. Mark each end of last row, then work 4 more rows.

Shape top
Next row K1, K2 tog, K to last 3 sts, sl 1, K1, psso, K1.
Next row P to end.

Rep the last 2 rows until 36 sts rem; end with a P row.
Next row K1, K2 tog, K13, K2 tog, sl 1, K1, psso, K13, sl 1, K1, psso, K1. Cont to dec in center of every 6th row twice more, and **at same time** cont to dec at each end of every other row until 14 sts rem; end with a P row. Bind off.

Collar
With RS facing, using No. 2 (3mm) needles and B, pick up and K 81[87:93: 99] sts around neck.
Next row K2, (P1, K1) 27[29:31:33] times, P1, turn.
Next row (K1, P1) 16[17:18:19] times, K1, turn.
Next row (P1, K1) 18[19:20:21] times, P1, turn.
Next row (K1, P1) 20[21:22:23] times, K1, turn. Cont in this way, working 4

more sts on each row until the row rib 73[75:85:87], turn has been worked.
Next row Rib to last 2 sts, K2.
Now work across all sts:
Next row K2, rib to last 2 sts, K2.
Rep last row until collar measures 2¼[2¼:2¾]in (6[6:7:7]cm) from beg of front edge. Bind off in ribbing.

Left front pocket
Using No. 4 (3¾mm) needles and A, bind off 26[26:28:28]sts. *Beg with a K row, work 4 rows stockinette st. Join in B and work 2 rows garter st. Change to A.*
Rep from * to * 3 times more, then rep first 2 rows again. Cont in patt. dec one st at beg of next and every foll 4th row until 21 sts rem; end with a WS row. Bind off.

Right front pocket
Work to match left front pocket, reversing shaping.

Front edges (alike)

Using No. 2 (3mm) needles, A and with RS facing pick up and K 80[86:92:98]sts along front edge between hemline marker and neck edge.

To finish

Join raglan seams, sewing last 4 rows of sleeve seams to bound-off sts at armholes. Join side and sleeve seams. Fold up hem at lower edge and hem in position. Sew in zipper. Sew on pockets. Make twisted or crochet cord in B and thread through hem.

Pants

Right leg

Using No. 2 (3mm) needles and A, cast on 90[96:102:108]sts and beg with a K row work 8 rows stockinette st. Mark each end of last row for hemline. Change to No. 4 (3¾mm) needles and cont in stockinette st until work measures 12[13½:15:16½]in (30[34:38:42]cm) from markers; end with a P row. Adjust length here if necessary.

Shape crotch

Bind off 4 sts at beg of next row, then 2 sts at beg of next 3 rows.
Next row K1, K2 tog, K to last 3 sts, sl 1,

K1, psso, K1.
Next row P to end.
Next row K1, K2 tog, K to end.
Next row P to end.
Cont to dec at front edge on every other row 1[2:3:4] times more and **at same time** cont to dec at back edge on every 4th row until 70[74:78:82]sts rem. Cont straight until work measures 7[8:8½:9½]in (18[20:22:24]cm) from beg of crotch; end with a K row.

Shape back

1st row P35[40:45:50], turn.
2nd and every foll alternate row K to end.
3rd row P28[32:36:40], turn.
5th row P21[24:27:30], turn.
Cont to work 7[8:9:10]sts less on alternate rows twice more, then P across all sts. Change to No. 2 (3mm) needles and work 8 rows. Bind off.

Left leg

Work to match right leg, reversing all shaping.

To finish

Press or block, according to yarn used. Join back, front and leg seams. Fold up hems and sl st in place. Turn last 8 rows at waist to WS and sl st in place. Thread elastic through hems at waist and ankles.

Technique tip

Making a twisted cord

This is a simple trimming that is ideal for ties, drawstrings and belts. Strands of yarn are twisted together to form a cord, the number varying according to the thickness of yarn used.

The strands of yarn should be three times the length of the finished cord. Tie a knot about ¾in (2cm) from each end. Insert a knitting needle through knots, and with the help of a friend, twist the needles in a clockwise direction.

Continue to turn the needles until the strands are tightly twisted.
Keeping the strands taut, fold them in half at the center. Without letting go of the ends, remove the needles and knot the two ends together.

Hold the knot and shake the cord, letting the cord twist back on itself.
Undo the original knots and even out the yarn in the tassel.
If the cord is to be used as a tie, sew the folded end to the garment or if it is to be used as a drawstring or belt, knot the other end of the cord and cut the fold to make a tassel.

EXTRA SPECIAL SEWING

Simply cut from rectangles of fabric, this two-piece suit is highlighted with bands of braid.

Braided beauty

Chris Harvey

Measurements

To fit sizes 10/12[14/16]. Finished waistband 26½in [30in] (67cm[76cm]). Adjust waistband measurement before cutting out, allowing 2⅜in (6cm) for seams and underlap at back fastening.

Note Measurements are for size 10/12, with measurements for larger size in brackets. If only one measurement is given, it applies to all sizes. ⅝in (1.5cm) seam allowances are included.

Suggested fabrics

Jersey, crepe, crepe-de-chine, fine woolens or cotton/wool blends.

Materials

  5yd (4.5m) of 36in (90cm)-wide
      fabric or
  2¾yd (2.5m) of 60in (150cm)-wide
      fabric
  8in (20cm) zipper; 3 hooks and eyes
  3 buttons ⅝in (1.5cm) in diameter
  3⅜yd (3m) of 1in (2.5cm)-wide braid
  2¼yd (2m) of medium-weight cord
  2 tassels to match cord
  ¼yd (.2m) interfacing
  ½yd (.2m) tape for skirt loops
  Yardstick, right triangle,
      tailor's chalk

Cutting out

1 Using a triangle, yardstick and tailor's chalk, mark the pattern pieces on the fabric, following the measurement diagram and cutting layout. Cut one front and one back tunic, curving the side seam outward as shown to ensure a smooth shoulder seam; cut two sleeves, one front skirt section, two back skirt sections, one waistband (check waist measurement before cutting out), one pair of cuffs, and bias strips 1¼in (3cm) wide to a total length of 2yd (180cm).
2 From interfacing cut one waistband piece, the same length as the waistband and ⅞in (2.2cm) wide, and two strips 1in by 9⅜in (2.5cm by 24cm) for cuffs.
3 Mark the underarm points on the front and back tunics. Mark the positions of the openings at back neck, back skirt and cuffs, and mark the center front and side points on the waistband. Measure in ⅝in (1.5cm) at one end and 1¾in (4.5cm) at other end to mark center back, then divide rest of the band into four equal parts as shown on the measurement diagram.

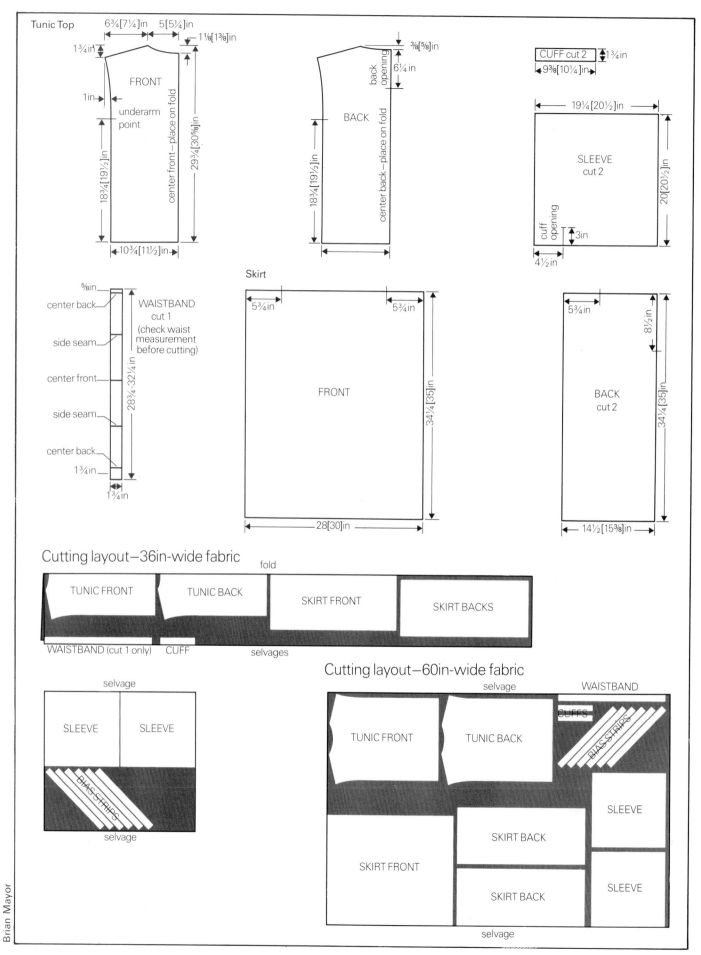

Tunic Top

FRONT

6¾[7¼]in 5[5¼]in 1⅛[1⅜]in
1¾in
1in
underarm point
center front–place on fold
18¾[19½]in
29¾[30⅝]in
10¾[11½]in

BACK

⅜[⅝]in
back opening
6¼in
center back–place on fold
18¾[19½]in

CUFF cut 2   1¾in
9⅜[10¼]in

SLEEVE cut 2
19¼[20½]in
20[20½]in
cuff opening
3in
4½in

WAISTBAND cut 1 (check waist measurement before cutting)
⅝in
center back
side seam
center front
side seam
center back
1¾in
1¾in
28¾–32¼in

Skirt

FRONT
5¾in   5¾in
34¼[35]in
28[30]in

BACK cut 2
5¾in
8½in
34¼[35]in
14½[15⅜]in

Cutting layout–36in-wide fabric

fold

TUNIC FRONT TUNIC BACK SKIRT FRONT SKIRT BACKS

WAISTBAND (cut 1 only) CUFF selvages

selvage

SLEEVE SLEEVE

BIAS STRIPS

selvage

Cutting layout–60in-wide fabric

selvage WAISTBAND

CUFFS

TUNIC FRONT TUNIC BACK

BIAS STRIPS

SLEEVE

SKIRT BACK

SKIRT FRONT

SKIRT BACK

SLEEVE

selvage

Brian Mayor

Tunic top

1 Following the markings on the back neck and sleeves, reinforce slit openings with a line of machine stitching, $\frac{3}{8}$in (1cm) wide at top and tapering to point of slit. Cut slit down marked lines, but be careful not to cut through the stitching.

2 Cut a piece of the bias strip for each opening, making each strip a little more than twice the length of the opening. With right sides together and edges of slit pulled out to form a straight line, stitch binding to opening as shown, positioning stitching $\frac{1}{4}$in (6mm) from raw edge of binding and working with right side of garment upward.

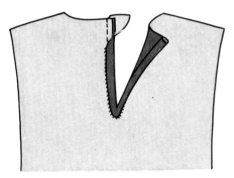

3 Press binding to inside, turn $\frac{1}{4}$in (6mm) along free edge of binding, and slip stitch in place close to line of machine stitching.

4 Push the fold at the point of the placket to the inside and machine stitch a diagonal line of stitching through the fold of the binding to hold it in place.
5 From bias strips, make a piece of tubing 8in (20cm) long for button loops.

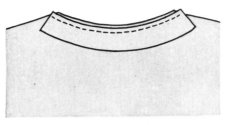

6 Using bias strips, with right side of strip to wrong side of neck opening and raw edges even, stitch facing to neck edges, $\frac{5}{8}$in (1.5cm) from edge. Trim seam and clip at intervals. Turn right side out; press binding and allowances away from bodice.
7 Understitch bias facing close to seam, working through seam allowances also (see Technique tip). Trim bias facing so that it measures $\frac{3}{4}$in (2cm) in width, and fold it over to right side of garment.

8 Baste facing to neckline. Cut a $2\frac{3}{8}$in (6cm) length of tubing and stitch to right back at top neck opening. Turn under ends of neck facing and baste them in place.

9 Pin, baste and stitch shoulder seams, wrong sides together and raw edges even. Press seams open.

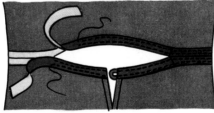

10 Starting from one shoulder, pin two strips of braid along shoulder seams and along neck edges, covering the seam allowances and the facings. This provides a neat finish along the seamline and facing, both inside and out. Make a small pleat in the binding at the angle between the shoulder seam and the neck edge. At the center back, turn under raw edges to finish. Topstitch braid in place.

11 With a line of basting, mark the position for one edge of the braid on the tunic top from the marked point on the front side seam, over the shoulder to the mark on the side seam on the back. Baste a piece of braid the same length as the basted line plus $1\frac{5}{8}$in (4cm) seam allowance and baste in place, matching one edge to marked line. At underarm points, fold braid under to meet edge of fabric at marked point as shown below.

12 Topstitch braid in place along edge nearer neck, and baste it along seamline. Repeat for other armhole. With right sides together and raw edges even, pin, baste and stitch side seams up to underarm point, enclosing ends of braid. Press seam open and finish raw edges.

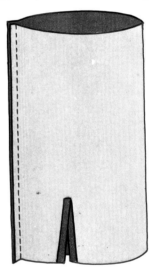

13 Stitch sleeve seams, right sides together, leaving a $\frac{5}{8}$in (1.5cm) opening at top of seam. Press seam open and finish seam allowances.
14 Run a line of gathering along wrist edge. Catch-stitch interfacing to cuff, matching one long edge and both short edges. Pull up gathering threads to fit cuff, allowing $\frac{5}{8}$in (1.5cm) at each end of the cuff. Tie gathering threads and distribute fullness evenly. Stitch one edge of cuff to edge of sleeve, right sides together.

15 Stitch tubing loop to front part of cuff. Fold cuff in half, right sides facing, and stitch ends. Turn cuff right side out, turn under raw edge and slip stitch fold to line of machine stitching.

16 With right sides together, pin and baste sleeve into armhole right sides facing, matching underarm point to sleeve seam.

17 Stitch armhole seam without stitching across underarm seam. Press seam allowances toward body of garment and baste in position. Topstitch basted edge of braid to tunic, catching in seam allowances at the same time.

18 Turn up a 1in (2.5cm) double hem all around lower edge of the tunic. Topstitch in place. Sew on the buttons to match the loops.

Skirt

1 Matching one edge of interfacing to one edge of waistband, catch-stitch interfacing to the wrong side of the waistband.

2 Mark four points, each 3½in (9cm) from side seam markings, on the wrong side of the waistband as indicated.

3 Stitch center back seam, leaving 8¾in (22.5cm) open for zipper. Press and finish seam allowances. Insert zipper by slot seam method (see Volume 4, page 68). Stitch side seams. Press and finish raw edges.

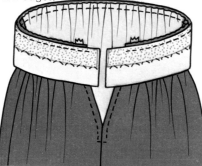

4 Mark points on top edge of skirt 5¾in (14.5cm) from side seams. Run two lines of gathering through top of skirt. Draw threads up to fit waistband, allowing 2⅜in (6cm) for seams and underlap. With right sides together, matching marked points on skirt to marked points on waistband and with interfaced edge of waistband to edge of skirt, pin and baste skirt to waistband. Allow a 1⅛in (3cm) underlap on right back. There will be more fullness at the front and back of the skirt than at the sides. Try for fit. Machine stitch in place. Catch in two 10in (23.5cm) tape loops at side seams for hanging. Grade seams and press upward.

5 Fold waistband on foldline and turn to inside. Turn under and press a ⅝in (1.5cm) seam allowance. Turn in ends of waistband. Slip stitch folded edges together and free edge to inside of skirt. Sew on three hooks and eyes.

6 Try for fit and turn up a 1in (2.5cm) double hem all around. Topstitch in place.

Technique tip

Facings

Facings are used to strengthen and finish raw edges, particularly when they are curved or shaped. Generally, facings are cut from fabric on the same grain as the edge to be faced and are shaped to match that edge. They are then attached to the edge to be faced, right sides together, and turned to the inside of the garment.

The facings on the tunic top are unusual in two ways.

They are cut from bias strips of fabric, which can be gently curved to match the neck edge, and they are sewn to the neck edge with right side of facing to wrong side of garment and turned to the right side of the garment.

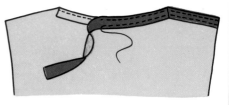

The facings are covered by a strip of braid, so that the edges are finished on both the inside and the outside.

Understitching

Understitching is a technique commonly used to give a crisp edge to a facing. First, stitch the facing in place (to either the right side or the wrong side of the fabric).

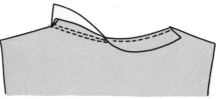

Press the facing and seam allowance away from the garment and baste ¼in (6mm) from the seamline. Stitch through the two seam allowances and the facing; then grade the seam allowances.

Press the facing back to lie flat against the garment and finish according to pattern directions.

Terry Evans

Night birds

This pretty nightgown can be made in two lengths, to wear with or without matching pajama pants.

Ross Greetham

Size
The outfits may be made in two sizes, 10/12 and 14/16.
Finished length of nightgown: 46[47]in (117[119]cm) (mid-calf). Finished length of top: $28\frac{1}{2}[29\frac{1}{2}]$in (72[75]cm). Finished length of pajama pants: 42[43]in (107[109]cm).
Measurements for the larger size are given in brackets []. If only one figure is given, it applies to both sizes. $\frac{5}{8}$in (1.5cm) seam allowances are included, with $\frac{1}{4}$in (6mm) seam allowance on bound edges.

Materials
Nightgown: $3\frac{3}{8}[3\frac{7}{8}]$yd (3[3.5]m) 36in (90cm)-wide fabric or $3\frac{3}{8}$yd (3m) 45in (115cm)-wide fabric
Pajamas: 4yd [$4\frac{1}{2}$]yd (3.6[4.1]m) 36in (90cm)-wide fabric or 4yd (3.6m) 45in (115cm)-wide fabric
$5\frac{1}{2}$yd (5m) 1in (2.5cm)-wide bias binding (optional)
$2\frac{1}{4}$yd (2m) $\frac{3}{8}$in (1cm)-wide eyelet edging (optional)
Waist measurement plus 1in (2.5cm) of 1in (2.5cm)-wide elastic (for pajamas)

1 Prepare fabric and cut out nightgown pieces, following appropriate cutting layout and measurement diagram.

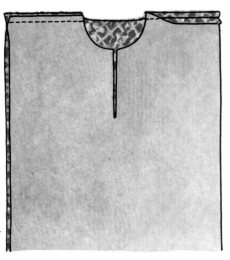

Terry Evans

2 With right sides together and raw edges matching, pin, baste and stitch shoulder seams. Press.

3 Cut a $3\frac{1}{8}$in (8cm) slit down center front on nightgown. If not using contrast binding for the neck, cut bias strips and join as necessary. Apply binding around neck edge and down neck opening.

Ross Greetham

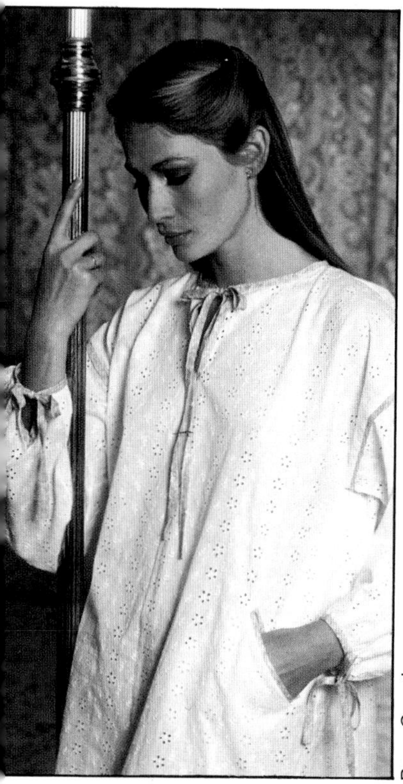

Ross Greetham

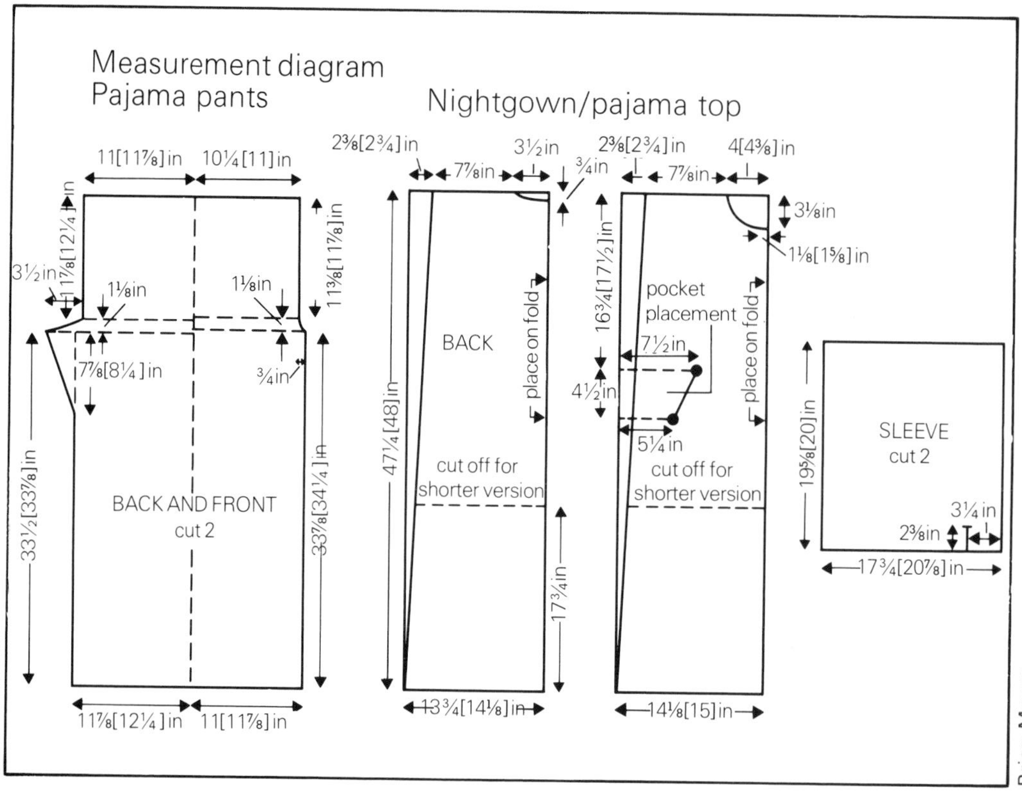

Measurement diagram
Pajama pants
Nightgown/pajama top
11[11⅞]in
10¼[11]in
1⅛in
1⅛in
3½in
7⅞[8¼]in
¾in
BACK AND FRONT
cut 2
33½[33⅞]in
33⅞[34¼]in
11⅞[12¼]in
11⅜[11⅞]in
11⅞[12¼]in
11[11⅞]in
2⅜[2¾]in
7⅞in
3½in
¾in
BACK
place on fold
cut off for
shorter version
47¼[48]in
17¾in
13¾[14⅛]in
2⅜[2¾]in
7⅞in
4[4⅜]in
3⅛in
1⅛[1⅝]in
pocket
placement
7½in
4½in
5¼in
16¾[17½]in
place on fold
cut off for
shorter version
14⅛[15]in
SLEEVE
cut 2
19⅝[20]in
3¼in
2⅜in
17¾[20⅞]in

Brian Mayor

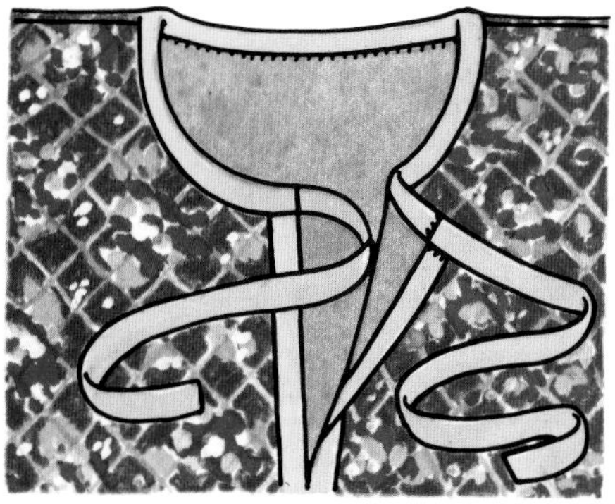

4 Make two 10in (25cm)-long tubing strips and attach to neck opening.

5 Make bound pockets as shown in Technique Tip.

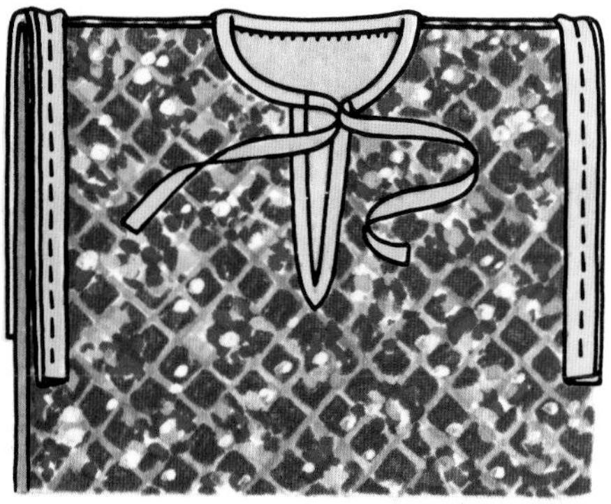

6 If using contrast binding, you can pipe the shoulder seam. Cut a 19[22]in (48[56]cm) length of binding for each sleeve cap. Fold contrast binding in half, wrong sides together. Pin and baste to right side of front and back of nightgown, over shoulder seam.

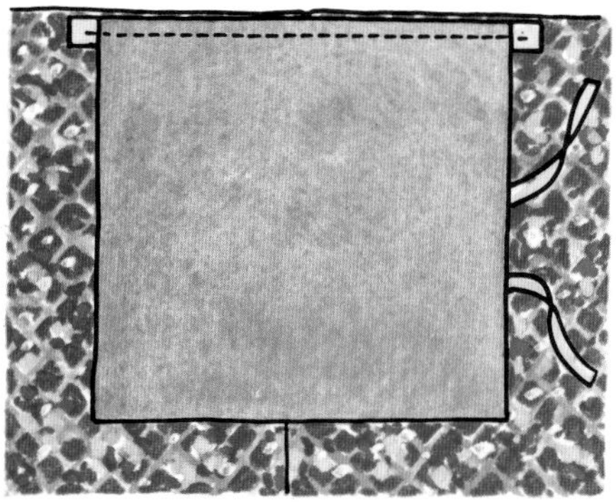

7 Position sleeve on nightgown, right side of sleeve facing right side of nightgown. Pin, baste and stitch, enclosing piping. Press. Finish seam allowances.

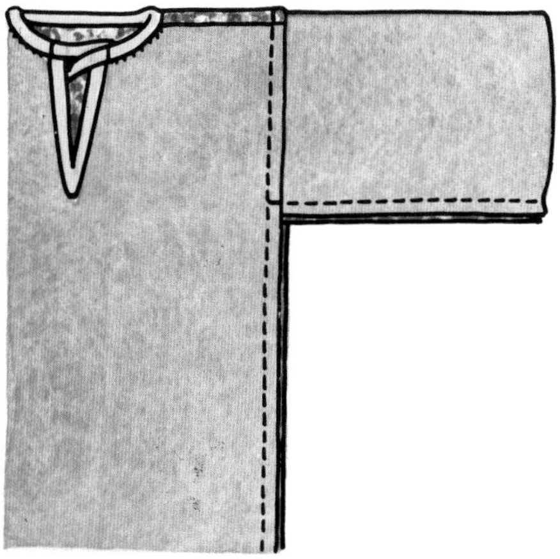

8 Stitch underarm seams and side seams, leaving a 3in (7.5cm) opening at bottom of side seams in the shorter version.

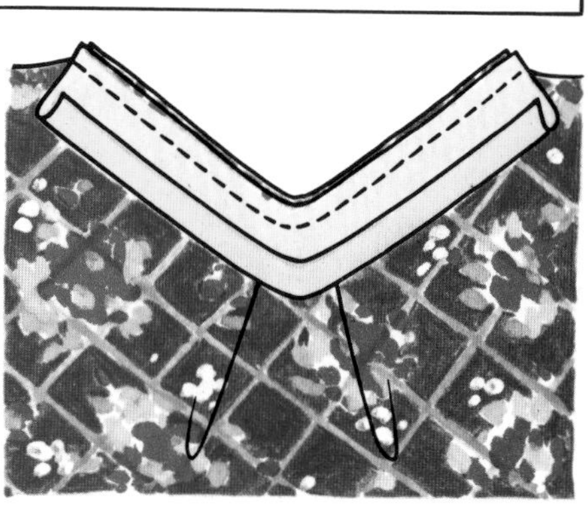

9 Attach a continuous strip binding to the slit in the sleeve (see Volume 5, page 63).

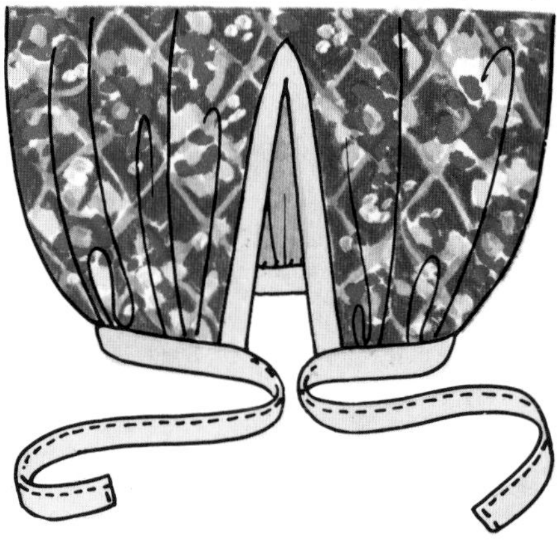

Terry Evans

10 Run a row of gathering stitches around lower edge of the sleeve. Cut two 31½in (80cm) lengths of binding to bind sleeve and make ties as shown.

11 Turn up and stitch a 3in (7.5cm) double hem around lower edge of nightgown, and up side slits on shorter version.

Cutting layout for pajama pants all sizes and widths

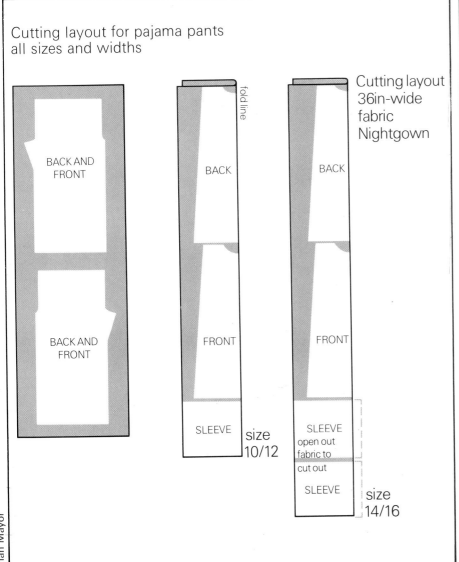

BACK AND FRONT

BACK AND FRONT

fold line

BACK

FRONT

SLEEVE

size 10/12

Cutting layout 36in-wide fabric Nightgown

BACK

FRONT

SLEEVE
open out
fabric to
cut out

SLEEVE

size 14/16

Brian Mayor

Pants

1 Cut out two pieces, following the measurement diagram. (This is easier if you cut a paper pattern first.)

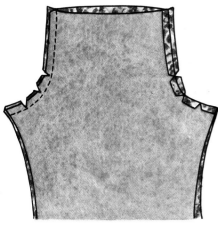

2 With right sides together and raw edges matching, pin, baste and stitch back and front crotch seams. Clip and press.

3 With right sides together, stitch inside leg seams.

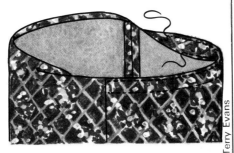

4 To make a casing, turn down $\frac{5}{8}$in (1.5cm) all around top, and then a further $2\frac{1}{4}$in (5.5cm). Pin, baste and stitch in place with two lines of topstitching, $\frac{1}{8}$in (3mm) from each fold, leaving a gap in the lower line of stitching.
5 Thread elastic through casing; try pants on. Stitch ends together securely. Slip stitch opening in casing.
6 Turn up a $\frac{3}{4}$in (2cm) double hem all around bottom of pants legs.

Terry Evans

Technique tip

Bound pockets

These pockets give a neat finish to any pocket opening which is not in a seam-line. The binding may be in matching or contrasting fabric.

Cut two bias strips, $1\frac{1}{4}$in (3cm) wide and 2in (5cm) longer than the marked pocket opening. Fold the two strips in half, wrong sides together, and trim so that the width of the binding when folded is exactly twice the width of the binding which will show when the opening is finished.

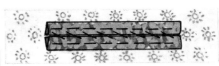

Positioning raw edges of binding along marked pocket line, pin and baste both strips to RS of garment. Secure raw edges temporarily with overcasting. Stitch down the center of each strip of binding, making the stitching line the same length as the pocket opening.

From the wrong side, cut the opening, cutting to $\frac{3}{8}$in (1cm) from each end. Snip diagonally into the corners.

Tuck raw edges of bindings, triangle of fabric and ends of bindings wrong side out. Stitch triangle of fabric to bindings by hand. Overcast folded edges of binding temporarily.

Pin and baste smaller pocket section to seam allowance of binding and pocket opening, right sides matching. Stitch close to existing stitching line. Repeat for larger pocket piece. Press both pieces in same direction.

To stitch pocket pieces together, start stitching at top of larger section, stitching side of pocket to ends of bindings, then stitch all around both pocket pieces, ending by stitching across bindings at other end. Overcast raw edges.

Needlework

EXTRA

Needleworkers' workbag

A patchwork parade of triangles goes around this pretty draw-string workbag. Inside, there are pockets to hold your needlework tools and materials.

Finished size The bag measures 8in (20cm) in diameter and in height. A ¾in (1cm) seam allowance is included.

Materials

⅞yd (.8m) of 36in (90cm)-wide printed cotton fabric

⅜yd (.3m) of 36in (90cm)-wide corduroy in a harmonizing color

Stiff cardboard 8×21in (20×53cm)

Piece of ¼in (5mm)-thick foam rubber 8in (20cm) square

Fabric glue

Matching sewing thread

1¾yd (1.5cm) of narrow cord to match the fabric

Compass; ruler

Right triangle

Craft knife (optional)

1 Using the compass, draw two circles on the cardboard, each 8in (20cm) in diameter. Cut them out carefully. (A craft knife is best for this, but if you are not experienced in its use, it's wise to get the help of an expert).

2 Using one of the circles as a pattern, draw a circle on the foam rubber and cut it out. Lay these circles aside.

3 From the remaining cardboard draw two right triangle templates, following the measurements shown on the diagram. Make sure the measurements are exact and cut out the templates carefully.

4 From the printed cotton cut the following pieces: a strip 25×2in (63.5×5cm), a piece 25×21½in (63.5×55cm), a circle 10in (25cm) in diameter and 26 triangles using the smaller template.

5 From the corduroy cut a 10in (25cm) diameter circle and 13 triangles, using the larger template and placing the diagonal side on the lengthwise grain of the fabric.

6 Place one small triangle on a large corduroy triangle, right sides facing and with the long side of the small triangle along one of the short sides of the large

triangle. Pin, baste and stitch in place. Open out the patches and press the seam allowances toward the printed patch.

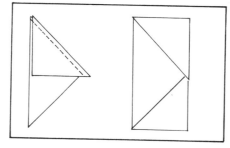

7 Similarly, join another printed patch to the other short side of the large triangle.

8 Repeat steps 6 and 7 to make 13 oblong patchwork shapes.

9 Pin, baste and stitch the oblongs together, right sides facing, with the point of each corduroy triangle toward the long side of the next, to make a strip measuring 4¾×25in (12×63.5cm).

10 On the large piece of printed fabric, turn one long edge 6in (15cm) to the wrong side and press along the fold. Stitch the two layers in place 4in (10cm) from the fold and parallel to it.

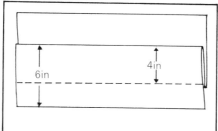

Ron Kelly

11 Press this fold upward, toward the larger section of fabric, as shown.

12 Divide this folded section into six equal parts and machine stitch parallel lines from the horizontal seam up to the folded edge to form the pockets.

13 Place one cardboard circle on the corduroy circle. Clip the edges of the corduroy and glue them in place on top of the cardboard.

14 Glue the foam circle lightly to the other cardboard circle, then cover the foam with the printed fabric circle, clipping the seam allowances and gluing them to the cardboard as for the first circle. Keep the foam compressed while you work and until the glue has dried.

Assembling the workbag

1 Pin, baste and stitch the narrow strip of printed fabric to one long side of the patchwork strip, right sides facing and edges matching.

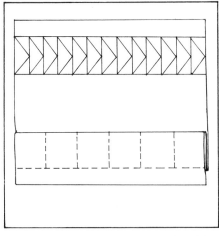

2 Join the pocket piece to the other side of the patchwork strip, right sides together, as shown. Make sure that the pockets point upward.

3 Place the two short edges of the bag together, right sides facing, making sure that the patchwork sections match neatly. Pin, baste and stitch. Press the seam open.

4 Turn the patchwork part of the resulting tube to the right side, so that the raw edges meet at the bottom. Overcast or zigzag stitch these edges together. Press the fold at the top.

5 Stitch along the fold, $\frac{3}{8}$in (1cm) and then $1\frac{1}{4}$in (3cm) from the edge, to form a casing.

6 Open the side seam on the right side where it crosses the casing, to make a hole for the cord. Cut a slit in the casing opposite the side seam and work buttonhole stitch around it to make a hole for the other cord.

7 Run a gathering thread around the lower edge of the bag and draw the thread up slightly. Place the padded circle inside the bag, fabric side upward. Adjust the gathers smoothly and glue the gathered fabric to the underside of the circle.

8 Glue the corduroy circle to the underside of the bag. When the glue has dried, slip stitch the edges of the corduroy to the printed fabric with tiny stitches.

9 Cut the cord in half, thread one piece through one hole, through the casing and out the same hole. Knot the ends together. Repeat with the other piece of cord, using the other hole.

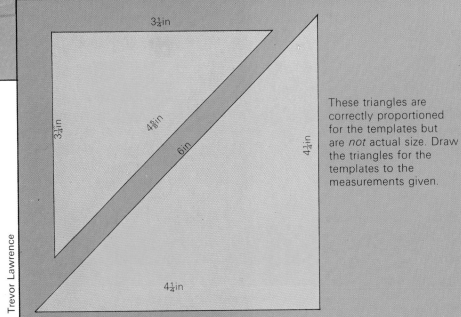

$3\frac{1}{2}$in

$3\frac{1}{4}$in

$4\frac{5}{8}$in

6in

$4\frac{1}{4}$in

$4\frac{1}{4}$in

These triangles are correctly proportioned for the templates but are *not* actual size. Draw the triangles for the templates to the measurements given.

Homemaker

Pop it in a pocket!

These bright and practical hold-alls provide easy storage in the bedroom, playroom or kitchen. Adapt the measurements to suit your needs.

Shoebag

Finished size
38in (96cm) long, 20in (51cm) wide. A seam allowance of $\frac{3}{4}$in (2cm) has been included unless otherwise stated.

Materials
$2\frac{1}{4}$yd (2m) of 45in (115cm)-wide printed cotton furnishing fabric
$1\frac{1}{8}$yd (1m) of 36in (90cm)-wide heavyweight iron-on interfacing
Matching thread
Two $1\frac{1}{4}$in (3cm) D rings

1 From printed cotton fabric cut out two pieces, each $39\frac{1}{2} \times 21\frac{1}{2}$in (100×55cm) for base back and front.
2 From iron-on interfacing cut out one piece the same size as base.
3 Place interfacing shiny side down on wrong side of one base piece, matching all edges. Iron the interfacing in place.
4 From printed cotton fabric cut out four pocket strips, each $38\frac{3}{4} \times 9$in (98×23cm).

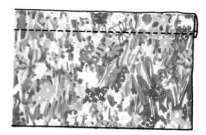

5 Hem one long edge of one pocket strip, turning under first $\frac{3}{8}$in (1cm) and then a further $1\frac{1}{4}$in (3cm). Press creases in place. Pin, baste and stitch down.

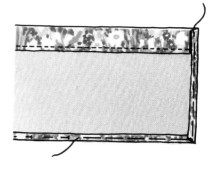

6 Turn under $\frac{3}{8}$in (1cm) on all remaining edges of pocket strip. Pin and baste these hems in place.
7 Repeat steps 5 and 6 to prepare the three remaining pocket strips.

Geoffrey Frosh

112

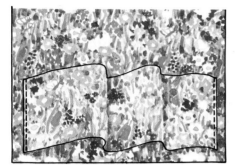

8 Position one pocket strip on interfaced base, with lower edge of pocket strip 1½in (4cm) up from lower edge of base and with side edges of pocket strip 1¼in (3cm) in from side edges of base. Pin, baste and stitch sides in place.

9 Working from the right-hand side, measure 4½in (11.5cm) along base from side edge of pocket and mark. Measure 9½in (24cm) along base edge of pocket strip and mark. Position pocket strip mark over base mark. Pin and baste. Run two lines of topstitching down pocket strip through interfaced base at this mark.
10 Repeat step 9 along the pocket strip to form three more pockets the same size, keeping the pocket strip parallel with and 1½in (4cm) from the lower edge.

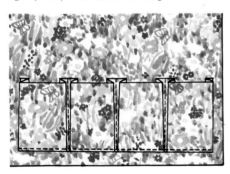

11 Press each pocket flat, forming 1¼in (3cm) inverted pleats at each side of each pocket. Pin and baste pleats down at lower edges. Stitch along base of pocket strip, to hold pockets in place.
12 Repeat steps 8 to 11 to form four more rows of pockets, the same size as the first, spacing the rows 1½in (4cm) apart.
13 For hanging loops, cut out one piece 8×3in (20×8cm) from remaining printed cotton fabric.

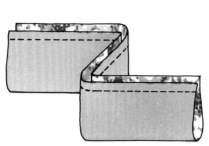

14 Fold loop strip in half lengthwise, with right sides together, matching edges. Pin, baste and stitch down the length, taking ⅜in (1cm) seam allowance. Trim and turn strip right side out. Cut the strip into two equal pieces.

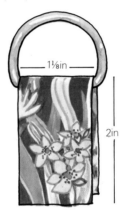

15 Thread one loop strip through one D ring and match raw edges together. Position strip at top corner of interfaced base, 1in (2.5cm) in from side edges. Pin and baste in place.

16 Repeat step 15, positioning second strip at opposite top corner.
17 Place interfaced base and other base piece together with right sides facing. Pin, baste and stitch around the edges, leaving 6in (15cm) open on lower edge.
18 Trim seams and cut diagonally across corners. Turn shoebag right side out. Turn in opening edges and slip stitch the folded edges together.

Child's shoebag

Finished size
20in (51cm) long, 9½in (24cm) wide. A seam allowance of ⅜in (1cm) has been included throughout.

Materials
¾yd (.7m) of 36in (90cm)-wide blue blue cotton poplin
⅜yd (.3m) of 36in (90cm)-wide red cotton poplin
⅜yd (.3m) of 36in (90cm)-wide heavyweight iron-on interfacing
1¾yd (1.5m) of ½in (1.2cm)-wide yellow bias binding
Matching and contrasting thread
12in (30cm) long red coat hanger

1 From blue poplin cut out two pieces, each 23½×11in (60×28cm), for base.
2 From iron-on interfacing cut out one piece the same size as base.

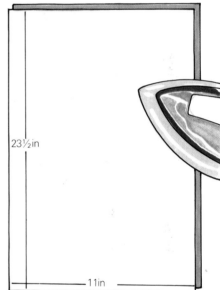

3 Place interfacing shiny side down on wrong side of one base piece, matching all edges. Iron the interfacing in place.
4 From red poplin cut three pieces, each 15×5in (38×13cm), to make the pocket strips.

5 Bind one long edge of one pocket strip. Fold bias binding in half evenly over one long edge. Pin, baste and stitch in place.

Terri Lawlor

6 Turn under ⅜in (1cm) on all remaining edges of pocket strip. Pin and baste these hems in place.

7 Repeat steps 5 and 6 to prepare the two remaining pocket strips.

8 Place one pocket strip on interfaced base, with side edges of pocket strip 1½in (4cm) in from base side edges and 1½in (4cm) up from lower edge of base. Pin, baste and stitch sides in place, using contrasting sewing thread.

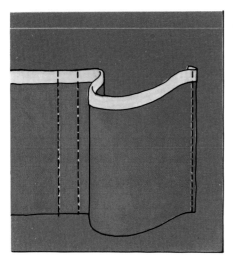

9 Working from the right-hand side, measure 3½in (9cm) along base from side edge of pocket and mark. Measure 6¾in (17cm) along base edge of pocket strip and mark. Position pocket strip mark over base mark. Pin and baste. Stitch down pocket at mark and again ¾in (2cm) along from mark, through interfaced base piece.

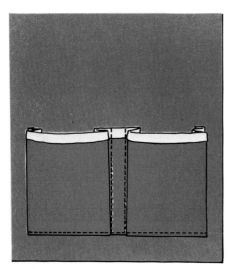

10 Fold pockets flat on each side of central stitching to form a ¾in (2cm) inverted pleat at each side of each pocket. Pin and baste pleats down at lower edges. Stitch along the base edge of pockets to hold them in place.

11 Repeat steps 8 to 10, stitching the two remaining pocket strips above the first pockets, spacing them 1½in (4cm) apart.

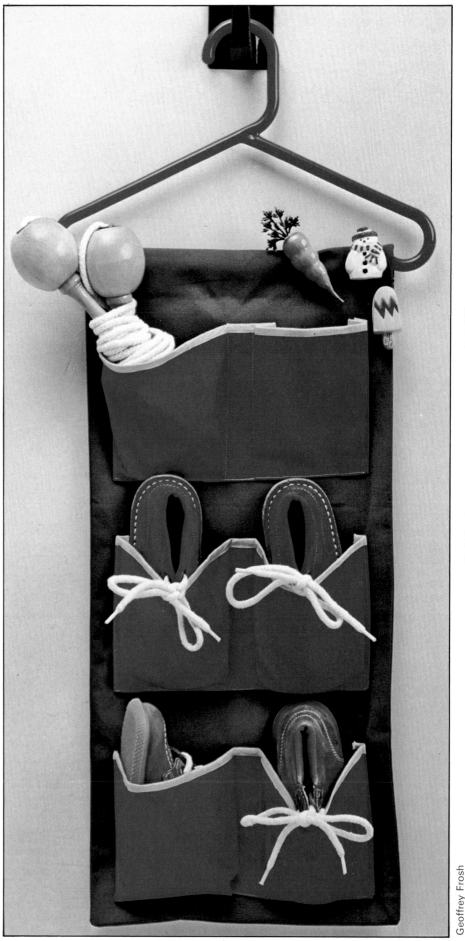

Kitchen holdall

Finished size

20in (51cm) long, 24in (61cm) wide.

Materials

1⅜yd (1.2m) of 45in (115cm)-wide
  check vinyl-coated fabric
1¾yd (.6m) of 36in (90cm)-wide
  heavyweight interfacing
½yd (.4m) of 50in (128cm)-wide
  clear plastic
2¼yd (2m) of ½in (1.2cm)-wide bias
  binding
Thread, eyelet and eyelet punch
25½in (65cm) of ½in (1.2cm)-
  diameter doweling
Transparent tape

1 From vinyl fabric cut two pieces, each
25×22in (64×56cm) for base.
2 From interfacing cut out one piece
the same size as base.
3 From clear plastic cut out two pieces,
each 38×6in (96×15cm), for pockets.

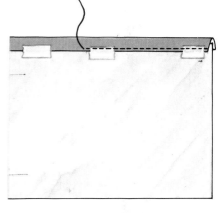

Terri Lawlor

4 Bind one long edge of one clear plastic
pocket strip with bias binding: fold
binding in half over one long edge of
pocket strip; hold in place with tape.
Stitch in place.
5 Repeat step 4 with other clear plastic
pocket strip.
6 Place one pocket strip on one base
piece with side edges of pocket strip
1¼in (3cm) in from side edges of base and
with lower edge 1¼in (3cm) up from
lower edge of base. Hold strip in place
with tape. Stitch down side edges of
pocket strip.
7 Working from the right-hand side,
measure 12¼in (31cm) on pocket strip
from side edge of pocket strip. Measure
6in (15cm) from side edge of pocket strip
on base. Hold these points together with
tape. Stitch down pocket strip twice
at these marks, using a large stitch.
8 Now measure off 9in (23cm) along
pocket strip and 5in (12.5cm) on base.
Place these points together and hold
them with tape. Stitch down pocket strip
again with two rows of stitching.
9 Repeat step to form another pocket
the same size.

12 Place the interfaced base and
remaining base together with right sides
facing. Pin, baste and stitch together all
around, leaving top edge open.
13 Trim seam and cut diagonally across
corners. Turn shoebag right side out.

14 Trim away ¾in (2cm) of back base
piece. Fold under ¾in (2cm) along top of
interfaced base. Slip this edge over
hanger. Pin, baste hem to back base.

and 4½in (11.5cm) on base. Stitch along lower edge of pocket strip as before, forming inverted pleats on each side of each pocket.

14 Place pocket base and other base together with right sides facing. Place interfacing on top, matching all edges. Stitch together around edges, leaving top edge open and also side edges, 3¼in (8cm) down from the top edge. Trim and cut diagonally across corners. Turn holdall right side out.

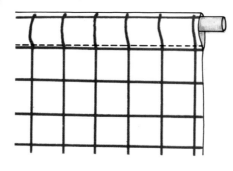

15 Cut 2in (5cm) off back base. Lap front base over back base. Stitch across holdall through all thicknesses to form a casing.

16 Thread dowel through casing.

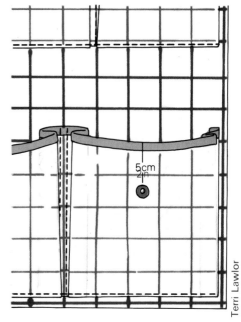

5cm
2in

17 Make an eyelet in the center of the bottom right-hand pocket, positioning it 2in (5cm) down from top edge.

10 Keeping the remainder of the pocket strip flat, measure along strip for 6½in (18cm). Topstitch twice down the center of last section to form two flat pockets.

11 Press first two pockets flat with the hands to form inverted pleats at each side. Hold the pleats in place with pieces of tape. Stitch along lower edge of pocket strip.

12 Position second pocket strip 3¼in (8cm) above first pocket strip, and stitch down side edges as before.

13 Stitch pocket strip to base, with intervals of 7½in (19cm) on pocket strip

Homemaker

All set for baby

Make a pretty bedding set from color-coordinated sheets for a baby's crib — bumpers for extra protection and covers and sheets to match.

Ron Kelly

Size

To fit a crib 15in (37.5cm) wide, 30in (75cm) long and 10in (25cm) deep, measured on the inside of the crib.

Materials

A floral-patterned twin-size sheet (A) (this will make two sheets and two crib quilts)
A twin-size sheet in a coordinating print (B) for bumpers
A solid-color twin-size sheet for mattress cover (C)
$1\frac{1}{2}$yd (1.3m) of 36in (90cm)-wide medium-weight batting
$13\frac{5}{8}$yd (12.5m) of $\frac{1}{2}$in (1.2cm)-wide harmonizing binding
Matching sewing thread

Bumper set

1 Cut out side and end pieces for bumpers from sheet B, following the cutting layout.
2 From batting cut out two pieces, each 30×10in (75×25cm), for side pieces and two pieces, each 15×10in (37.5×25cm) for end pieces.

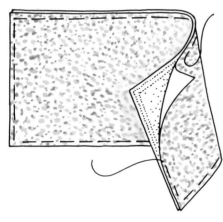

3 Place batting side piece in between two fabric side pieces, matching outer edges and with right sides on the outside. Pin and baste together with large stitches.

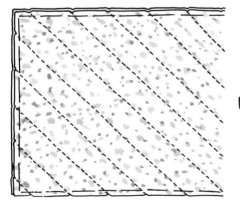

4 Work diagonal lines of stitching across the side piece, through all three thicknesses, spacing the lines of stitching 2in (5cm) apart.

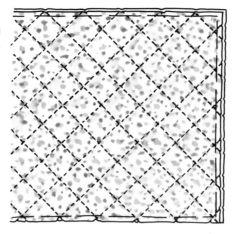

5 Work diagonal lines of stitching across the side piece, perpendicular to the first rows of stitching, to form a quilted diamond effect.
6 Repeat steps 3 to 5 to make the second side piece in the same way.
7 Repeat steps 3 to 5 to make the end pieces in the same way.
8 For ties, cut eight 12in (30cm) pieces of bias binding.

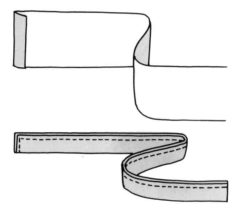

9 On one tie piece, fold in one short edge for $\frac{3}{8}$in (1cm) and baste. Fold the tie piece in half lengthwise, wrong side inside. Baste and stitch together down complete length.
10 Repeat step 9 to make seven more ties in the same way.

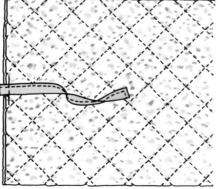

11 Place raw short edge on one tie in the center of each short side of each bumper piece. Pin and baste in place with tie facing in toward center of piece.

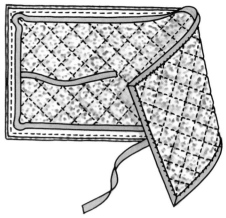

12 Pin, baste and stitch one side of bias binding all around the outer edge of side piece, with right sides together and raw edges even, catching in ends of ties. Miter the corners and join the short edges of bias binding together to fit.
13 Fold binding over the outer edge; pin, baste and slip stitch to the stitching line on the opposite side.
14 Repeat steps 12 and 13 to bind the outer edge of second side piece in the same way.
15 Repeat steps 12 and 13 to bind the outer edge of both end pieces in the same way.
16 Place the bumpers inside the crib, and tie them in place at each corner.

Sheets

1 Cut out both sheet pieces from sheet A, following the cutting layout opposite. These measurements include seam allowance.
2 Turn up a double hem of $\frac{3}{8}$in (1cm) and then $\frac{3}{4}$in (2cm) all around the edge of each sheet. Pin and baste in place, mitering the corners. Stitch in place.

Mattress cover

1 For mattress cover cut one piece 71×19$\frac{3}{4}$in (180×50cm) from sheet C.

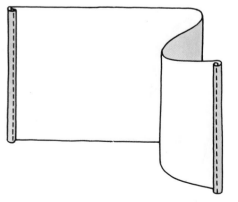

2 On each short side of the mattress cover turn under a double hem, $\frac{3}{8}$in (1cm) and then $\frac{3}{4}$in (2cm) deep. Pin, baste and stitch both hems in place.

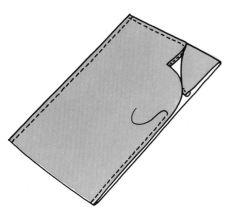

3 To form tuck-in, measure 30in (76cm) in from one short side and pin to mark. Fold fabric at this mark, wrong sides together. Turn the 8¾in (22cm) of excess fabric inside. Pin, baste and stitch down each long side, taking ⅜in (1cm) seam.

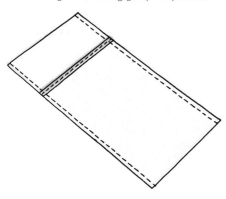

4 Re-fold the mattress cover wrong side out. Pin, baste and stitch down each long side again, this time taking ¾in (2cm) seam allowance.
5 Fold cover right side out. The tuck-in allows the mattress cover to be easily removed for washing.

Quilts

1 Cut out quilt pieces from sheet A following cutting layout.
2 From batting cut out one piece 20×15in (50×37.5cm).

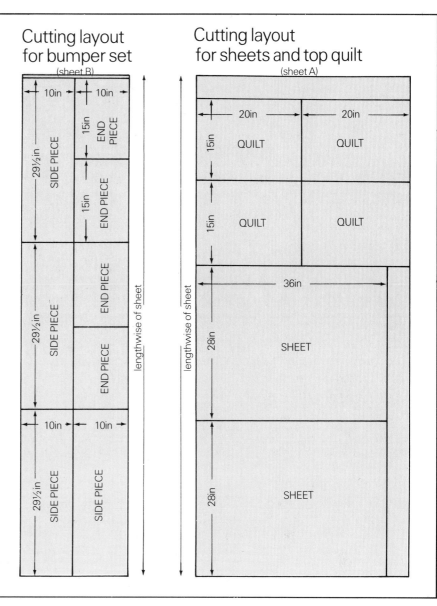

Cutting layout for bumper set
(sheet B)

10in	10in
29½in SIDE PIECE	15in END PIECE
	15in END PIECE
29½in SIDE PIECE	END PIECE
	END PIECE
29½in SIDE PIECE	END PIECE
10in	10in
29½in SIDE PIECE	SIDE PIECE

lengthwise of sheet

Cutting layout for sheets and top quilt
(sheet A)

20in	20in
15in QUILT	QUILT
15in QUILT	QUILT
36in	
28in SHEET	
28in SHEET	

lengthwise of sheet

John Hutchinson

4 Work diagonal lines of stitching across the fabric, through all thicknesses, spacing the lines 2in (5cm) apart.
5 Work diagonal lines of stitching across the fabric perpendicular to the first lines

with right sides together and raw edges even. Miter the corners and join the short edges of bias binding together to fit. Stitch the first side of the bias binding in place.

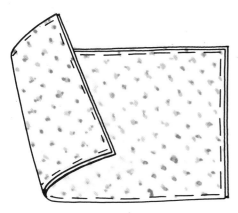

3 Place batting piece between the two fabric pieces, matching all outer edges and with right sides out. Pin and baste together.

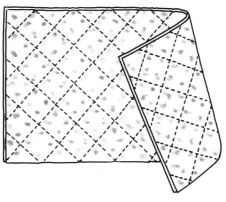

of stitching to form a quilted diamond.
6 Pin and baste one side of the bias binding all around the outer edge of quilt,

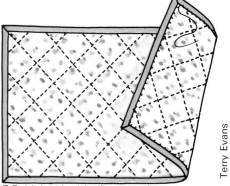

7 Fold the bias binding over the outer edge of the quilt; baste and slip stitch the remaining edge of the bias binding to the stitching line on the opposite side. Repeat steps 2 to 7 for second quilt.

Terry Evans

119

Homemaker

Sleeping partners

These endearing sleeping bags, in the form of a fox and a rabbit, will make nap-time fun.

Mr Rabbit

Size
About 65 × 26in (165 × 66cm). ¾in (2cm) seam allowances are included.

Materials
3⅞yd (3.5m) of 36in (90cm)-wide printed cotton fabric
2¾yd (2.5m) of 36in (90cm)-wide solid cotton fabric for lining
2¾yd (2.5m) of 36in (90cm)-wide muslin
2¾yd (2.5m) of 36in (90cm)-wide medium-weight polyester batting
⅝yd (.5m) of 48in (122cm)-wide white fleece fabric
12in (30cm) square of pink felt
Scraps of light and dark brown felt for eyes
Tracing paper; thread

1 Using tracing paper and a sharp pencil, trace pattern pieces for rabbit shown on pages 124 and 125. Cut out pieces.

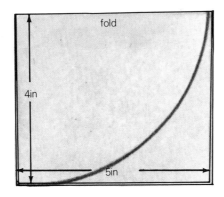

2 To make pattern for tail, from tracing paper cut out a rectangle 8 × 5in (20 × 12cm). Fold paper in half widthwise. Draw a curve on pattern from fold to side edge. Cut along curved line. Open out.
3 From printed fabric cut four paws and four legs. From fleece cut two heads, two ears and two tails. From pink felt cut two ears. Cut one tail, two heads, two paws, two legs and two ears from batting. Cut eyes from brown felts.
4 For main sleeping bag/body cut out two pieces, each 50 × 27in (127 × 69cm), from printed cotton fabric.
5 Repeat step 4 to cut two pieces from batting, muslin and solid cotton for lining.

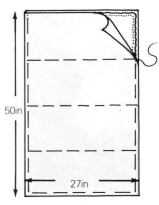

6 For front body, place one batting piece and then one muslin piece on wrong side of one printed body, matching all edges. Pin and baste together all around edges, and across fabric at intervals, to hold.

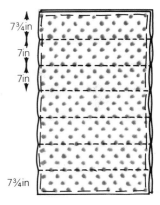

7 Quilt across the front body with lines of stitching, the top and bottom lines 7¾in (19.5cm) from the edge and the remaining lines just under 7in (17.5cm) apart.
8 Repeat steps 5 and 6 to assemble; then quilt the back body in the same way.

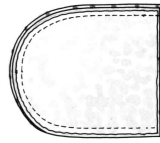

9 Place two fabric paws together with right sides facing and edges matching.

Place one batting paw on one side of fabric paw, matching all edges. Pin, baste and stitch around the paw, leaving straight edges open. Trim seam allowance. Turn paw right side out.

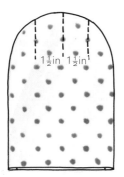

10 Mark the claws on the paw with three lines of topstitching, using a contrasting sewing thread.
11 Repeat steps 9 and 10 to make the other paw in the same way.
12 Repeat step 9 to make the legs in the same way. Topstitch leg markings.

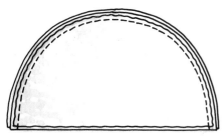

13 Place tails together with right sides facing and edges matching. Place batting tail on one side of fabric tail, matching edges. Pin, baste and stitch around the tail, leaving straight edges open. Trim seam allowance and turn tail right side out.

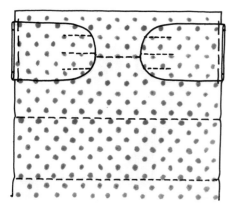

14 Place paws on right side of front body with straight edges aligned and upper edges of paws 1½in (4cm) down from top edge.
Pin and baste paws in place.
15 Place legs on right side of front body with straight edges aligned and heels positioned 1¼in (3cm) up from the lower edge.
Pin and baste the legs in place.

16 Place tail on right side of front body, centering it on the lower edge and aligning the straight edges. Pin and baste in place.
17 Place back and front body pieces together, right sides facing. Pin, baste and stitch all around body, leaving top edge open and catching in paws, legs and tail. Trim seam allowances and cut across corners. Turn body right side out.

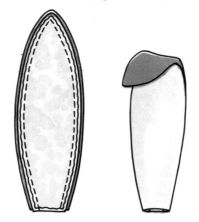

18 Place one felt ear and one fleece ear together with right sides facing. Place one batting ear on one side of fabric ear. Pin, baste and stitch ears together, leaving straight edge open. Trim seam and turn ear right side out.
19 Repeat step 18 to make the other ear in the same way.
20 Lightly pencil the mouth, nose and outer eye on one fabric head – the front.

21 Place the two inner eyes on the two outer eyes; pin and baste. Place eyes on front head over marked outer eyes. Pin, baste and stitch combined eyes in place on head.
22 Place two batting heads behind front head; pin and baste in place.
Topstitch along marked feature lines, using matching thread for eyes and contrasting sewing thread for nose and mouth.

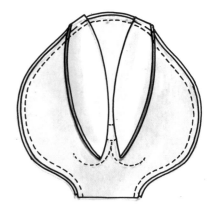

23 Position ears on front head between small x's, with ears pointing inward and raw edges aligned. Pin and baste in place.
24 Place back head and front head together with right sides facing. Pin, baste and stitch around head, catching in ears and leaving neck edge open. Trim seam and turn head right side out.

25 Center the head on top edge of back body with back of head against right side of quilted fabric, so front head will face toward the front.
26 Place lining body pieces together with right sides facing and edges matching. Pin, baste and stitch side edges.

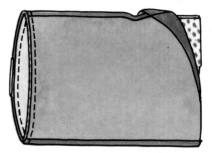

27 Slip lining body over body with right sides facing, matching side seams and raw edges. Pin, baste and stitch around top edge, catching in head at the back.
28 Pull lining up. Turn in lower raw edges and pin, baste and stitch across lower edge.
29 Push lining inside main bag. Tack it in place at bottom corners.

Terry Evans

Mr Fox

Size
About 65×26in (165×66cm). ¾in (2cm) seam allowances are included.

Materials
- 3⅞yd (3.5m) of 36in (90cm)-wide plaid printed cotton fabric
- 2¾yd (2.5m) of 36in (90cm)-wide solid cotton fabric for lining
- 2¾yd (2.5m) of 36in (90cm)-wide muslin
- 2¾yd (2.5m) of 36in (90cm)-wide medium-weight polyester batting
- ⅝yd (.5m) of 48in (122cm)-wide white fleece fabric
- Scraps of green and brown felt
- Length of brown yarn
- Tracing paper; thread

1 Repeat step 1 of the instructions for Mr Rabbit to cut out pattern pieces.

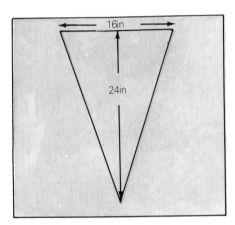

2 For bib front, on tracing paper draw a line 16in (40.5cm) long and mark the center. Draw a line 24in (61cm) long at a right angle from the center point. Join the end of the longer line to the two ends of the shorter line to form a triangle.

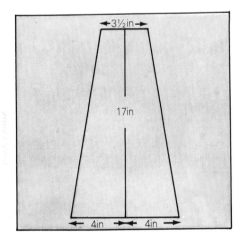

3 For tail piece, draw a line 3½in (9cm) long on tracing paper and mark center. Draw a line 17in (43cm) long at a right angle from center and another at the end of it, at a right angle, extending 4in (10cm) to each side. Join parallel lines.

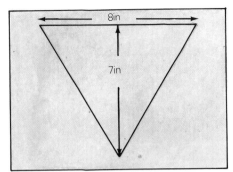

4 For tail tip, draw a line 8in (20cm) long on tracing paper and mark center point. Draw a line 7in (18cm) long at a right angle to center point. Join tip of center line to outside points to form triangle.

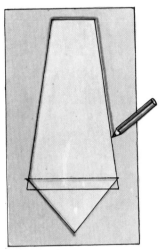

5 For batting tail pattern, place main tail on tracing paper. Place tail tip pattern against it, overlapping edges to eliminate seam allowances. Draw and cut out.
6 From plaid or print fabric cut two heads, four outer ears, four paws, four legs and two main tail pieces. From fleece cut one bib front, two inner ears, two outer eyes and two tail tips. From batting cut out one tail piece, two heads, two paws, two legs and two ears. From green felt cut two middle eyes. From brown felt cut one nose tip and two inner eyes.
7 Repeat steps 4 to 8 of Mr Rabbit instructions to make body pieces.

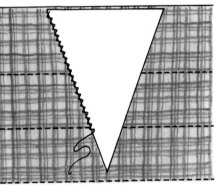

8 Center bib front on body front, matching top edges. Pin, baste and machine stitch bib in place, using zig-zag stitch.
9 Repeat steps 9 to 12 of Mr Rabbit instructions to make paws and legs in the same way.
10 Place one main tail on one tail tip, matching straight raw edges. Pin, baste and stitch together. Repeat, to make the other side of tail.
11 Place tails together with right sides facing, matching outer edges and tail tip seams. Place batting tail on one side of fabric tails, matching outer edges. Pin, baste and stitch around tail, leaving top edge open. Trim and turn tail right side out.
12 Repeat steps 14 to 17 of Mr Rabbit instructions to assemble body.
13 Center two inner ears on two outer ears; pin, baste and zig-zag stitch in place. Lay one combined ear on one plain ear, with right sides together and edges matching. Place one batting ear on one side of fabric ears, matching edges. Pin, baste and stitch around ear, leaving lower edge open. Trim and turn ear right side out.
14 Repeat step 13 for other ear.
15 Repeat steps 20 to 29 of Mr Rabbit instructions to complete Mr Fox. Topstitch nose in place and sew nose outline in brown yarn, using backstitch.

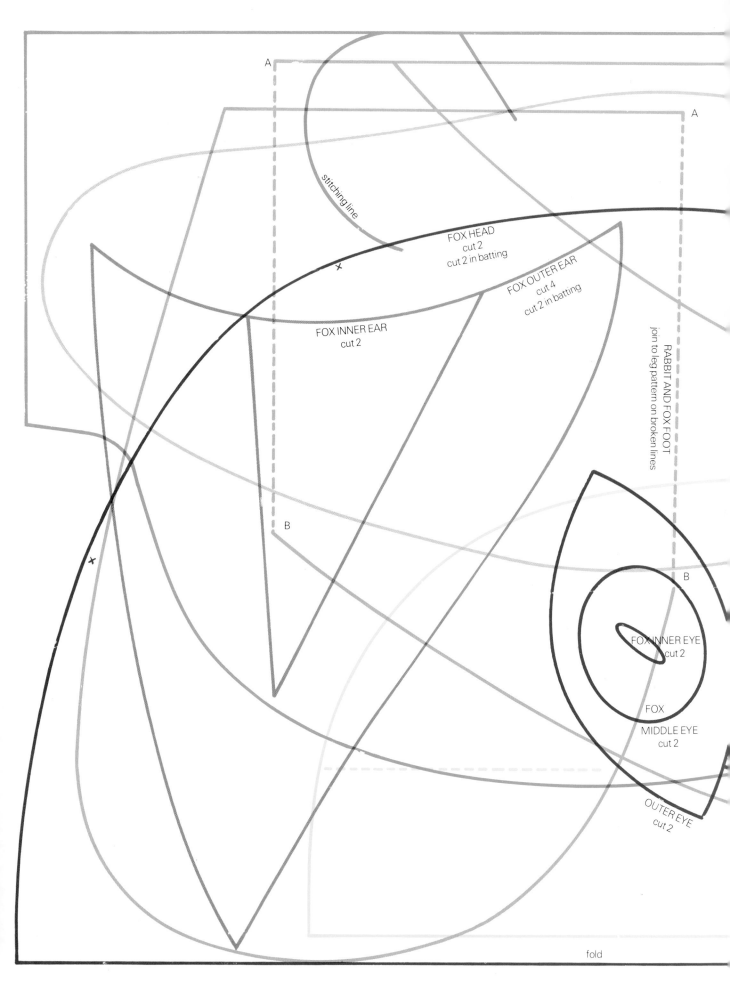

A

A

stitching line

FOX HEAD
cut 2
cut 2 in batting

x

FOX OUTER EAR
cut 4
cut 2 in batting

FOX INNER EAR
cut 2

RABBIT AND FOX FOOT
join to leg pattern on broken lines

B

x

B

FOX INNER EYE
cut 2

FOX
MIDDLE EYE
cut 2

OUTER EYE
cut 2

fold

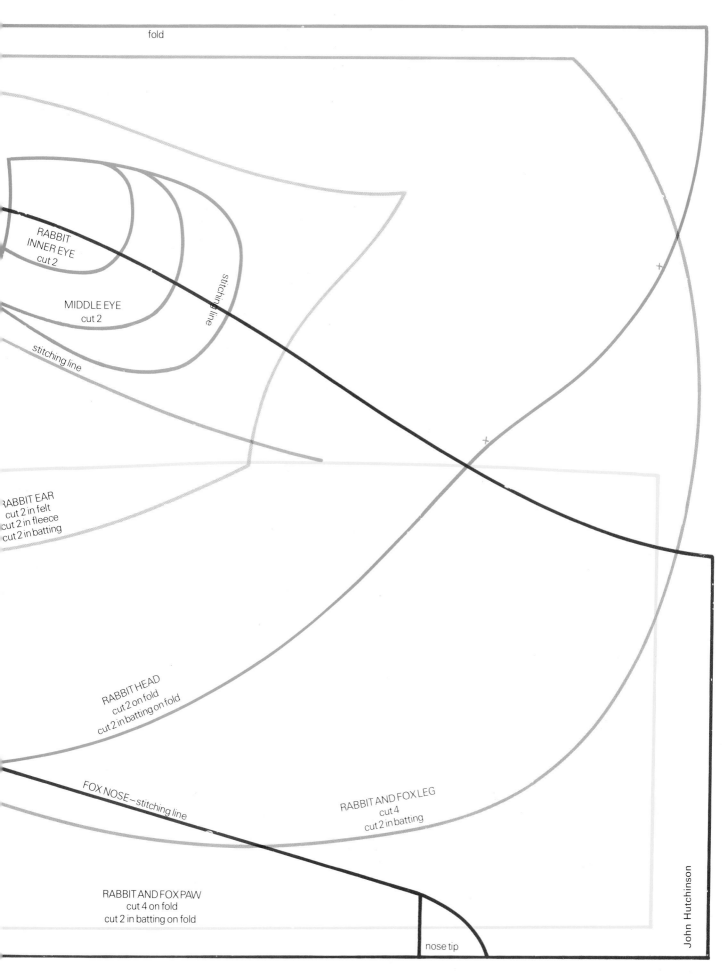

fold

RABBIT
INNER EYE
cut 2

MIDDLE EYE
cut 2

stitching line

stitching line

RABBIT EAR
cut 2 in felt
cut 2 in fleece
cut 2 in batting

RABBIT HEAD
cut 2 on fold
cut 2 in batting on fold

FOX NOSE – stitching line

RABBIT AND FOX LEG
cut 4
cut 2 in batting

RABBIT AND FOX PAW
cut 4 on fold
cut 2 in batting on fold

nose tip

John Hutchinson

Special settings

These beautiful hand-sewn place mats and napkins—decorated with fine lawn appliqué—will bring a touch of elegance to your table.

Size
Place mat is $13\frac{1}{2} \times 9\frac{1}{2}$in ($34 \times 24$cm).
Napkin is 15in (38cm) square.

Materials for each setting
$\frac{1}{2}$yd (.4m) of 36in (90cm)-wide fine white cotton lawn
Lawn in three colors—two harmonizing and one contrasting; a piece $\frac{1}{2}$yd (.5m) square in one color and scraps of other colors
Small amount of medium-weight iron-on interfacing
Medium-size crewel needle
Stranded embroidery floss in two of the three colors; sewing thread
Tracing paper

Place mat

1 From white lawn cut a piece $13\frac{1}{2} \times 9\frac{1}{2}$in ($34 \times 24$cm). From square of contrasting lawn cut $1\frac{1}{2}$in (4cm) bias strips and join to make a piece 47in (120cm) long.

2 Fold under $\frac{1}{4}$in (5mm) on edges of bias strip; press. Press in half lengthwise.
3 Starting at one corner, place the wrong side of the binding under the edge of the place mat with the edge at the center fold of the binding.

4 Fold binding over raw edge of place mat Miter the corners as shown. Fold binding

at a right angle at each corner, then fold upper edge of top binding to right side; pin. Fold under adjacent length. Baste and stitch up to 3in (8cm) of first corner.

5 At the first corner, cut the first end of binding to fit exactly the edge of the place mat. Trim the opposite end of binding so that it extends $\frac{3}{8}$in (1cm) past edge of place mat.

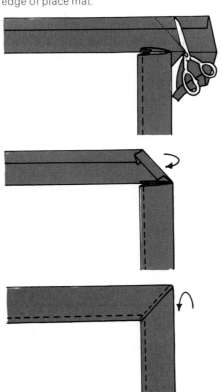

6 Trim the free end at a 45° angle as shown, allowing $\frac{1}{8}$in (3mm) for turning under. Turn under this amount on front and back, then fold the binding around the edge of the place mat to make a mitered corner matching other three.

7 Place one corner of the place mat over the flower design on page 128, $1\frac{1}{4}$in (3cm) from the bound edges. Lightly draw positions of stems and petals on the place mat.
8 Trace the patterns for the interfacing beside the motif and cut them out.
9 Using these patterns cut out interfacing pieces the number of times stated.
10 Place interfacing pieces on wrong side of three colored lawn fabrics, the number of times shown, leaving $\frac{1}{2}$in (1cm) between each piece. Iron on.
11 Cut out each interfaced fabric piece leaving $\frac{1}{4}$in (5mm) extra all around.

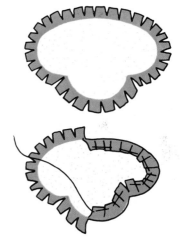

12 Snip into the margin all around one interfaced fabric piece. Fold the clipped fabric to the wrong side. Pin and baste neatly in place.
13 Repeat step 12 to finish the edges of each petal and leaf.
14 Group the petals and leaves together on the corner of the place mat in the positions marked. Pin and baste in place.

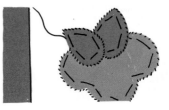

15 Using matching thread, neatly slip stitch each piece in place, overlapping the petals where shown.

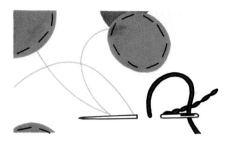

16 Using three strands of embroidery floss, work the stems and stamens in back stitch over the pencil lines.

17 Using contrasting embroidery floss, work French knots at the end of each stamen.

18 Remove all the basting threads and press the place mat carefully on the wrong side.

19 Repeat steps 1 to 18 to make more place mats in the same way.

Napkins

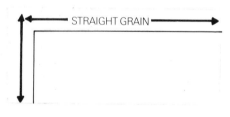

1 From white lawn cut out a piece of fabric 16in (40.5cm) square, aligning the sides of the square with the selvage or straight grain of the fabric.

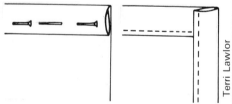

Terri Lawlor

2 Turn under a ½in (1.2cm) double hem on all four edges. On each edge turn under ¼in (5mm) and press, then turn under another ¼in (5mm); baste. When folding the corners make sure they are crisp and neat. Press.

3 Stitch around the hem, close to the turned-under edges.

4 Repeat steps 7 to 18 of the place mat directions to appliqué the flower motif onto one corner of the napkin, about 1¼in (3cm) from the edges.

5 Repeat steps 1 to 4 to make more napkins in the same way.

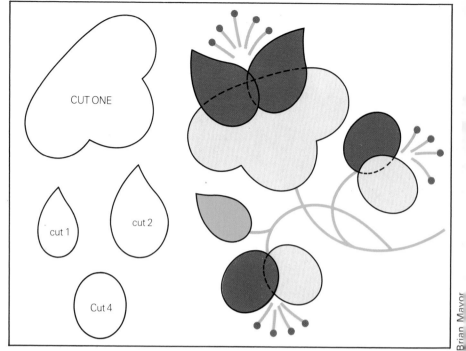

CUT ONE

cut 1

cut 2

Cut 4

Brian Mavor

Spike Powell